Brazilian Mosaic

Political Map of Brazil (courtesy of the Brazilian-American Chamber of Commerce)

Brazilian Mosaic

Portraits of a Diverse People and Culture

Edited by

G. Harvey Summ

A Scholarly Resources Inc. Imprint
Wilmington, Delaware

Acknowledgments

The help of Daniel Gross, Jane Malinoff Kamide, Conrad Phillip Kottak, Wayne A. Selcher, Thomas E. Skidmore, and Andrew Steigman is gratefully acknowledged. The choice of selections and the judgments herein, however, are entirely those of the editor.

First published 1995
Printed and bound in the United States of America

Scholarly Resources Inc.
104 Greenhill Avenue
Wilmington, DE 19805-1897

Frontispiece: Political map of Brazil. Courtesy of the Brazilian-American Chamber of Commerce.

Library of Congress Cataloging-in-Publication Data

Brazilian mosaic : portraits of a diverse people and culture / edited by G. Harvey Summ.
p. cm. — (Latin American silhouettes)
Includes bibliographical references (p.).
ISBN 0-8420-2491-3 (cloth). — ISBN 0-8420-2492-1 (pbk.)
1. National characteristics, Brazilian. I. Summ, G. Harvey.
II. Series.
F2510.B72 1995
306.4'0981—dc20 94-42343
CIP

♾ The paper used in this publication meets the minimum requirements of the American National Standard for permanence of paper for printed library materials, Z39.48, 1984.

In memory of

Charles Wagley

Friend, mentor, brother-in-law

About the Editor

G. Harvey Summ was director of the master's program in Latin American studies and professorial lecturer in international affairs at Georgetown University. He was chairperson of the advanced area studies course on Brazil of the Foreign Service Institute of the Department of State. A retired foreign service officer, he was director of research for Latin America and served in Brazil, Portugal, and Angola. He is the coeditor of *The Good Neighbors: America, Panama, and the 1977 Canal Treaties* (1988).

Contents

Introduction

A mosaic revealing many aspects of Brazilian culture emerges from comments made over the last two centuries by foreign visitors to Brazil and by Brazilians themselves. Mosaic is a particularly apt term to describe the totality of these observations. Just as the viewing of one piece of tile is meaningless, reading one observation in isolation sheds little light on Brazil. When they are combined, however, an image emerges. This volume consists of thirty-five observations by foreigners, supplemented by those of nine Brazilian writers.[1]

A caution is in order here. Foreign travelers, since the observers of ancient Greece, have characterized others in terms that result in unfortunate and improper stereotypes. In the selections that follow, such travelers in the nineteenth century often reflect and reveal the cultural, ethnic, racial, and geographic bias of their European origin when they comment on the people of Brazil. The Brazilian is often described as "he"; Brazilian women have not received equal attention. Moreover, not every Brazilian shares all or even any of the characteristics described; many have traits at odds with these generalizations. Nevertheless, when we look beyond their prejudices of place, race, and religion, these observers can provide useful clues, insights, and explanations for the behavior of Brazilians.

Many foreign observers have labeled sensibility—"a capacity for emotion or feeling"—as the key to explaining the "passionate" Brazilian.[2] As stated in Selection 6, "the heart is the measure of all things." The joy and satisfaction derived from the warmth and friendliness of interpersonal contact, from getting up close to each other when speaking, from playing the "let's-be-friends" game are important to Brazilians (Selection 33), and they value congeniality highly—"a smile wins, a frown loses" (Selection 28). Emotion can catch up a worker watching a soccer game, to the point where he is watching "the world's best *futebol*, and the players are himself" (Selection 36); at a soccer game, "what's important is life, the game being played, the presence of other people" (Selection 42).

Sensibility in Brazil also has its dark side. We are told in Selection 3 that melancholy—fundamental to the national character—arose from a combination of early settlers' greed for quick riches and lust for Indian and African women. Moreover, as noted in Selection 25, morbid and melancholy sadness are as Brazilian as the "joy, happiness, and smiles at Carnival." The colonial past figures in the description of Brazilians as "three sad races": the Portuguese mourn the homeland they left behind; the Indians yearn for the world that whites took from them; and the Africans lament their loss of freedom (Selection 39). This melancholy often takes the form of *saudade*, a Portuguese trait defined as a soft, sentimental, fatalistic, and even morbid sadness, with elements of homesickness and nostalgia (Selection 6).

To other observers, Brazilian emotion is tempered with pragmatism. The people are described as "sweet-tempered, witty, and patient" (Selection 30), while the phrase "finesse and avoid commitment" is used to summarize the techniques employed by contemporary Brazilian diplomats to deal with their country's mixed First World, Third World status (Selection 38). Slum dwellers, who describe themselves as a people of feeling, also experience *saudade*; they are "sensual, vibrant, deeply sentimental, melancholy, sad." In their milieu, however, they have learned to express their feelings cautiously, as excess emotion can bring misery and suffering (Selection 44).

Another characteristic, suspicion, surfaces in Brazilian humor. Those same slum dwellers, who refer to themselves as "nobodies," turn to ironic, absurdist black humor to swallow and deflect their anger at exploitation by elites. Intellectuals use fanciful humor to cover up deep anxiety. Sly self-criticism and the keen and cynical pointing out and discussion of others' mistakes and shortcomings, rather than the guffaw and the belly laugh, are staples of this humor (Selection 7).

Because of the elite's racial prejudice and the recognition that much of the country is nonwhite, "each Brazilian daily presents himself for careful inspection and classification by those he meets" (Selection 39). Brazilians have yet to find a clear-cut racial and national identity. They believe that man is evil unless proved to the contrary, that ceremoniousness and apparent cordiality might mask shyness and distrust, allowing Brazilians to escape the ridicule they fear, or may serve as a technique for gaining advantage (Selection 7).

The colonial experience helps to explain Brazilian distrust. Portuguese settlers lived in relative solitude in a vast, sparsely populated, demanding, and unfamiliar tropical forest. Contending with "the awesome obstacles of mountains, jungles and vast distances," marauders, tax collectors, adventurers, and greedy merchants, they suffered from "cosmic terror" (Selection 7). With little confidence in the future, they learned to practice discretion, bide their time, and wait for opportunities.

In a similar vein, one might say that the Brazilian works hard, but not cooperatively (Selection 2). Lack of social solidarity has deep colonial roots. A small elite of self-sufficient and slave-owning landowners, presiding over immense tracts—captaincies granted by the Crown—had little reason to cooperate with one another against largely ineffectual colonial bureaucrats. Important ties were vertical; support for patriarchal leaders tended to take on a personal character. In temporary danger, a provincial leader's independence and courage, rather than his ideas, might draw support around him, but, when the danger was over, anarchic individualism prevailed. Few self-governing institutions emerged.

During the empire, Karl Friedrich Philipp von Martius described Brazil as lacking what he called the broader "civic virtues"—love of country, courage, constancy, industry, fidelity, and prudence (Selection 12). In the period of the republic, elected leaders—and even more so, occasional dictators—tended to draw support around their persons. In contemporary Brazil, there is little sense of community participation (Selection 35), despite broad voluntary associations, including political parties.

Of equal interest is the contrast between apparent Brazilian indolence and extraordinary reserves of periodic energy. In colonial times, manual labor was beneath the Portuguese, who aspired to be gentlemen; Indians wanted to hunt, fish, and fight while leaving agriculture to women; and to the African, hard work was linked with the shame of being a slave. Colonists might be excellent woodland guides or tamers of the desert, capable of determined effort involving self-denial and courage in pursuit of a goal that they deemed worthy. However, they exhibited these qualities only when necessary, as a way of economizing effort in a difficult climate and environment.

Such behavior has persisted. In the early days of the empire, Brazilians tended to abandon useful enterprise (Selection 10). Forty years later they demonstrated that they had "lofty impulses" but lacked persistence (Selection 16). At the beginning of the republican era, an alternation between impulse and apathy was noted (Selection 20). More recent observers have found them capable of determined, though irregular, effort.

Although most Brazilians work hard to make ends meet, an individual is believed more likely to succeed through luck or connections. Speculative profit is prized more than persistent toil (Selection 4). The young man's dream is a well-paying government or white-collar job, involving minimal work or effort (Selection 33). Boom-and-bust cycles have reinforced on-again, off-again behavior. Thus, economic growth in the 1970s led some members of the elite to believe that their country was on the verge of attaining great-power status. The 1980s, however, brought debt, inflation, and disillusionment.

Another facet of the Brazilian mosaic is the *jeito*, a literally untranslatable but widespread and highly prized term, roughly equivalent to "a way around." The practice dates back to the colonial era, when "circumventing legal but unrealistic obligations" was necessary to avoid complying with confused and contradictory decrees (Selection 5). In the imperial period, Hermann Burmeister noted, differences in circumstances and deeply rooted customs created "a law much more rigorous than the written law, which the Brazilians know how to ignore when it suits them" (Selection 13). Other nineteenth-century observers were less charitable, using the phrases "an adroit and skulking depravity" (Selection 9) and "trickery, cheating, and debauchery" (Selection 14) to describe Brazilian practices. Corruption continued during the empire and the republic, and current scandals indicate that such practices still prevail.

In its modern guise, *jeito* involves "bypassing the system." The author of Selection 31 humorously describes the good sense used by a Brazilian consul in Europe—which any Brazilian would "understand and support"—in arbitrarily reclassifying a foreigner's profession in order to issue him a visa. Shantytown dwellers also admire *jeito*; to them, it is "badness," a display of "sexual allure, street smarts, and wit" (Selection 44). They approve of those who have it and pity the weak and hopeless who do not.

In Selection 21, Rudyard Kipling remarks upon another Brazilian characteristic, namely, to seek "a mutual accommodation from highest to humblest." Subtlety—taking the form of delicate, but not always sincere, courtesy—may hark back to Iberian courtliness in colonial times, and its practice in Brazil may have been accentuated after the Portuguese court arrived in the early nineteenth century. Independence came about through accommodation and involved no rupture with the past when the Portuguese monarchy, in exile in Brazil after fleeing Napoleon's occupation of the Iberian peninsula, established a separate branch there. Other landmark events, including the abolition of slavery and the shift from an empire to a republic at the end of the nineteenth century, also followed a peaceful pattern.

Nineteenth-century observers ascribed amiable, imaginative, and lighthearted qualities to Brazilians (Selections 8, 11, and 15); twentieth-century observers used similar expressions, including affable, intuitive, and cordial (Selections 22, 23, and 24). A fatalistic belief in miracles and in luck—the lottery and the *bicho*, or "animal game" (Selection 25) are examples—may be connected with the Portuguese messianic cult of Sebastianism. Sixteenth-century King Sebastião I disappeared in Morocco but, according to Brazilian as well as Portuguese myth, would return someday to redeem his people.

Race and class, intimately entangled with one another, have profoundly affected Brazilian culture. Since most early settlers did not bring wives, racial mixing between Portuguese men and native Indian women, and later with slaves brought from Africa, was common in the colonial period. Slavery reinforced the class distinctions and submissiveness of the Portuguese patron-client system. Masters might exercise authority haughtily and oppressively but also might capriciously reward humble, obedient, and loyal slaves and other clients (Selection 17). In the mid-nineteenth century, the importance of "long-standing differences of color, position, and wealth" did not wane (Selection 13). In a social structure narrow at the top and broad at the base, slaves were at the bottom.

After abolition and the advent of the republic, social mobility continued to grow slowly. Upper-class Brazilians adopted a European-influenced "whitening" ideology (Selection 19). To Gilberto Freyre (Selection 18), "Luso-tropical civilization" would feature a new multiracial "Brazilian type of man and woman" in a "racial democracy." However, an "obsession with whiteness and blackness" is closer to current reality (Selection 37). Disparities of wealth and income widened further in the more recent military period, as measures to reduce social inequities were hardly tried or they failed. Women, too, have suffered from a double standard since colonial times, although they now have more educational and professional opportunities. In Freyre's view, Brazilians "liberated themselves more quickly from racial prejudice than from that of sex."

Status is important at all levels. The phrase "Do you know who you're talking to?!" is cited (Selection 32) as the Brazilian way of expressing the need for everyone to know his or her place. Hierarchical relationships coexist in tension with affectionate ties between individual descendants of planters and former slaves. Servile slum dwellers, even when disillusioned with bad bosses, still find the idea of a benefactor soothing. In southern Brazil, one observer noted (Selection 26) a tone of social egalitarianism among European immigrants. Servility and haughtiness are absent, as a result of rapid economic change, industrial development, and immigration.

The family, perhaps Brazil's most important institution, has played a dominant role in the country's history, with the clan or the extended family as the only form of social solidarity that Brazilians really feel and practice (Selection 2). As Freyre put it (Selection 18), Brazilian civilization resulted more from "familistic organization" than from the "achievement of state or church, of kings or military leaders." Although the family is of less importance at lower social levels, it can serve as a model for other segments of society.

The extended kinship network described in Selections 34 and 40 is a tightly knit unit with a strong sense of mutual loyalty and obligation. Within it, the "civic virtues" to which Martius referred are practiced. An element of being Brazilian is the ability to say, "I am loyal to my friends and can deny nothing to my family" (Selection 32). By extension, the family can be seen as being at the core of the political system. As pointed out in Selection 41, an adaptable and resilient political elite, interacting through close personal relationships of friends, associates, and supporters, has governed Brazil in a flexible and pragmatic "patrimonial" system for almost five hundred years.

Of the hundreds of writings by foreign observers available on Brazil, those included in this volume provide—in the editor's opinion—the most meaningful interpretations of the people. Twenty of the forty-four observers are American; five are British, three are German, and two are French. Ten nationalities in all are represented, including Austrian, Ghanaian, Hungarian, Italian, and Spanish. Nine authors are Brazilian. Five, all Americans, are female. One, the Ghanaian, is black. Eleven wrote in the nineteenth century, ten in the first half of the twentieth century, and twenty-three in the second half. By profession they are anthropologists, attorneys, authors, businessmen, diplomats, doctors, folklorists, historians, journalists, naturalists, poets, political scientists, psychologists, sociologists, and specialists in Brazilian literature.

Many nineteenth- and early twentieth-century observers came from temperate climates and were often overwhelmed by the luxuriance and denseness of the exotic tropics. Several of their observations about the fauna and flora of Brazil have turned out to be priceless. Their writings about the people, however, frequently reflect colonialist, racist, and sexist attitudes. Many who visited Brazil for very short periods, such as Kipling or the Spanish journalist Ricardo Baeza, had contact primarily with members of the elite, and their perceptions are often colored by this privileged group's viewpoints.

An outstanding nineteenth-century exception was Auguste de Saint-Hilaire, who wrote nine books in which he recorded extensive details about every conceivable aspect of Brazil, including insightful comments made in passing about the culture. German zoologist Burmeister had the misfortune to break his leg in a small town, which allowed him to train his keen powers of observation on local customs for three months. Distinguished British naturalists Henry Walter Bates and Alfred Russel Wallace traveled long and widely enough to be exposed to all elements of the country's society.

German naturalist Martius came to Brazil as a very young man in the 1820s, but he remained in touch with the country for the rest of his life and was highly respected by Brazilians. His contribution was the only foreign one included in a special issue of an 1844 Brazilian scholarly journal. He aimed at persuading future historians to get away from a dry, monotonous, pompous chronicle of "sterile citations" of "insignificant facts of slight historical importance" and "dubious historical authenticity." He recommended instead that they study blacks and Indians as well as the white population; that they take regional differences into account; and that they recognize that "the upper class is developed from elements of the lower class, vitalized and strengthened by them."

Other early commentators were European and American men who occasionally were shocked by—but for the most part took for granted—a heavily male-dominated society. Slavery made strong impressions on almost all of them, notably the Englishman Henry Koster and the American Herbert Smith. Boston-born Elizabeth Agassiz, coauthor, with her husband Louis, of *A Journey in Brazil*, made incisive comments on the status and education of women. Later nineteenth-century female observers of Brazil included Maria Graham, who served briefly as governess to the children of the emperor just after Independence; Ida Pfeiffer, an Austrian and inveterate world traveler; and May Frances, a young Englishwoman who lived briefly in Rio Grande do Sul at the end of the century. Their comments on Brazil, however, like those of hundreds of their male counterparts, were mainly superficial.[3]

In the twentieth century, particularly after 1950, most foreign observers were American, a consequence largely of two factors: increasingly close Brazilian-U.S. relations during and after World War II, and U.S. government sponsorship of academic research that fostered area studies programs—including Latin American studies—at American universities. Thus, many of the more recent selections, including four by female observers, are from writings of trained social scientists whose very function is the objective and systematic study of human behavior and social organization.

In particular, the two most recent selections, from Daphne Patai and Nancy Scheper-Hughes, have begun to fill in missing elements in the mosaic. Their research, dealing mainly with poor black women, casts doubt—for Brazil, at least—on the Oscar Lewis view that in modern nations "poverty creates a subculture of its own that cuts across regional, rural-urban, and even national boundaries."[4] Rather, the characteristics that they portray as applying to the vast poor and nonwhite majority of the Brazilian population—women as well as men—seem similar, in greater or lesser degree, to those of the affluent and the relatively small middle class.

Of other recent foreign observers, William Lytle Schurz incorporates and confirms many of Fernando de Azevedo's views on Brazilians and describes them as "unconventional individualists." Pulitzer Prize-winning poet Elizabeth Bishop touches on many aspects of personal and family relationships, although she came to hate the book she wrote for the Life World Library series because of the way the editors softened her prose to provide a more optimistic picture of Brazil. Charles Wagley's piece is a unique attempt to analyze strengths and weaknesses of the society from his vantage point of "if I were a Brazilian." David Maybury-Lewis examines the lack of community spirit, political factiousness, and the patron-client relationship.

Brazilian observers of their own countrymen began to make their mark in the twentieth century. Many of them took Martius's advice. Beginning with Euclides da Cunha's classic *Os sertões* in 1902, the selections of the nine Brazilians included in this volume match in quality those of the best foreign analysts. All comment on the persistence of one or more traditional traits of the Brazilian; none of their approaches is in basic conflict with the others.

Azevedo provides the best overall portrait. Freyre, who was educated in the United States and specialized in race relations, may overemphasize the racial and cultural adaptability of the Portuguese in the tropics. Francisco José de Oliveira Vianna's main contribution is his analysis of the historical origin of Brazil's lack of social solidarity. Sérgio Buarque de Holanda looks carefully at what he called the "cordial man." Clodomiro Vianna Moog believes that the Brazilian's "dislike for useful work" is at the root of the country's underdevelopment. Roberto da Matta, whose comments included in this volume are mainly on the hierarchy, is now an academic in the United States, where he continues to interpret many aspects of his countrymen's contemporary behavior.

Brazilian observers of Brazil, Freyre in particular, draw heavily on nineteenth-century writings by foreign visitors; conversely, twentieth-century foreign observers have relied to a considerable degree on their Brazilian counterparts. The latter have been at least as critical of their countrymen as have foreigners. They have translated English, French, German, and Italian travelers' accounts into Portuguese. Some of those accounts, although negative in tone, are included in this volume.

The most recent selections place less emphasis on regional differences. Improved nationwide transportation and communication since 1950 have tended to blur regional aspects of the Brazilian mosaic. Accelerated migration from rural to urban areas, as well as within and between regions, and the homogenizing influence of Globo, probably the largest television network in the world, have had a striking effect. A focus on differences among Brazilians in the country's five regions would have to try to answer questions such as the following in order to fit regional differences into the mosaic.[5]

Do recent migrants to the Center-West and to the North from other regions resemble the residents of the Amazon described by Bates and Wallace in the late nineteenth century? Does the Mineiro, regarded by many Brazilians themselves as the prototypical Brazilian, have the same traits as described by Burmeister in the mid-nineteenth century, or have Mineiros migrated to so many different regions of the country that they no longer have specifically identifiable characteristics?

How deep is the influence of the significant late nineteenth- and early twentieth-century Italian immigration to São Paulo? Do residents of the two southern states of Rio Grande do Sul and Santa Catarina—about whom relatively little has been written by foreigners—display distinct characteristics as a result of German migration to those states?

Are the foresters in Scheper-Hughes's study typical of the northeastern backlands from which they came, or the coastal Northeast shantytowns in which they now reside? Do the "ordinary" women interviewed by Patai, mainly from the urban Northeast and Rio de Janeiro, have characteristics in common deriving more from their ethnic origins and life experiences than from their places of origin?

What are the characteristics of residents of Brasília, the capital founded in 1960? Has the typical Carioca changed now that Rio is no longer the capital? Was, for example, former President Fernando Collor de Melo typical of Rio de Janeiro (where he was brought up), Brasília (where he went to school), the Northeast of his father, or the South of his maternal grandfather? And finally, do 1994 presidential candidate Luiz Inácio ("Lula") da Silva and former São Paulo Mayor Luiza Erundina da Silva have characteristics of the Northeast from which they came or the Southeast to which they migrated?

The earliest selection in this volume was drawn from an observer who wrote in 1816, a few years before Brazilian independence; the last appeared first in 1992. Although Brazil's 300-year colonial past has had a lasting and overwhelming influence on the nation, the selections, after a brief historical overview, have been arranged into four historical parts: the colonial era, the empire, the republic, and the military period.

The observations of Azevedo and Oliveira Vianna in Part I are the most general of the readings, and they serve to describe topics introduced in greater detail in Parts II-V. The selections in Part II were written in the twentieth century but deal primarily with aspects of the Brazilian character in colonial times. Parts II-V are each prefaced by a short historical sketch of the period, followed by one (or in Part IV, two) twentieth-century selection that sets the scene for the whole period. Otherwise, readings in these parts are in chronological order.

Each piece is preceded by a note that summarizes the observer's main theme. In some cases, a selection is drawn from two or more works by the same author. Editorial liberties were taken; for example, paragraphs have been shortened and punctuation and spelling changed when necessary to increase clarity. Every effort was made to retain the original substance and flavor of the comments.

Finally, I cannot conclude any better than Elizabeth Agassiz, who wrote in 1868: "Will my Brazilian friends who read this summary say that I have given but grudging praise to their public institutions, accompanied by an unkind criticism of their social condition? I hope not. I should do myself great wrong did I give the impression that I part from Brazil with any feeling but that of warm sympathy."[6]

Notes

1. Other studies of the Brazilian national character by foreign observers include:

James Bryce, *South America: Observations and Impressions* (New York: Macmillan Company, 1916). Bryce is the same British historian who wrote perceptively on the American character.

Richard F. Burton, *Exploration of the Highlands of Brazil: With a Full Account of the Gold and Diamond Mines. Also, Canoeing Down 1,500 Miles of the Great River São Francisco* (New York: Greenwood Press, 1869). Burton, the famous British explorer, described the residents of Minas Gerais.

James C. Fletcher and Daniel P. Kidder, *Brazil and the Brazilians Portrayed in Historical and Descriptive Sketches* (Boston: Little, Brown and Co., 1867). American Protestant missionaries, the authors were widely read in the United States in the late nineteenth century.

Hugh Gibson, *Rio* (New York: Doubleday, 1937). Gibson, the American ambassador to Brazil, observed Cariocas insightfully.

Hermann Keyserling, *South American Meditations on Heaven and Hell in the Soul of Man* (New York: Harper and Brothers, 1932). Keyserling, a Russian philosopher, remarked perceptively on Brazilian *delicadeza*.

In addition, Brazilian psychologist Dante Moreira Leite cataloged Brazilian writings on the national character in *O carater nacional brasileiro: História de una ideologia* (São Paulo: Livraria Pioneira Editora, 1976).

2. *Webster's Third International Dictionary* (1964).

3. Maria Graham, *Journal of a Voyage to Brazil and Residence There, During Part of the Years 1821, 1822, 1823* (London: John Murray, 1824); Ida Pfeiffer, *A Woman's Journey Around the World from Vienna to Brazil, Chili [sic], Tahiti, China, Hindostan, Persia, and Asia Minor* (London: Nathaniel Cooke, 1854); May Frances, *Beyond the Argentine: or, Letters from Brazil* (London: W. H. Allen and Co., 1890).

4. Oscar Lewis, *Five Families* (New York: Basic Books, 1959), 2.

5. Brazil's twenty-seven states are divided into five regions: the North (Acre, Amapá, Amazonas, Pará, Rondônia, Roraima, Tocantins); the Northeast (Alagoas,

Bahia, Ceará, Maranhão, Paraíba, Pernambuco, Piauí, Rio Grande do Norte, Sergipe); the Center-West (the Federal District, Goiás, Mato Grosso, Mato Grosso do Sul); the Southeast (Espírito Santo, Rio de Janeiro, Minas Gerais, São Paulo); and the South (Paraná, Rio Grande do Sul, Santa Catarina).

6. See p. 76 in this volume.

I

The Brazilian People: Products of Their Past

After the Portuguese discovery of Brazil in 1500, settlers encountered a harsh tropical environment, with mountainous terrain, droughts, and torrential rains. Adapting, in the words of Brazilian sociologist Fernando de Azevedo, with "a kind of resigned capitulation to nature," they temporized and felt their way with subtle cunning (sometimes described in Portuguese as *jeito*, or a way around).

Portugal's decline in the first century and a half after the discovery, its lack of manpower to either settle or supervise the new colony, and its involvement in its other overseas possessions resulted in neglect of Brazil. Realizing that they could not rely on support from the mother country, Portuguese colonists became skeptical and distrustful of government officials, adventurers, and merchants.

Colonial landowners, under captaincies established by Portugal, were granted the responsibility to administer their territories by virtue of detailed decrees from Lisbon, but they received little financial help. The local bureaucracy, preoccupied with sinecures and maintaining appearances, devised elaborate legalistic and formalistic trivia. Hangers-on who followed the royal family to Brazil before Independence in the early nineteenth century vastly expanded opportunities for, and the legitimacy of, the bureaucracy. Foreign travelers to Brazil in that period commented on widespread venality and the lack of civic virtues.

The captaincies broke up into mutually isolated regional entities, resistant to centralized power. Large-scale miscegenation among the racially tolerant Portuguese, internal migration, freedom of movement in the vast hinterland, and an independence of spirit generated by distance and isolation encouraged an easygoing egalitarianism. Similarly, the emotional, colorful, often messianic religiosity of folk Catholicism allowed for a kind of backlands democracy.

Law enforcement was corrupt and uneven. Clever and adaptable colonists—encouraged, paradoxically, by Portugal's so-called law of good sense—easily avoided compliance. Other aspects of the captaincy system led to a top-down, patron-client class system controlled by large landholders. The state became the ultimate patron, and later, in independent Brazil, the emperor became the ultimate patriarch.

Voluntary cooperation existed both in the Portuguese and in the native Indian tradition, but according to sociologist Francisco de Oliveira Vianna, "social solidarity was extremely rare" in Brazil. Landowners for the most part could take care of themselves. Land struggles between elite families often degenerated into local conflict, making for solidarity within the extended family rather than outside it. Patriarchs engaged in favoritism and nepotism in protecting their families.

There was little loyalty to the body politic. Local landowners and political bosses dominated and united an essentially individualistic society. The pattern of absolute rule by the distant Portuguese monarchy was duplicated by these men who exercised unquestioned and unlimited, although temporary and sentimental, authority over groups of families and retainers, both free and slave. Serious threats from either internal or foreign enemies were few, and when the threats ended and the purpose for cooperation no longer existed, factionalism replaced solidarity. Similarly, political parties or groups formed for humanitarian, moral, recreational, or other purposes were artificial and did not last long.

Three hundred years of slavery intensified tendencies toward arrogance, selfishness, servility, and offended pride. Occupations considered menial because of their association with slavery, and the concept of useful work, were, and tend to be, more than a century after abolition, scorned by both ex-masters and ex-slaves. A complex system of racial categories, based on both race and class, has governed relations between haves and have-nots and has marked the search for a viable Brazilian identity.

1 *Fernando de Azevedo* ◆ Altruistic, Sentimental, and Generous

Fernando de Azevedo was born in Minas Gerais in 1894. He began his career as a journalist and professor and became director of public education in Rio de Janeiro, at which time he proposed fundamental reforms in the educational system. Azevedo moved to São Paulo, where he was one of the founders of the University of São Paulo and the first dean of its Faculty of Philosophy and Letters. He authored books on education, Brazilian history, Brazilian and Roman literature, and the natural and social sciences. Azevedo died in 1974.

This wide-ranging excerpt on characteristics growing out of the Brazilian colonial period is adapted from Azevedo's monumental A cultura brasileira, *originally published in 1943. The book brings together all of the disciplines of his distinguished career, including history, education, and the arts and sciences.*

The emotional, the irrational, and the mystical predominate and are sometimes considered the very key to the Brazilian character. Those traits have infiltrated the structure of every spiritual being. The intelligence of Brazilians is emotional in its essence and is charged with imagination. Sensibility, imagination, and religiosity are intense and strong. Culture merely raises them from the primitive and the gross to higher and more delicate forms.

Sentiment intervenes constantly in Brazilians' judgments and opinions and reasoning is emotional; they easily believe and spread news of all things strange and miraculous and are not interested in objectivity. All of these factors translate into a tendency to put and resolve everything in personal terms, as "friend" and "enemy." In all social classes Brazilians conceive of authority as founded on man's sentimental faith in the superiority of a chieftain or of a group.

Brazilians are not in revolt but are resigned and docile. They submit to physical and moral tricks of fate, which they have learned to endure with courage, bowing their heads to these tricks, but without bitterness, recognizing that they have no defense against them. The Brazilian attitude toward life—a mixture of indulgence, piety, and irony—is a kind of resigned capitulation to hostile and unconquerable nature. From

From *A cultura brasileira*, 5th ed. (São Paulo: Edições Melhoramentos, Editora da Universidade de São Paulo, 1971), 211–26, 230. Translated and adapted by G. Harvey Summ.

experience, they know the violence of nature and have learned to face it—almost always without support, relying on themselves alone in their attempts to tame the land.

~ The kindness of Brazilians, both a strength and a weakness, is perhaps one of their most distinctive traits; it stands out immediately. It appears to spring from the soul and the temperament of the people. Sensitivity to the suffering of others, ease in forgiving and forgetting offenses, a certain shame about one's own selfishness, absence of racial pride, rejection of radical solutions, tolerance, hospitality, liberality, and generosity: these are manifestations of the strongly marked emotionalism in the national character.

This kindness is not politeness, which is the product of refinement and civilization, and which is acquired rather than natural. It is uncalculated, disinterested, and delicate. It is frank, naive, and primitively simple. At times it is rustic, but it is frequently tender and limited by timidity and discretion. It transcends class and race. It withdraws, as if offended, when faced with violence and brutality. It makes the Brazilians easy to lead when you appeal to their reason and, above all, to their sentiments, but difficult to move by force.

~ Natural reserve and distrust, defense mechanisms that history explains, modify the characteristic Brazilian hospitality. Great though their hospitality may be, Brazilians, even loquacious and communicative northerners, do not open up easily or totally. In a sparsely populated new country, influenced by different races assimilated slowly into the original core of settlers, men living alone were exposed to extortions by the treasury, encirclement by adventurers, and the greed of merchants. They had to live constantly on the alert and perpetually in distrust. Even when Brazilians opened the gates of their houses, they would close those of their intimacy and of their heart.

Distrust, however, is neither aggressive nor incompatible with hospitality. Rather, it is linked to other traits, such as reserve in speech, dissimulation, and an apparent incontinence in language that permits one to speak a great deal without saying anything, or at least without opening one's heart.

Nature, apparently easy and opulent, in fact distributed its wealth with deceptive greed and inconstancy. The unfavorable environment that it created imprinted indulgent skepticism in the Brazilian character. The Brazilians adapt easily to new situations, but prudently and astutely. They protect themselves by distrust, doubt, and irreverence, and by watchful waiting. This skepticism, which manifests itself in complacency, in good humor, in piety, and in irony toward life, turns out to be one of the liveliest traits of a simple and young people, still in the process of formation.

~ Primitively simple, and easily satisfied in material needs, Brazilians have the sobriety of inhabitants of a country that has poor cultivable land. Their farmlands need to be occupied continuously and worked incessantly to maintain their value. They had to get used to mountainous, tropical, hard, and savage terrain. Slopes, prolonged droughts, and torrential rains are obstacles to cultivation. Frugal in food and in other ways, Brazilians are not and never have been tormented by the thirst for gold. Avidity for gain and preoccupation with the future are certainly not characteristic of Brazilians. Calculation is not the essence of these people. What is beyond the present hardly exists for them—the present is what counts.

Lack of foresight is linked to constant instability in our society. Economic uncertainty, and the destruction of old fortunes and the creating of new ones, led to dissipation of wealth. Reliance on miracles and sudden turnabouts of fortune outweighed confidence in the continuity of work. Education became a sign of class distinction, rather than something that had practical or moral value. Not that Brazilians lacked interest in things of the mind: their delicate and excitable sensibility, keen intelligence, the ease with which they adapted to material scarcity, and their religious traditions gave them a lively understanding of the need to subordinate material to moral values and strongly inclined them toward matters of the spirit.

Brazil's culture is generally literary and superficial. It comes from a centuries-old tradition, Iberian-influenced, scholastic, verbal, and dogmatic. This tradition kept Brazilians distanced from a positive spirit, from objectivity, and from exactness. It rendered them uninterested in ideas and easily impressed and charmed by form, by language, and by pompous erudition. The Brazilians' sensibility, combined with a vivacious and keen intelligence, held them back from philosophical speculation and scientific investigation, which require rigorous technique and strong discipline of thought. Neither penetration nor vigor nor profundity characterizes the people of Brazil, but rather facility, grace, and brilliance. They grasp things quickly but totally lack exactness and precision; they have a talent for indirection.

Influenced by the three races that make up the people, by the physical environment and climate, and by their history, Brazilians are subject to an irregular and offbeat rhythm, to depressions and recoveries, and to indolence and impetuosity. Despite the appearance of laziness, lassitude, and indifference, an explosive will and an ability to maintain reserves of energy—to be released when needed or when Brazilians are shocked emotionally—clearly show a marked preponderance of sensibility over intelligence.

The acts of Brazilians generally are not premeditated or reflective. They are made up of sometimes violent—yet passing and discontinuous—impulses. It is an illusion to see weakness in an air of indifference and a lack of concern. Indolence is rather an "economy" of force, a defense against the climate and the environment. The capacity for great but irregular effort is astonishing. Although they conceal and casually husband their capacity for violence and readiness for combat, Brazilians appear to delight in mobilizing and then unleashing their energies when faced with an emotional shock.

Individualism is one of the most active elements in that singular mixture of virtues and defects that make up the Brazilian character. Iberian in origin, it turned to aggressiveness under favorable conditions in the backlands and later on the southern frontier. It became an effective instrument for defense and loosened restrictions allowing society to prevail over the individual. On the other hand, it served as a disciplinary agent when the prestige of the law and institutional authority did not work well or were endangered.

It is not creative like Anglo-Saxon individualism, nor does it possess the same social significance or content. Rather, it tends to be negative. Only the individual counts. This rude individualism implies an extremely active feeling for the importance of the person and for an individual's autonomy. It does not, however, always involve respect for life, for one's fellowman, and for the proper worth of a human being. Individualism rewards individual boldness, courage, and arrogance, but it emphasizes individual competition, dispersion, and lack of discipline, which are sources of rivalry and conflict.

Add another phenomenon—regionalism—to destructive and anarchical individualism. Regionalism resulted from the political breakup of the colonies into the "captaincies"—a mutually distant and isolated multitude of little cells or collective individualities. Individualism and regionalism led to centrifugal power, which in turn created a lack of social cohesion, as well as active and passive resistance to centralized political power. The essential theme of Brazilian history for more than three centuries, strongly noticeable during the empire and the republic, was this combination of individualism and of particularism. The latter, in turn, resulted in the juxtaposition of small and large states, out of contact with each other and subject to diverse geographic and social influences. The outcome: the absence in Brazilians of a spirit of cooperation.

~ Of all of the social institutions, the family shows the greatest solidity and cohesion. Domestic society is a refuge and redoubt where individuals can unite and resist disintegrating influences. In general, what counts is not the individual, but the institution: the family. That institution became a basis of support and protection for the individual, and above all for women—kept in seclusion—wherever the law and the state were weak. In the social sphere, where political power was slow to arrive, the family acquired authority and strength.

Thus there was formed a domestic particularism that turned into centuries-long struggles between families in the backlands about land disputes or personal differences, degenerating into conflict. The influence of this particularism extended to a political life monopolized by great families and took the form of parasitical favoritism and nepotism. This led to the moral solidarity and cooperation of the Brazilian family. The slogan "one for all and all for one" became the fundamental principle by which the family defended both itself as an institution and the individuals within it.

Individualism was reduced by the efforts of common enemies, Indians, or foreigners to conquer and occupy Brazil. These threats tended to unify the people. However, common undertakings demanded the unquestioned and unlimited authority of a chieftain. At first glance this deep-rooted phenomenon, which might seem to reveal a spirit of cooperation, in fact demonstrated the opposite. Cohesion through a chieftain's unlimited power dominated and united society superficially in the face of common danger but society remained essentially individualistic. Sporadic and transient groups—organized out of necessity for limited purposes—soon dissolved. They left no vestige in society in the form of permanent institutions or associations.

Individualism and particularism encouraged democratic sentiment and egalitarianism. Other factors leading toward egalitarianism and democracy included: contact between races; large-scale miscegenation; internal migration; pastoral nomadism; the general freedom of life in the backlands; and a spirit of independence generated by distance and isolation. But if one looks behind these spontaneous and vigorous tendencies, one better understands the institutions, the customs, and the men who make up political "forces."

Individualism, the spirit of freedom, and traditional local influences led men to band around persons rather than ideas. Parties became less able to serve as instruments of the public interest. Little by little they turned local loyalties into instruments of servitude. Individualism gave group struggles a personal character. Even when Brazilians believe they are applauding or combating ideas, they are really idolizing or rejecting the individuals who incarnate those ideas. Brazilians generally cannot separate persons from their ideas.

~ To sum up, Brazilians are altruistic, sentimental, and generous, capable of impulsive passions, violent but not very tenacious, lovers of life more than order, peaceful, hospitable but suspicious, and tolerant both by temperament and by lack of concern. They are hard workers, endowed with vigorous pioneer individualism, but without a cooperative spirit. Beneath a disagreeable exterior of indolence and indifference, they have extraordinary reserves of energy. Acting impulsively and discontinuously, they appear to save their strength and react periodically, both on an individual and social basis. Brazilians have an acute sensibility, a rare intellectual vivacity, and an imagination rich in invention, which predisposes them more to letters and the arts than to the sciences.

2 *Francisco José de Oliveira Vianna* ◆ A Wealth of Incalculable Spiritual Attributes

Francisco José de Oliveira Vianna, born in 1883, was from a traditional rural family in Rio de Janeiro state. After first studying engineering, he received a law degree in Rio de Janeiro and became a professor as part of the law faculty of the University of Brazil. His many books and articles dealt with corporation and labor law, Brazilian history, political and constitutional questions, social psychology, and race. During the Estado Novo corporatist period of Getúlio Vargas in the 1930s, he was a consultant to the Ministry of Labor. He died in 1951.

The following excerpts are taken from his first book, Southern Populations of Brazil, *which is subtitled "Rural Populations of the Center-South." Its central theme is the influence of the rural aristocracy on the Brazilian political system and social institutions during the colonial period.*

Institutions of social solidarity among our people are extremely rare. In general, here, man lives isolated within large rural properties or his family circle. The scope of social unity is highly restricted.

From *Populações meridionais do Brasil* (1920; reprint ed., Rio de Janeiro: Editora Paz e Terra, 1973), 155–63, 266–69. Reprinted by permission of Editora Paz e Terra. Translated by G. Harvey Summ.

This absence of institutions of solidarity and cooperation, principally at the neighborhood level, so common and numerous among older Western peoples, is much more surprising because the Portuguese, whose civilization absorbed that brought by the Indian and by the Negro, possessed and still possess various forms, and not a few, of neighborhood solidarity. The old medieval "councils," with their basic charters and their fine defensive organization, popular and civic in nature, disappeared completely after being transplanted here with the first colonizers. Not even the granting of special rights to certain towns and cities in the colonial period succeeded in imparting life to those esteemed Portuguese institutions.

Likewise, other seats of social cooperation that flourished in the Portuguese tradition did not take root here. Such was the case with the fine village festivals, the harvests, and the stamping of the grapes, which on the Peninsula took place with the assistance of neighbors. Neither the cotton harvest in the north and the coffee harvest in the south nor the rice or corn harvests brought about similar kinds of neighborhood cooperation. All these activities here are burdensome and sad and are undertaken by the families of small farmers themselves or on large properties by slave labor, but always without the festive atmosphere of joy and sociability that characterizes this work in the Lusitanian countryside.

Only in regions where there are large holdings, where pastures are the rule—on the pampas of the south and the scrub country of the north—can some rudiments of solidarity and cooperation be made out. In the south, the "rodeos," and in the north, the noisy "roundups," give us examples of organized, neighborly oneness; both broaden the area of social solidarity a little beyond the family nucleus. Real, traditional cooperation of neighbors exists there.

In the agricultural zones, where large independent holdings are common, even this rudimentary solidarity diminishes and disappears; lack of unity is complete. No kind of association among neighbors for a common purpose can be discovered there. Everything gives us the desolate impression of disarticulation and disorganization.

Other examples of solidarity among neighbors are the custom of helping the sick and the pious tradition of "sitting in the room" of the dead, an action which, in rural areas, bears the holiness of sacred obligation. But those expressions of neighborhood solidarity, unknown in large urban centers, come only from the impulses of affection and moral delicacy that are so common among our race; they are not really forms of social cooperation, of joint action for a common purpose.

In hamlets, villages, and towns of the backlands, there is another example of this kind of association: local "philharmonic" groups. These bodies, however, are temporary in nature, and really only last when rivalries among them result in organizing factions or "parties," the only type of association that the "herd spirit" inherent among the lower class allows to be formed among us, outside the planter clans.

These, in truth, are our only displays of solidarity, the only typical forms that our people have succeeded in organizing during our four centuries of history. This lack of solidarity results from the fact that, out of these multiple agents of social synthesis, so decisive in integrating European societies, in our whole history not even one of these factors drew our rural clans toward concentration and solidarity. On the contrary, since our first century these clans have kept their initial isolation, the product of the system of large independent landholdings, and even today they have not succeeded in raising their social organization above the small human group that makes them up.

Over this long period of four centuries, foreign enemies, in effect, were not a serious problem. Furthermore, there were no serious threats from internal enemies, either from aborigines or slave rebellions.

Another agent of solidarity, hostility between classes, so efficient in the organization of Western peoples, likewise did not function here. That integrating force was missing in our plantation nobility. No class could turn on the landowners, because all classes, through the simplifying factor of the large landholding, were attracted to the rural aristocracy and allowed themselves to be absorbed by it. Meanwhile, class struggle was not only one of the greatest forces for solidarity among Western peoples, but it was also the best school of civic education and political culture. In our history class conflicts were extremely rare. When they did break out, they were invariably ephemeral, occasional, discontinuous, and local.

All of it did not remotely compare with the secular, if not millennial, struggles of social classes in the West. Our insignificant struggles pale in comparison. They lasted a very short time, took place in very restricted areas, and had entirely negative effects on the political and social development of our nation.

Moreover, our rural nobility never suffered the tyrannical pressure of power like its European counterparts. Our nobility was harassed, subjected to extortion, and even blocked in its attempts at gaining power, but that harassment, that extortion, and those obstacles only resulted in the resentment of rural magnates against Crown officials; it did not reach the point of forcing them into permanent defensive concentrations, as in the case of the Saxon barons at the time of the Magna Carta.

So neither battles with external enemies, the most important impetus toward social cohesion since the troglodyte hordes; nor the struggle with the unconquerable aborigine, so efficient for the unification of small Saxon settlements on the Atlantic coast of North America; nor a reaction against

Negro assailants hiding at the edge of the forest; nor defense against a powerful dynasty, which so strengthened the character of embattled aristocracies of the Old World, were sufficient to implant the habits and customs of solidarity and cooperation in the social traditions of the rural nobility. No powerful pressure—coming from above from the powerful, coming from below from a lower class, coming from outside from an internal or foreign enemy—forced our tame and honest backwoodsmen, from the first century of colonization until now, to bond their efforts together in an undertaking of common defense. In sum: *except for the local solidarity of the rural clan, the unity of neighbors, especially that of the great chieftains of the rural world—the planters—never became necessary.*

Here there is no *society*; at most there exist certain rudiments of *sociability*. That great agent of gregariousness—the struggle against the common enemy—is undertaken neither against regional groups nor against the whole nation. Objectively, then, solidarity is reduced to the simple rural clan, and, subjectively, it is limited almost purely to family solidarity.

In truth, the Brazilian backwoodsman, as the development of four centuries illustrates, has not been able to achieve, politically, the conscience of *village solidarity*, like the Hindu pariah, or *tribal solidarity*, like the shepherd of the steppes of Pamir—because he never really felt the need for the "village" or the "tribe."

Political systems to which he has been subject or that he has tried to adopt assume that his mind-set contains a "local, a provincial, and a national consciousness." However, in his psyche, the rancher in the backlands, the farmer in the woods, or even the city dweller does not reach the point where he feels a part of his local community—unlike the citizen of the Greek "city," the burgher of the medieval "commune," or the resident of the old "council" of the Iberian Peninsula.

In addition to these cases of forced solidarity, defensive solidarity, and solidarity imposed by the instinct of self-preservation, there also exist peaceful solidarity, voluntary solidarity, and solidarity for the conquest of a common interest.

In order to ensure safety of transport, we have seen that peoples of the East and West have resorted to impressive measures to ensure their unity. Desert Arabs, for example, trading between Asia and the African shore of the Mediterranean, across the Sahara, formed large and strongly organized caravans to protect themselves against attackers, who gathered in frightening hordes. Similarly, to carry their products from the remote stretches of the North and Baltic Seas, the great German traders of the Middle Ages organized themselves into powerful groups.

Our large rural landowners never felt this urgency. Not only large ranchers, who transported their herds themselves, but all other landowners had, on their own properties, ways of moving their products safely to coastal trading centers. They organized and sent numerous expeditions to the coast with rustic leather bags full of cereals, coffee, or sugar—and they did not fear anything. Their own police actions early on contained and destroyed the banditry of runaway slave groups.

Since the earliest settlements, therefore, transport from production centers to coastal consumption centers was not subject to serious, general, or permanent obstacles that could have generated or established noticeable traditions of cooperation and joint effort in our rural population.

Nothing, therefore, in our history, national or local, has forced sugar and coffee planters—that is, the great heads of rural clans—to engage in the prolonged and habitual practice of cooperation and solidarity. On the contrary, everything tended to disunite, to separate, to disintegrate, and to isolate them. In vain will you look among them for those private associations for moral or social purposes so common in Germanic peoples, especially among the Anglo-Saxons of three continents.

These forms of voluntary solidarity, of free and spontaneous cooperation, only appear among us as the result of great collective enthusiasms: in cold blood we do not create them nor do we ever maintain them instinctively and automatically as do the Anglo-Saxons. Political parties, humanitarian groups, associations formed for moral ends, or recreational clubs—all these forms of joint action are artificial and of short duration among us. Once organized, they are soon dissolved, either because of internal bickering or because we quickly forget their original purposes. On other occasions, they are simply abortive attempts, which break up and disappear shortly after launching, smoothly and silently—which proves their lack of foundation in the normal psychology of the people. Normally the circle of our active interest does not effectively go beyond clan solidarity. That is the only form of social solidarity that we really feel, the only one we really practice. . . .

The distinctive characteristic of the English people is really a multi-century struggle between royalty of foreign origin, violent and extortionary, and a people profoundly conscious of its traditional liberties.

Among us, those splendid rights and liberal guarantees are only the literary conquests of an aristocratic minority of orators, publicists, and thinkers. Our people never fought for them, or at least we never fought intrepidly and gallantly, like the English, to defend those rights against the violence and the arbitrariness of their kings. Unfortunately, there never fell among us that "lasting blessing" [in English in the original]—a succession of bad governments and tyrannical princes. We have always lived in an atmosphere of diffuse semiauthoritarianism of sentimental petty tyrants, some of them even spineless, inconsistent, fiberless, and amorphous.

This singular absence of oppressive and cruel tyrants, this nonexistence of selfish and exploitative oligarchies, this lack of class or race conflict, this peace, this tranquility, this moderation that so characterizes our political history and distinguishes it from the political histories of other peoples—naturally, for all this, extremely complex and multiple factors are responsible. But there is no doubt that all these singularities will remain inexplicable, if, to explain them, we do not introduce, along with the above-mentioned historical and social factors, the effect of another, extremely special ingredient, which is imponderable and subtle but powerful—the *nature of the people*.

This system of misgovernment, which prevents neither order nor progress, is explained by the nature of the people, by their imprecise spirit of equity, justice, and moderation and by their fine moral sensibility, extremely rich in noble and gentlemanly attributes. In any other part of the world, such a system, in which all give orders and no one obeys, would have degenerated into Mexican anarchy or Argentine turmoil and would have made society return to the era of the caveman.

On the contrary, the generous and affectionate sentiments of our people and their fundamentally sweet and soft temper have made our historical environment unfit in any way for the birth of those cruel and bloody tyrants that we see, for example, in Hispanic-American republics. That sadistic need for revenge and persecution that characterizes tiger-like dictators is morally impossible among us. Given the extreme delicacy of our spiritual sensibility, such reactions are repugnant to us.

In this sense, we are among the most generously endowed people of the world. What we lack in political ability is more than made up for by the wealth of incalculable spiritual attributes. These correct, attenuate, or even reduce the inconveniences and evils that the dearth of the other characteristics should bring.

II

The Colonial Era (1500–1822): A Patriarchal and Hierarchical Society

In 1500 a Portuguese expedition under Pedro Alvares Cabral discovered Brazil. For almost a century daring Portuguese navigators had been exploring the Atlantic as well as the shores of Africa and Asia. Portugal, one of the world's leading empires of that era, was interested in conquest, plunder, and trade and had neither the population nor the inclination for settlement.

In Brazil the Portuguese found a hot and humid tropical forest inhabited by native Indians, numbering over two million, living as hunters and gatherers in small, scattered tribes with no form of intertribal political organization. Many of them fled rather than adapt to the regular labor for which the Portuguese sought them. They were further decimated by their resistance to the Europeans and by disease.

Brazilwood, the dyewood that gave the new colony its name, offered only modest prospects to the settlers. Private merchants, licensed by the Portuguese Crown, exported the wood until the supply gave out, and they also engaged in other small-scale agricultural activities. The economy depended upon the export of a succession of primary products. After dyewood and sugar in the sixteenth century, colonists found gold and diamonds in the late 1600s. Later, coffee and rubber were principal export crops. The vagaries of worldwide demand, other European countries' more modern production methods, and/or exhaustion of the supply of minerals led to frequent boom-and-bust cycles.

Beginning in the 1530s, the Crown, an absolute monarchy, granted huge captaincies—hereditary tracts extending inland from the coast—to royal favorites. In turn, those large landholders granted smaller concessions to other colonists. The captains were held responsible to the Crown by virtue of a series of detailed decrees from Portugal, but they received little financial help.

Whether on their self-sufficient plantations or living as absentee landlords in nearby towns, planters and ranchers acted as employers, patrons, and heads of large clans or extended families. They recruited settlers, enacted laws, provided for armed forces, levied and collected taxes, ruled the native population, and engaged clergy for religious duties. Their writ was often so vast as to be unenforceable over large, outlying parts of their territories. The captaincies of Pernambuco in the Northeast and São Paulo (originally called São Vicente) in the Southeast were the more successful ones.

In 1549, Portugal revoked or cut back on many of the captaincy grants and created a central colonial administration under a governor-general based in Salvador, Bahia. The captaincies then evolved into provinces. Royal governors and, at times, local chieftains, organized the population to help fend off hostile raids and the occupation of coastal areas by French and Dutch forces, but the colony experienced no serious threats from foreign enemies, native tribes, or civil unrest. Royal supervision provided jobs for colonial bureaucrats, but enforcement over most provinces was lax, particularly from 1580 to 1640, when Portugal was occupied by Spain. The adaptable colonists devised ingenious ways to avoid complying with the mass of the mother country's confused and contradictory decrees aimed at enforcing mercantilist policies and levying heavy taxes. Few institutions of self-government emerged.

After quickly exhausting the native population as cheap labor, the Portuguese, a people of mixed cultural and racial heritage, turned to the African slave trade. About 3.5 million blacks were transported from Africa to Brazil, by far the largest number to be taken to any destination in the New World. Because most of the first settlers did not bring women, widespread racial mixing began early. Slavery affected Brazilian customs and attitudes profoundly, and the treatment of slaves varied widely. Humble, obedient, and loyal house slaves were sometimes granted their freedom. On the other hand, beginning in the sixteenth century, unplanned fugitive slave communities called *quilombos*, formed in reaction to harsh discipline, injustice, and mistreatment, sprang up in rural areas.

To protect morals and preserve values, Portuguese Catholic missionaries accompanied the discoverers from the earliest days of settlement. A few courageous Jesuit missionaries tried—with limited success—to defend Indians from exploitation. However, pressure from landowners prevented the clergy, many of whom were ignorant and corrupt, from launching similar efforts to protect African slaves. Folk festivals, processions, shrines, pilgrimages, and millenarianism, typical of Portuguese Catholicism, as well as a willingness to syncretize African religious practices, characterized Catholicism in Brazil.

Beginning in the 1600s, groups of *bandeirantes* (flag-carrying frontiersmen) set out on westward expeditions, mainly from São Paulo, into the *sertão* (backlands) in search of gold, precious metals, Indian slaves, and souls to convert. The small frontier posts established by the *bandeirantes* (some of mixed race) helped to extend Brazil's boundaries westward. The discovery of gold and diamonds in the late 1600s led to a mining boom and to growth in Brazil's stature and in its confidence in its destiny. Interior urban settlements grew, principally in Minas Gerais and São Paulo provinces. Brazil's center of gravity moved southward, and the port of Rio de Janeiro, accessible to both those provinces, became the capital in 1763. However, as the mining boom petered out and Portugal's decline continued, insurrections began in the colony. The seed of Brazil's independence movement was sown by a rebellion (the so-called Inconfidência Mineira) in Minas Gerais in the late 1700s that was put down brutally by colonial authorities.

Thus, Brazil's later development as a patrimonial state—that is, a highly flexible and paternalistic public order under the tutelage of a small political and economic elite—was the result of the captaincy system established in the colonial period. Other legacies of the captaincies included a landowner-dominated patriarchal and hierarchical society, a slave-owning and highly unequal plantation economy, an extractive get-rich-quick mentality, submissiveness, and the avoidance of manual labor.

3 *Paulo Prado* ◆ Essay on Sadness

Paulo Prado, a coffee planter and exporter from a distinguished Paulista family, was born in 1869. After earning a law degree, he traveled widely in Europe. He was one of the principal sponsors of the famous Modern Art Week of 1922 in São Paulo and a leader of the Brazilian "modernist" movement of the 1920s in art and literature. In addition to his Retrato do Brasil *(Portrait of Brazil), published in 1928, from which this selection is taken, he wrote a history of São Paulo, entitled* Paulística. *He died at the age of seventy-four.*

"Essay on Brazilian Sadness" is the subtitle of Prado's Retrato do Brasil. *This excerpt summarizes the book's main theme, that the Portuguese discoverers' sensuality and insatiable lust for gold and rapid enrichment were responsible for the sadness in the Brazilian character.*

In a radiant land there lives a sad people. The discoverers who opened that land to the world and settled it bequeathed to it that melancholy. . . .

Just as the primitive, individualistic, and anarchic settler, avid for pleasure and an unfettered life, came to us from the Europe of the Renaissance so also came the Portuguese government official and the clergy. He was the colonizer. He was our European ancestor. At the first contact with the physical and social environment in his exile, new and extremely varied influences took possession of him and changed him into a new being, neither the same nor different from the man who had left the mother country. Two tyrannical sentiments dominated him: sensuality and passion for gold. The history of Brazil lies in the way that the disorderly development of those obsessions subdued the spirit and the body of its victims. Three factors contributed as accomplices to that exaggerated eroticism: the climate, the land, and the native or African slave woman.

In the virgin land everything stimulated the cultivation of sexual vices. At the end of a century of discovery, what we know of the beginnings of the then-existing society is a testimony to erotic madness. From these excesses of sensual life there remained indelible traces in the Brazilian character. The effects of exhaustion were not limited to sensory and vegetative functions; they extended to the realm of intelligence and feelings. They produced somatic and psychic disturbances in the organism, accom-

From *Retrato do Brasil: Ensaio sobre tristeza brasileira*, 6th ed. (Rio de Janeiro: Livraria José Olympio Editora, 1962), 3, 99–103. Translated by G. Harvey Summ.

panied by profound fatigue, that easily took on pathological aspects ranging from disgust to hate. In addition, another sentiment springing forth from this passion rose in the soul of the conqueror and settler, one which spoke of his materialistic sterility: a fascination for gold, to the point of madness.

A representative and picturesque example of the excitement to which these violent passions led was Sebastião Pinheiro Raposo, an explorer. Coming from São Paulo, he ranged through the backlands of the North and the Northeast with his band of comrades and Indian and Negro slaves, leaving everywhere a bloody trail and a legend of wealth. A band of slave women, with whom he had numerous children, accompanied him. On one occasion two of them, exhausted by the mountainous journey, fell dead by the side of the road. The explorer had them thrown off a precipice, because "he did not want to leave them alive to serve anyone else." He was reputed to be extremely rich, with his leather bags always full of gold; they were his "sacks of money," it was said. They called him the King of Gold and Lust.

In the struggle between these appetites—undertaken and continued without any other ideal, either religious or aesthetic, without any political, intellectual, or artistic concern—over the course of centuries, a sad race was created. The melancholy of those afflicted with venereal disease and those who lived with the fixed idea of enrichment—in the purposeless absorption of these insatiable passions—formed deep tracks in our racial psyche. These passions developed here from a pathogenic origin, doubtless provoked by the absence of higher-level affection. The inhabitant of the colony was born, lived, and grew in that special atmosphere.

From the weakening of physical energy, from the absence or diminishing of mental activity, one of the characteristic results among both men and groups is undoubtedly the development of a propensity toward melancholy. *Post coitum animal triste, nisi gallus qui cantat* [after intercourse animals are sad, except for the cock who crows], says the old medical adage; that is, the doctors say "collapse," or physical and moral depression, temporary under normal conditions, is continuous in the case of repeated excess. In Brazil sadness followed the intense sexual life of the settler, for generations diverted toward erotic perversion. For its part, greed, with its own symptoms, causes, and development, is a morbid state, a sickness of the spirit. It can absorb all of one's psychic energy, with no remedy or cure for its evils. Among us, for centuries it was an unsatisfied passion that became a fixed idea because of the very disappointment that accompanied it. Greed absorbed all the dynamism of the adventurous settler whose desire for riches or the simple tranquility of a goal achieved was never satisfied. In its hungry anxiety, in the disillusionment of not finding gold, this feeling is also melancholy because of the uselessness of the effort and the rancor resulting from disillusionment.

Lust, greed: melancholy. In groups, just as with individuals, it follows a psychopathic course: physical and moral depression, fatigue, insensibility, apathy, and sadness. In turn, sadness, by slowing down vital functions, brings weakness and changes the amount of oxygen that gets to the cells. This produces more aggravation of the disease, leading to agitation, lament, and violent convulsions. Was melancholy caused by the climate, living habits, food, or the healthy or poor functioning of the endocrine glands (which science is beginning to study)?

4 *Preston E. James* ◆ The Brazilian El Dorado

Preston E. James, a prominent American geographer specializing in Latin America, was a professor at the University of Michigan and at Syracuse University. He made many field trips to Brazil and was a consultant to the Brazilian government. James wrote extensively on Latin American geography and was a leader in academic circles in organizing geographic activities in the Americas and in the United States. James's works include the classic Latin America *(1942),* Brazil *(1946), and* American Geography: Inventory and Prospect *(1954). Here, he examines the get-rich-quick aspect of the Portuguese colonial period.*

None of the many advantages and disadvantages inherent in the physical makeup of Brazil have real significance for us in terms of human settlement until we know about the people and their way of living. Perhaps nowhere on the earth is there a greater mixture of different kinds of people than in Brazil. The primary ingredients are Portuguese, Indian, and Negro, but during the past century the population has been much altered by the arrival of millions of immigrants from Europe and Asia. All these elements have mixed freely, for one of the important traits brought by the Portuguese was the absence of any taboo against race mixture, except among the aristocracy. Each ingredient, therefore, has given certain easily observable physical characteristics to the new race of Brazilians, and has contributed numerous culture traits to the Brazilian civilization.

From *Latin America* (New York: Lothrop, Leed, and Shepard Company, 1942), 399–400.

The Indians who inhabited Brazil in 1500 were chiefly of Tupi-Guarani stock—a linguistic group to which the Indians of Paraguay also belong. In almost every respect these Indians of eastern South America were a contrast to the Quechuas of the Andes. The Tupi-Guarani tribes were hunters, fishers, collectors, and shifting cultivators. They lived in small, scattered groups with no form of intertribal political organization. Their basic food crop was manioc rather than maize. It is estimated that the Indian population of 1500 in all of Brazil was only about eight hundred thousand.

As a source of labor, the Tupi-Guarani proved quite inadequate. In the first place, great numbers of them died of European diseases in the early years of the conquest. Those who survived were handicapped by the traditional Indian attitude toward work. Agriculture was left to the women; the men devoted themselves to hunting, fishing, and fighting. The men could not adjust themselves to the agricultural work demanded by the Europeans. Free intermarriage, however, between the Portuguese men and the Indian women introduced many of the physical and psychological traits of the Indians into the resulting population.

Negroes, also, made an important contribution to the composition and character of the Brazilian people. Beginning in 1538, Negro slaves from Africa were brought across the ocean, especially to the Brazilian Northeast, where there was a demand for field hands in the new sugar industry. The Negro was not only a good worker, but he also possessed a knowledge of technological processes which has often been overlooked. The Negroes of the Sudan, it should be remembered, were the inventors of the process of iron smelting. This technological ability they brought with them to Brazil, along with their rhythmic music and their superstitions. The Negro foremen on the plantations, or later in the gold mines, knew more about the technological processes than did many of the Portuguese owners. From the seventeenth to the nineteenth century, agricultural and mining enterprise in Brazil owed a large debt to the Negro laborers and technicians.

From the Portuguese, however, came the main characteristics of the Brazilians. Even before their departure from Europe, the Portuguese were already made up of a most remarkable variety of racial and cultural elements, inherited from the various peoples who had successively conquered the Iberian Peninsula. Like the Spaniards, they included ingredients of Celtic, Nordic, and Mediterranean origin; and especially in the south of Portugal, around Lisbon, there was a large mixture of Moorish blood and of Moorish and Semitic culture traits. Moreover, the Portuguese from Lisbon were familiar with the use of Negro labor, for slaves had been brought to this part of Portugal in considerable numbers during the period of Moorish rule. Like the Spaniards, too, the Portuguese had the traditions of feudalism and of large private estates—traditions which profoundly influenced the relations of people to the land throughout Latin America.

The Portuguese had long been accustomed to commerce and to adventuring in distant places when they came to America in search of quick wealth. Like most of the Europeans who came to the New World—including the English—the foremost objective was to loot the rich resources of a virgin land. The Portuguese were much less interested than the Spaniards in implanting their institutions in America; they had little of the fanatical zeal for the spread of Christianity that their Spanish brothers possessed. They were attracted less by the prospects of earning a living by persistent toil than by the opportunities for speculative profit. As one Brazilian writer [Sérgio Buarque de Holanda (see Selection 24)] puts it, the ideal was "to collect the fruit without planting the tree." Whereas some of the peoples of America have been led by force of circumstances to be content with less spectacular returns from more intensive forms of economy, the Brazilians, with their huge land area, their superlative resources, and their small numbers, are still seeking new ways for the speculative exploitation of the treasures stored up in nature. This is the Brazilian variation of the theme of El Dorado.

5 *Keith S. Rosenn* ◆ Circumventing Legal but Unrealistic Obligations

Keith S. Rosenn is associate dean and professor at the University of Miami, where he has been a member of the faculty of the law school since 1979. He formerly taught law at Ohio State University and was a project associate for the Ford Foundation in Rio de Janeiro from 1966 to 1968. He specializes in Latin American law, particularly the systems in Brazil, Argentina, and Chile. Rosenn's Foreign Investment in Brazil *(1991) expands on a report prepared while he was a consultant for the World Bank; it deals comprehensively with the foreign investment climate in that country.* Regulation of Foreign Investment in Brazil: A Critical Analysis *(1983) deals in more detail with the regulatory aspect of foreign investment. Other works include* Law and Development in Latin America: A Case Book *(1975) and* Law and Inflation *(1982). In this selection, Rosenn discusses*

From "The Jeito: Brazil's Institutional Bypass of the Formal Legal System and Its Developmental Implications," *American Journal of Comparative Law* 19 (Summer 1971): 515–26, 528–31, 534–35. Footnotes omitted.

in detail the Brazilian paralegal institution known as the jeito, *a legacy of the colonial period.*

Brazilian laws and regulations are regularly twisted to the demands of expediency by government officials and private citizens alike. Brazil is not unique in this respect; bending of legal norms to expediency occurs in all countries, be they developed or developing. . . . But what is striking about Brazil is that the practice of bending legal norms to expediency has been elevated into a highly prized paralegal institution called the *jeito*. The *jeito* is an integral part of Brazil's legal culture, and in many areas of the law it is employed normally rather than exceptionally.

The *jeito* is easier to describe than to define, for the Brazilians use the term and its diminutive, *jeitinho*, in many different senses. . . . For analytic purposes the *jeito* can be broken down into at least five different kinds of behavior frequently observed in Brazil:

1) When a public servant deviates from his legal obligations because of private pecuniary or status (friends, family, or clique) gains. *E.g.*, a government contract is awarded to the highest briber.

2) When private citizens employ subterfuges to circumvent legal obligations which are sensible and just (in an objective sense). *E.g.*, a few essential parts are removed from an illegally imported car, which is reported to the authorities as contraband; when the car is sold at public auction, as required by law, the smuggler, who is the only one with the missing parts, is the only bidder, thus enabling him to sell the car with a clear legal title.

3) When the speed with which a public servant performs his legal obligations depends upon private pecuniary or status gains. *E.g.*, a passport application remains unprocessed for months unless the applicant knows or tips someone in the passport office.

4) When private citizens employ subterfuges to circumvent legal obligations which are unrealistic, unjust, or wasteful (in an objective sense). *E.g.*, real property is transferred by an agreement of sale rather than by deed to avoid capital gains taxation on nominal profits rendered largely illusory by severe inflation.

5) When a public servant deviates from his legal obligations because of his conviction that the formal norms are unrealistic, unjust, or wasteful. *E.g.*, a labor inspector condones the failure of a marginal firm in an area of high unemployment to pay the official minimum wage on the theory that strict enforcement

would likely throw many employees out of work and perhaps shut down the plant altogether.

The first two elements constitute the dishonest behavior benefiting an individual at the expense of the state—the conventional conception of corruption. The third element may also be labeled corruption by conventional standards, though most people, particularly in Brazil, would consider this kind of behavior less morally offensive than the first two forms of corruption. It is the fourth and fifth components, which illustrate behavior in which public purposes are served by evading legal norms, that bear no stigma and have made the *jeito* into such a highly prized national institution.

Obviously these categories are not mutually exclusive. Some civil servants become aware of a law's uneconomic or unjust aspects only after their palm has been greased. Occasionally, public officials cooperate with private citizens in legitimizing or facilitating vitiation of legal norms by subterfuge, such as occurred with Brazil's rent control. Residential rents remained frozen during a seventeen-year period in which the cost of living rose at an annual average of more than 22 percent. The statutes prohibited the landlord from raising the rent or evicting the tenant, but permitted the landlord to retake the premises for his own use or that of his family. Many landlords simulated a personal need for the leasehold in order to secure an under-the-table rent increase or evict an undesired tenant. Recognizing the injustice created by the statutes, the courts facilitated this simulation by placing the burden of proving the insincerity of the request upon the tenant, a priori an almost impossible task. This type of *jeito* incorporates both the fourth and fifth elements of the above schemework. . . .

The Colonial Background of the *Jeito*

The development of the *jeito* cannot really be understood without a brief historical background. The roots of the *jeito* run deep into the Portuguese past, which still conditions Brazilian attitudes toward governmental functioning. . . .

The Legacy of Administrative Chaos. Portuguese rule was essentially authoritarian, paternalistic, particularistic, and ad hoc. Scanning the confused and contradictory mass of statutes, orders, opinions, regulations, decrees, edicts, and instructions . . . through which the sovereign's will was transmitted to the Brazilian colony, one is amazed that the administrative machinery functioned at all. Equally astonishing is [an] extraordinary preoccupation with trivia. . . .

The Portuguese did bequeath the Brazilians a canon of statutory interpretation that is but a step removed from the *jeito*. The *Lei da Boa Razão* (Law of Good Sense), enacted on August 18, 1769, . . . directed the judiciary to apply Roman law to fill legislative lacunae only when it accorded with "good human sense." . . . It encouraged judges and lawyers to look to common sense and the spirit of the law as the basis for decision. . . . Thus, the Brazilian custom of reinterpreting laws in the light of good sense has enjoyed a respectable and long-standing heritage in Portuguese positive law.

The Weakness of Portuguese Control. With a population estimated at only one million in the fifteenth century, Portugal lacked sufficient manpower to enforce rigid controls over its widespread empire. . . . Moreover, Portugal ceded more extensive jurisdictional powers to Brazil's original colonizers than did other colonial powers and subsequently had great difficulty reestablishing the authority of the Crown over the great landholders. Particularly in the backlands, Portuguese administration was ineffective. Justice (what there was of it) was in practice administered by large landowners who controlled the military in their area. . . . Additional flexibility and autonomy for colonial administrators resulted from the Iberian practice of encouraging all officials and even the meanest vassal to appeal directly to the king if they disagreed with the order or policy of a superior.

The reputation of the colonial judiciary was one of inefficient venality. . . . Justice was regularly bartered like any other commodity, though delivered more slowly. Judicially collecting a debt was an extremely onerous, time-consuming, and expensive proposition, subject to many exceptions and much paperwork. Supervision over the notaries and judicial clerks was practically nil. Since these offices were frequently leased or subleased, sometimes for more than the position's salary, the investment in the office was commonly recouped through acceptance of bribes. . . . Though the statutes prohibited Brazilians from serving on the high courts and in other judicial capacities, in practice these statutes were continually bent to permit Brazilians to hold these posts. That most colonists preferred the justice of their own (or hired) hands, family, or friends to that of the king's magistrates was hardly surprising.

Several other factors contributed to the disregard for law that prevailed in colonial Brazil. Portugal punished serious crimes with exile to Brazil, making the colony a dumping ground for a sundry collection of social misfits, whose respect for law and order was attenuated prior to arrival. . . . The strict mercantilist policies and heavy taxation imposed by Portugal gave the Brazilians strong economic incentives for devising ingenious techniques to avoid compliance. As in other colonies, smuggling became a way of life. . . . Even if Portuguese law had been crystal clear and appropriately designed for Brazilian conditions, and the powers that were had been inclined to enforce it, a gap between the law on the books and practice would certainly have resulted from the lack of effective communications. One of the most striking features of Brazil is the enormity of its land mass. . . . Given the extreme precariousness of communications, decision makers have had to fall back on improvisation.

The Legacy of Portuguese Character

. . . One such legacy is a poorly developed expectation of honest, public-serving behavior by government officials. . . . The Portuguese also bequeathed the Brazilians a weak sense of loyalty and obligation toward the body politic, and a strong sense of loyalty and obligation toward family and friends. . . . The dominant attitude is reflected in the familiar Brazilian maxim: For friends, everything; for strangers, nothing; and for enemies, the law. . . .

A corollary of this stressing of direct personal relations might be termed the *coitado* complex, the compassion and sympathy which Luso-Brazilians so readily extend to those in unfortunate circumstances. If forced to opt between helping someone whom he pities and respecting a legal norm, the Luso-Brazilian frequently chooses the former. . . . The *coitado* is someone to be befriended, and once befriended, that direct, personal obligation rises above the impersonal, abstract legal norm. This national sentimentalism tends to soften the law's rigors and multiply instances of the *jeito*. . . .

Another important legacy has been Catholicism. . . . With its rigid dogmas, moral intolerance, great formalism, and slowness to change, Catholicism has stimulated considerable *jeito*-like behavior. More than 90 percent of Brazil's population is Catholic, but the great bulk are Catholic in name only, paying lip service to the precepts of the Church in much the same fashion as they pay lip service to much of the laws. . . .

The ability to conciliate and compromise has been developed into an art and a tradition by the Brazilians. This may have resulted from the natural obstacles encountered in colonizing such a vast territory with so few people and so little might. The history of Brazil is replete with examples of crises surmounted by resort to good sense and compromise instead of abstract philosophic doctrine. . . . The *jeito* is simply one manifestation of this proclivity, inherited from the Portuguese, for finding pragmatic ways out of impasses.

The Legal Culture

The paternalism which stemmed from the Portuguese monarchy, the Catholic Church, and the extended patriarchal family still permeates Brazilian society. It is commonly expressed in the *patrão* (patron) complex of traditional Brazil. In return for fealty and service the *patrão*, a member of the local elite, customarily looks after the interests of his employees, tenants, or debtors. The *patrão* plays the role of protector, interceding with the authorities when any of his flock is in trouble. This aspect of the *patrão* system serves to personalize and particularize legal relations for the lower class.

The ultimate *patrão* is the state, from which the Brazilians seem to expect just about everything. . . . Authority is tightly concentrated in Brazil, and there is a great reluctance to delegate it. . . . Because the government's view of what is best for the people does not always correspond with what the people view as best for themselves, Brazilians have been prone to act according to an old adage: He who can, gives orders; he who wants to, obeys.

The Brazilian culture is highly legalistic; that is, the society places great emphasis upon seeing that all social relations are regulated by comprehensive legislation. There is a strong feeling that new institutions or practices ought not [to] be adopted without a prior law authorizing them. . . . There is a "horror of a legal vacuum." Brazil has reams of laws and decrees regulating with great specificity seemingly every aspect of Brazilian life, as well as some aspects of life not found in Brazil. It often appears that if something is not prohibited by law, it must be obligatory.

Lawmakers are generally not content to set out desired conduct in general terms. In many areas they seem constrained to try to preregulate all possible future occurrences with detailed, comprehensive, and occasionally incomprehensible legislation. Situations that would typically be left to judges or administrators in other countries to work out on a case basis under the rubric of "reasonableness" are preordained by statute in Brazil. . . .

Legalism has contributed to the *jeito*'s popularity in two basic ways. It has led to a superabundance of regulatory legislation and a failure to build sufficient flexibility into that regulation. The *jeito* can be viewed as a legalistic response to both problems.

Closely related to legalism is the exaggerated concern with legal formalities. . . . The presumption appears to be that every citizen is lying unless he produces written, documentary proof that he is telling the truth. The formal legal system, whether ascertaining criminal guilt or issuing employment benefits, displays a decided tendency to believe only documents and not people. . . .

Another facet of formalism is the obvious discrepancy between concrete conduct and the legal norms designed to regulate such conduct. Brazilians commonly refer to laws in much the same manner as one refers to vaccinations. There are those which take, and those which do not. . . .

Many factors explain the prevalence of formalism in Brazil. . . . Independence brought little relief from legislation ill-suited to the demands of Brazilian society. In general, Brazilian laws have not been autochthonous; most have been imported wholesale from Europe or the United States with little, if any, consideration given to their suitability for implantation in Brazilian soil. This in turn is largely attributable to the way in which the legislative process functions. Most Brazilian legislation has been drafted by distinguished jurists or law professors in an atmosphere far removed from the clamor of special-interest groups. The draftsmen have typically consulted the various solutions to the problem that have been enacted abroad and tried to select the one that, as an abstract proposition, appears best, rather than seek a rule which crystallizes custom or practice. Seldom has there been a fact-finding inquiry about the peculiarly Brazilian nature of the economic, social, political, or administrative problems involved. . . .

The Bureaucratic Imbroglio

Intertwined with the problem of formalism and essential to a comprehension of the persistence of the *jeito* is the nature of the Brazilian bureaucracy. Historically, the bureaucracy has served as a means of employing educated persons whom the private sector could not absorb. This practice has imparted a "make work" character that has continued to the present day. . . . Voters are readily attracted by the promise of governmental jobs, and the Brazilians have humanely refrained from dismissing civil servants when regimes change. . . .

Political clientage, whose roots go back to the *patrão* system of colonial Brazil, still dominates the bureaucratic structure. One who owes his job to political clientage is less likely to be averse to doing favors for family or friends. Moreover, the influx of large numbers of untrained and unqualified personnel has itself generated more red tape, partially to give superfluous employees something to do, and partially to diffuse responsibility so that fixing blame for incompetence becomes more difficult. . . .

Bureaucratic practices could hardly be designed more appropriately to promote administrative inefficiency. Many departments are open but a few hours a day. A plethora of documents are required for any claim. . . . As a general rule, a person is compelled to run from place to place and endure the customary slow-moving lines many times before he has arranged all the necessary pieces of paper. Then he may be forced to wait weeks, months, or years while the process is sent up for "higher consideration."

In this setting it is relatively simple for civil servants to rationalize levying direct taxes upon those members of the public requiring their services. Brazilians complain, not without justification, that "they create difficulties in order to sell facilities."

6 *Stuart B. Schwartz* ◆ The Portuguese Heritage: Adaptability

Stuart B. Schwartz has been a professor of history at the University of Minnesota since 1967. He has also held visiting professor positions at the University of California and the Federal University of Bahia, Brazil. Schwartz has written mainly on colonial Northeast Brazil, with special emphasis on the social structure, slavery, sugar, peasants, and the judiciary. His books include: Sovereignty and Society in Colonial Brazil: The High Court of Bahia and Its Judges *(1973);* Early Latin America: A History of Colonial Spanish America and Brazil *(1983);* Sugar Plantations in the Formation of Brazilian Society, Bahia, 1550–1835 *(1985); and* Slaves, Peasants, and Rebels: Reconsidering Brazilian Slavery *(1991). In the excerpt that follows, Schwartz examines the Portuguese heritage in the country, knowledge of which he deems "crucial for an understanding of Brazil's past and present."*

There is a famous painting by Maria Margarida entitled *Tres Meninas da Mesma Rua*, which is often reproduced in books on Brazil. This painting symbolically depicts three beautiful girls representing each of the three major racial components of Brazilian society: Indian, Negro, and white. Anthropologists and other social scientists, perhaps lured by

From "The Uncourted *Menina*: Brazil's Portuguese Heritage," *Luso-Brazilian Review* 2 (Summer 1965): 67–80. Footnotes omitted.

the exotic, have ardently courted the first two young ladies in the sense that much attention has been given to the Indian and Negro elements in Brazilian society. The white girl, however, has been neglected. This is especially true of the Portuguese element of Brazil which is obviously so crucial for an understanding of Brazil's past and present. . . .

The Portuguese heritage of Brazil can be examined on two different levels. One is the administrative, official aspect which amounts to the history of Portuguese colonial control of Brazil. The other is the social and cultural heritage transferred not by the government of Portugal, but by the Portuguese people. The two are at many points difficult to separate, but it is the social and cultural tradition which will be discussed here. What were the characteristics of the Portuguese colonizers? What aspects of Brazilian life are the result of Lusitanian influence? These are the primary questions. Almost everyone who writes on Brazil agrees that the common denominator of Brazilian culture is basically Portuguese. There remains to be studied, however, what these elements are, what changes they underwent, and how they were integrated into Brazilian culture.

Certainly, the starting point of an examination of Brazil's cultural debt to Portugal must be a discussion of the development and character of the Portuguese people. The Portuguese at the time of the conquest of Brazil were not a racially homogenous group and their culture was a result of a variety of contacts and developments. The original Lusitanians had, through contact with Phoenicians, Romans, French and English knights, Moors, Jews, and Negroes, acquired a complex of traditions and values which formed the basis of Portuguese society. In a sense the Portuguese were a people of mixed cultural and racial heritage, a fact that would be important in their settlement of Brazil. . . .

The Portuguese have been called a mixture of dreamers and of men of action who do not lack a practical side to their nature. They can be extremely pragmatic and adaptable when faced with a problem that calls for a practical solution. This plasticity and adaptability has been considered by some to be the basic key to the success of Portugal in creating a lasting civilization in Brazil. As an active dreamer, the Portuguese, if given an ideal, is capable of great efforts through determined and persistent action involving self-denial, sacrifice, and courage. When, however, the task is mediocre and does not arouse his interest, he lacks initiative. . . . It was the stimulation of his imagination and interest for the glory of conquest and battle, the lure of wealth, and the service of religion which motivated the Portuguese in the Age of Discovery.

The heart is the measure of all things for the Portuguese and he is basically human, amorous, and affectionate. . . . The Portuguese has a strong belief in miracles and in the stroke of luck, as is evidenced by the popularity of the lottery in Portugal and as has been shown in the past by the cult of Sebastianism. This belief in miraculous solutions appears to have been inherited by the Brazilians, who have developed a *Deus é brasileiro* [God is Brazilian] attitude toward their problems. This attitude has been reinforced, however, by Brazil's own peculiar history, especially in view of its economic cycles and boom-bust-boom experience. . . .

An aspect of Portuguese character which the people of Portugal like to claim as theirs alone is that of *saudade*. *Saudade* is an untranslatable word which seems to be a combination of sentimentality, homesickness, and nostalgia. This *saudade*, this sadness of character, is a current which runs deeply throughout Portuguese literature. At times it can become fatalistic and even morbid. The soul-rending *fado* heard in Lisbon originated as an expression of the *saudade* of the Portuguese colonizer in Brazil for his homeland. This longing for Europe, for the metropolis, which characterized many Portuguese in Brazil during the colonial period, has been viewed as one of the worst aspects of the Portuguese heritage of Brazil, for its result was the *mazombismo* of Brazil which depreciated things Brazilian and looked toward Europe, first Portugal and then France, for a model. No less a friend of the Portuguese than Gilberto Freyre has said, "Since the end of the sixteenth century the Portuguese has lived parasitically on a past whose splendor he exaggerates." *Saudade*, however, in its less malignant aspects, is soft and sentimental—which is quite understandable when it is remembered that for the Portuguese the heart is the measure of all.

The penchant of the Portuguese for display and ostentation has been noted by many writers. Though there might be little to eat at home, there was always an air of pomp and gentry. . . . It seems, however, that this ostentation was not a matter of personal luxury and comfort but rather of imagination. Jorge Dias has noted that the Portuguese have the hardest beds in Europe, while the streets are filled with automobiles. Poor people who lack the least comfort in their home appear in the street in elegant dress. A similar situation was noted in colonial Brazil and still exists today in rural areas, where women whose dress at home may be ragged appear at Mass in finery to which all attention is given. This "Sunday best" is known in Brazil as *traje domingueiro* or *roupa de ver-a-Deus*. Gilberto Freyre, using Thorstein Veblen's term, has called this ostentation "conspicuous waste," and has noted that in the colonial period women who had so many jewels they could not wear them all at the same time often put them on the slaves who followed their mistresses to church.

Coupled with the ostentation of the Portuguese has been his attitude toward work. There existed, during the period of conquest, a depreciation of manual labor. Peasants, although they labored hard, shared the *fidalgo* ideal with the nobility. This attitude was found among the Spaniards as well. The Iberian hoped to get rich quickly, perhaps to own land, but not to labor. Work was for the slave. In fact, in Portugal the verb "to work," *trabalhar*, was often replaced with *mourejar*, "to work like a Moor." Perhaps this attitude of antipathy to manual labor was due to the fact that work indicates the submission of the individual will to an external force, and the Iberian with his emphasis on the individual could not condone this. The result in Brazil was a "*bandeirante* spirit" in which all energy was devoted to the quick profit. Even in agriculture the emphasis was on the large profit, and at times the Portuguese government had to legislate to force plantation owners to grow food crops. The result of this attitude was the development in Brazil of a "gentleman complex" which depreciated manual labor and emphasized nonfunctional education as a sign of breeding to be coupled with wealth. Even among the Brazilian lower classes the idea of the quick fortune is pervasive, and men in the Amazon often desert farming in hopes of a rapidly amassed fortune in rubber-hunting. In the mind of the Portuguese productive activity has had much less value than contemplation and love, and a dignified idleness always seemed more noble than the "insane struggle for the daily bread."

The most important aspect of Portuguese character, or at least the most often discussed, is his adaptability. The Portuguese lacks the flame and orthodoxy of the Castilian; rather, he is a compromiser without immutable prejudices who has been able to adapt to climates, occupations, cultures, and races in an exceptional manner. The quality of flexibility and tolerance of other races led in Brazil to miscegenation of an unprecedented extent. . . .

Much has been written on the capacity of the Portuguese people to mix with other races. . . . However, the scarcity of women may have had much to do with the extent of racial mixing, and in instances of colonization in Brazil in which the colonist was accompanied by his wife, as in Santa Catarina, much less miscegenation took place. Slavery, of course, played a role in the process of race mixture in Brazil. . . . The result of lasting importance was the creation of a psychological and cultural unity of the Brazilian people. . . .

The family in Brazil has been considered the most important institution in the history of the nation and has played a dominant role in the course of Brazil's history. . . . The prescribed roles of men and women in both the Brazilian and the Portuguese family are based on the virility/virginity complexes. The woman is expected to lead a secluded life, never appearing in public unless properly accompanied. . . . After marriage the woman is expected to be mother and housekeeper, not a companion to her husband. Virginity is a primary requisite before marriage, and should the bride be found lacking in this respect the groom has proper grounds for annulment of the marriage. Any extramarital relations on the part of the woman are considered grounds for separation. It is common, however, for a husband to kill both the unfaithful wife and her lover and then claim temporary insanity. This is expected and accepted community behavior.

In contrast to the female role in the upper-class Brazilian family is the virility complex of the male, which encourages sexual contact at an early age, ridicules male chastity, and considers extramarital sexual relations permissible. Within the home, however, the male is expected to act as guardian and protector. The males of the family are also expected to be avengers of the family's honor, especially that of its female members. This attitude in Brazil has been reinforced by immigration from Portugal, Spain, and southern Italy. Thus far, the above description can be applied to both Brazilian and Portuguese upper-class families.

The lower-class Brazilian family places much less emphasis on the virginity/virility complex. Marriage is far less stable, and extended kinship groups are not viewed as of great importance . . . the patriarchal, extended family lessens in importance as one descends the social scale. . . . The rural Brazilian family is weak, for it can offer little, and its children tend to leave the paternal home to seek better-paying jobs. . . . The original Portuguese family structure did not remain unchanged in Brazil but was altered to meet ecological, human, and economic conditions, and due to these new changes new structural organizations developed.

The patriarchal family usually attributed in its origins to Portugal must undergo some review, since it has been discovered that in some regions the patriarchal family is not as dominant an institution as had been thought. . . . In Brazil, similar developments can be noted which seem to be exceptions to the patriarchal generalization. Women in Sao Paulo of land-holding but not of planter-class families often raise their own produce and sell it, keeping the profits themselves. Occasionally, these women engage in speculative loans. These economic activities indicate a degree of independence not usually associated with the Brazilian woman. . . .

It is in the everyday life of the Brazilian, especially the rural Brazilian, that the Portuguese heritage is to be seen. The language of Brazil is Portuguese and the style of life of the Brazilian reflects the Portuguese heritage in a hundred ways. For example, the *mutirão*, or mutual work party, although found among Africans and Indians, can be seen in Alentejo, Beira, and Minho. The festivities in Brazil following a *mutirão* are found only in Portuguese origins. Here is but one more example of the duration of the Lusitanian element in Brazil.

The aspect of the Portuguese heritage of Brazil which is most apparent in everyday life and is probably easiest to study is that of the popular folk traditions of Brazilian society. Certainly, the administrative actions of the metropolis during the colonial period played an important role in the formation of Brazilian society just as the church did in conjunction with the Jesuit Order. But it is the popular rather than the official traditions to which I am referring. . . . Folk tales and folk songs, as well as *louvores populares* to the Virgin, can serve as a basis for tracing the transmission of Portuguese popular cultural elements to Brazil, especially since much work has been done on both sides of the Atlantic in collecting these songs and stories. . . . It seems that the custom of the *desafio*, the improvisation of verses by two contending balladeers so clearly explained by Euclides da Cunha in *Os sertões*, is a Lusitanian custom. . . . From infancy, the Brazilian child is exposed to the Portuguese heritage of his nation. The Brazilian's first games and playthings and even the bogeymen used to frighten him are of Lusitanian origin. . . .

Certainly, one of the most enduring aspects of Portuguese cultural heritage in Brazil is that of Catholicism: that special brand of Catholicism characteristic of Portugal. The agony-torn Christs of Spain and the soaring Gothic Spanish cathedrals are lacking in Portuguese Catholicism, which was and is a humanistic form of Christianity with anthropomorphic tendencies, often giving special importance to saints associated with love and agricultural fertility. . . . The parallelism and the cultural borrowing of Brazilian Catholicism from its Portuguese antecedents is extensive. The importance of shrines, pilgrimages, and the ceremony of the blessing, all so important in Brazilian Catholicism, stem from the Catholic traditions of Portugal. In both countries the June cycle of the three major saints—St. Anthony, St. John, and St. Peter—is a high point of the religious calendar, even though in Brazil June is a winter not a summer month as it is in Portugal. In Brazil and Portugal St. Anthony is a *santo pândego* or *santo folião*, a patron of revelry, a forgiver of human weakness, and a noted matchmaker to whom ribald songs are often sung. Also, saints' images are often treated like human beings and are punished or rewarded as their case may merit. It has been noted that Portuguese seamen who have prayed for a favorable wind and fail to receive it lash the saint's effigy to the mast and flog it. In Brazil a noncompliant saint's image may be put uncomfortably near a fire or even pounded to dust in a mortar.

[The] list of particularly Lusitanian features of Brazilian religion, especially in its folk manifestations, could be extended to great lengths. The impact of the Portuguese form of Catholicism on Brazilian religious and social life is undeniable. It must be remembered, however, that contact of Portugal with Brazil was a historical process extending over at least three centuries, and that the element of change is a part of this process. . . . To continue the analogy made at the beginning, the third *menina* deserves to be courted, for she comes from a fine old family which has left her a rich inheritance.

III

The Empire (1822–1889): No Real Rupture with the Past

Events elsewhere led to Brazil's independence. When French troops under Napoleon invaded Portugal in the Peninsular War, the royal family, escorted by the British navy, fled to Brazil in 1807–08 to avoid capture. In 1816, King João VI succeeded to the throne in Rio de Janeiro. After Napoleon's defeat and after dynastic struggles in Portugal had been resolved, João left Brazil in 1821 to resume his throne in Libson. To retain close ties between mother country and colony, he advised his son, Pedro, to remain, even if it meant creating a monarchy separate from the one in Portugal. However, with the support of proindependence Brazilian political leaders, Pedro forced a break with Portugal, which was in no position to resist, and declared the colony independent on September 7, 1822.

Brazil's very birth as a nation was thus a landmark that involved no real rupture with the past. Similar watershed events in its national life were the abolition of slavery in 1888, the shift from monarchy to republic in 1889, the overthrow of the republic in 1930, the seizure of power by the military in 1964, and the return to civilian rule in 1985. All came about by accommodation and with little violence, and without the implementation of dramatic economic or social reform. Pedro I, the first emperor of newly independent Brazil, working with a constituent assembly composed of provincial political leaders, produced a constitution for the new country in 1824. The empire was a centralized state, with tight restrictions on the right to vote based on property. A key constitutional clause allowed the emperor to exercise a "moderating power" to "oversee the independence, equilibrium, and harmony of the other political powers"—that is, the legislative and judicial branches of government.

After a relatively brief period, Pedro's arbitrariness and personal peccadilloes caused his initial popularity to quickly dissipate during power struggles with the Brazilian elite. In 1831 he abdicated and returned to Portugal, leaving behind his five-year-old son, who later became Pedro II. For the next nine years, however, Brazil was governed by a regency.

Young Pedro impressed political leaders sufficiently well that they crowned him emperor in 1840 at the age of fourteen. He assumed the broad powers granted him in the constitution and ruled conscientiously, soberly, and moderately for almost fifty years. He served as a respected symbol of national unity, enabling Brazil to survive separatist challenges and to halt a drift toward social revolution. So-called liberal and conservative ministers, members of a small, oligarchic, and unrepresentative elite, alternated in control of the parliament. Their policy differences were relatively unimportant. The mass of the population was ignored.

Brazil had about four million inhabitants at Independence. Roughly one half were slaves of African birth or descent. The economy was mostly agricultural, and sugarcane was the largest crop. The relatively few literate, cultured, and prosperous landowners, merchants, lawyers, and other professionals lived mainly in the cities—which were little more than small towns—and dominated society. Public life rested on ties between patrons and clients. A retinue numbering in the thousands had accompanied the royal family, and many were rewarded with government sinecures, vastly expanding the intrigue-filled and already cumbersome bureaucracy.

The vast majority of Brazilians, both free and slave, were illiterate, short-lived, and exploited by the small ruling minority. The presence of the expatriates from Portugal brought about glimmerings of culture, including the first printing press. In the 1840s the first university-level institutions were founded: law schools in Olinda and São Paulo and medical schools in Rio de Janeiro and Salvador.

The Brazilian social structure was narrow at the top and broad at the base. Derived from the Portuguese system of patron and client linked by mutual obligation, it was hierarchically, although not rigidly, based on race, wealth, and occupation. Land barons and their extended families, usually white, ruled from the plantation *casa grande* (big house) and from their houses in town. Next on the social scale, either white or of mixed race, were bureaucrats, priests, soldiers, artisans, smallholders, and peasants. Slaves were at the bottom.

Race in Brazil was not purely a biological matter; it was also a social concept, open to interpretation. Individuals often could not be labeled as being of one race or another. The poor were usually black, and blacks were usually poor, but a successful black might be considered white, while a poor white might be treated hardly better than a black. The blurred line between race and class allowed mulattoes and some blacks opportunities for upward mobility—usually through patron-client relationships—but also militated against the development of black solidarity. Some slaves possessed job skills. Freed slaves and a large mixed-blood population had some social mobility and thus were able to establish themselves economically.

In the midnineteenth century, a fundamental transition in the economy was one of several factors that eventually contributed to the end of the empire. Coffee production flourished, particularly in São Paulo. Paulista planters faced resistance from their counterparts in the economically decadent Northeast when they sought slave labor. By the 1880s they had launched a major effort to attract immigrants to work their plantations. Millions of European, mainly Italian, and later Japanese workers were brought in for coffee plantations in southern Brazil.

The abolition of slavery also hastened the empire's end. Great Britain, the dominant outside power after Brazil became independent, had pressed abolition on resistant slaveowners for over a half-century. The slave trade effectively ended in 1850, and a series of laws in the 1870s and 1880s further weakened slavery. To transform the country's retrograde slave-holding image in Europe, political leaders moved increasingly toward pro-abolition positions. Since slavery was nationwide, the abolition movement did not lead to sectional conflict.

The empire was further weakened as republicanism made inroads among the younger, university-educated sons of planters, merchants, and professional men. Abolitionist and pro-republican sentiment, provincial demands for autonomy, and impatience with an empire that increasingly seemed an anachronism led Brazilian politicians to favor a U.S.-style federal republic in place of an English-style constitutional monarchy.

After the War of the Triple Alliance (1865–1870), Brazil's only nineteenth-century foreign conflict, the army emerged as a factor in politics and contributed to the decline of the empire. At the start of the war the armed forces were mainly state militias, and a national army barely existed. Brazilians bore the brunt of the fighting, in which their country, Argentina, and Uruguay conquered an expansionist dictator of Paraguay. Postwar discontent in the army, neglected by Pedro II, led many officers to enter politics. Upwardly mobile army officers were frustrated by slow peacetime promotion prospects and meager appropriations for modernization and were convinced that their assignments in various parts of the country gave them a unique national perspective on Brazilian problems. They became especially receptive to abolitionist and pro-republican views.

French intellectual influences, strong in Brazil in the nineteenth century, also played a part in ending the empire. In particular, positivism, conceived by French philosopher Auguste Comte in the first half of the century, appealed to Brazilian reformers. Positivist doctrine called for a regimented social order based on "scientific" laws, and it maintained that history evolved in stages until it reached its final, "positive" one. In its authoritarian Brazilian form the doctrine had overtones of a civic religion. It penetrated faculties of higher education, especially military colleges, in the late nineteenth century. The reformers blamed Brazil's lethargy on its racially mixed underclass and its tropical setting. They defended individual liberties and condemned slavery. Insisting that order was necessary for progress, they fervently advocated a "republican dictatorship"—under their leadership—to bring about that progress and, in fact, were responsible for the motto "Order and Progress" on the new republican flag.

To Pedro II's critics, the latter stages of his reign seemed mediocre, tradition-bound, and bureaucratic. He had no male heirs, and toward the end of his rule did little to try to stem growing dissatisfaction with the empire. In 1888 the parliament voted overwhelmingly for abolition. In the following year, when military plotters, abetted by civilians, demanded that the emperor step down, he and his family left for exile in Portugal.

7 *Clodomiro Vianna Moog* ◆ José Dias: Cultural Symbol

Clodomiro Vianna Moog, born in 1906 in the southern state of Rio Grande do Sul, received his law degree at the age of twenty-four. He held various civil service positions, mainly in his home state, and became a journalist and novelist. An expert on Brazilian literature, he was elected to the prestigious Brazilian Academy of Letters in 1945. Moog traveled and lectured in the United States in 1942, and in subsequent years he served as a member of the Brazilian delegation to the United Nations and other international organizations and conferences, principally in the cultural field.

Moog wrote books on Brazilian history and Brazilian and Portuguese literature and also used the forms of biography and political analysis. His best-known book is Bandeirantes e pioneiros *(*Bandeirantes *and pioneers), originally published in 1954, which contrasts the Portuguese colonization of Brazil by* bandeirantes *(flag-bearers) with the English pioneering settlement of the United States. In this selection, Moog examines Brazilian institutions after the abolition of slavery and the end of the empire and attributes the country's economic backwardness to the continuation of traits introduced by the Portuguese during colonial times. He finds a cultural symbol in José Dias.*

After the impact of the first moments of Brazilian history, all was desire for quick riches, addiction to the past, dreams of returning to Europe, aggravated individualism, lack of concern with the moral aspects of life, and prejudice against useful labor. These factors and the lack of faith in human perfectibility left deep scars. For good or ill, they are still prominent among Brazil's social attributes.

To the American, profoundly Jeffersonian, man is generally good, and is bad only when he does not find conditions that permit him to be good. To the Brazilian, man is generally evil unless he proves the contrary. Doubts and distrusts not justified by his own experience or his own past cannot be removed.

The consequences are, in the United States: optimism, sympathetic receptivity, understanding, and goodwill toward men; in Brazil: the "foot behind" (as they call it), reserve, vigilance, and a diffuse ill will that polished words and emphatic declamations cannot disguise.

From *Bandeirantes e pioneiros*, 2d ed. (Porto Alegre, Brazil: Cia. Editora Globo, 1955). Translated by L. L. Barrett and published as *Bandeirantes and Pioneers* (New York: George Braziller, 1964), 202, 206–14, 222–24, 229–31. Adapted by G. Harvey Summ.

In the United States: stimulus, a good reception to initiative. In Brazil: distrust, discouragement, suspicion of hidden selfish interest in the highest purposes. In the United States: life understood as integration in a duty or a dream. In Brazil: life viewed as pursuit of wealth and pleasure, as a "wearisome trade," something quite irremediably prosaic.

In the United States, where the climate permits greater expenditures of energy: life facilitated and smoothed. In Brazil, where the climate requires conservation of strength: marches and countermarches to obstruct the simplest civil, commercial, and administrative operations.

In the United States: progressive capitalism, more and more conscious of its social responsibilities. In Brazil: capitalism which still believes in trusts and cartels, in small production and high prices, and which in its relations with its workers still battens on the feudal, paternalistic concepts of the eighteenth century.

In the United States: the good side of human nature being able to develop itself fully. In Brazil: backbiting, suspicion, fear of ridicule—that stupid Brazilian fear of ridicule—discouraging the positive qualities to the benefit of the negative.

In the United States: belief that goodness will win out over evil in the end, and health over sickness. In Brazil: doubts and mental reservations of every kind.

The differences between Brazilians and Americans in facing the essential problems of life and death, of joy and grief, of sickness and health, are endless. The insouciance with which Americans proclaim their states of gaiety, and the shamefaced way in which Brazilians conceal their fleeting states of happiness! They hide them as if they constituted scandalous monstrosities, real provocation to the gods. Scarcely does someone perceive their intimate joys when Brazilians shrink into themselves, grow serious, taken aback like a criminal caught red-handed. When they ought to laugh out loud, they barely smile. That broad guffaw that Homer passed down to Rabelais, the healthful belly laugh of the apogee of the Middle Ages and the Renaissance, is scarcely to be found among Brazilians. Their smile is rather the smile that Machado de Assis admittedly received from Lucian of Samosata, a smile that comes more from others' mistakes and ridiculous actions than from the euphoria of one's own joys.

But how loquacious, how prolix Brazilians are in their grounds for grief, their reasons for disquiet! Their susceptibilities, their idiosyncrasies, their moral and physical allergies, their sufferings—these they have not the least constraint in exhibiting, turning them over and over, discussing them, dissecting them in broad daylight. It is their weak point. They display those things in their talk, in their constant sighing, in eruptions of their prudery. Because the pearl is the oyster's disease, not to be sick of some real or imaginary disease is among Brazilians almost proof of poverty of spirit, a lack of self-respect, so much so that being sick is the general rule among them.

Is the conversation forced, does it fail to take shape, must it be enlivened at any cost? Why, you need only mention sickness. Then it becomes delirious. The flame of the mind, which was flickering, and the conversation, which was dragging, take on new life. The gathering becomes lively, fuses together new personal attractions, is prolonged until late into the night, and does not end before the last guest has exhausted, with luxuriant detail, his latest sufferings or his latest convalescence.

Fill out the framework of the story with details, deepen the colors of the dramatic passages, heighten the anguish of family and friends in the proper places, conjecture endlessly about analogous diseases and their specifics, in the style of instruction leaflets that accompany patent medicines, exaggerate the doctor's learning and his personal devotion (personal attention is particularly important, more important sometimes than his knowledge of his specialty). You will have an oral novelette certainly as successful among Brazilians as the stories of poor boys in which all turns out well are among Americans.

And here we come to the last of the fundamental outlines of Brazilian culture—the dislike of useful work and all that is connected with it: initiative, organization, cooperation, and the technical and scientific spirit.

After four centuries of exploration and patriarchalism, has the Brazilian attitude about creating a propitious atmosphere for technical and useful work been substantially and definitively altered? However much things have changed, Brazilians still cling to the prejudices of the past. How slow their evolution has been! Incredible as it may seem, not even the abolition of slavery changed things definitively and radically for the better, when everyone was hoping for miracles. In many ways, abolition actually aggravated the situation.

It was inevitable. On May 13, 1888, slavery was abolished in Brazil only legally and in very limited aspects. The United States enjoys all the economic advantages of abolition in the labor market, but maintains in the South the same racial prejudices as before. Brazil, on the other hand, enjoying all the consequences of abolition in terms of racial equality, forgot that emancipation could only be consolidated by raising the dignity of labor, and still nourishes absurd prejudices against work in many of its forms. Innumerable forms of work, instead of dignifying the individual, were held to lower and debase him.

The former masters and their descendants wanted to keep conceiving of life patriarchally, awaiting (and expecting) new privileges. Freedmen and descendants of freedmen, lacking better examples and better images, tried to conceal their origins. They held to the same reservations as their former masters about constructive, not merely ornamental, occupations: labor, craftsmanship, trade, specialization, mechanization, industry, and science. There would be no compromise with subordinate forms of labor necessary to industry, commerce, and farming. Such activities, everything other than the functions for which the *bandeirante* or the patriarch had some consideration—soldier, physician, lawyer, bureaucrat, priest, writer—if it was not becoming to people of high society with many centuries of real or supposed nobility in their veins, it was not becoming to the ex-slave.

Thus, in an essentially agricultural country, slave labor, the basis of Brazil's patriarchal economy, was abolished. The corresponding appreciation of free labor was not promoted. Not mechanics, engineers, chemists, agronomists, artisans, qualified skilled labor, and specialists: rather, thousands of law graduates with a ring on their finger to prove at a glance that they do not work with their hands; thousands of literary men filling public offices with stale air; thousands of candidates for the sinecure and the coveted title of *malandro* (sponger or cadger).

Instead of devotion to duty, lack of dedication by individuals toward tasks and occupations in their care; poor service, ill-finished work, inefficiency, deterioration, lack of punctuality, procrastination; work regarded as a dishonoring stain. In an atmosphere not propitious to belief in perfectibility, where skepticism and defeatism are the rule, nobody is satisfied with what he has, few put their hearts into what they do, all feel more or less robbed in what they have lost or in what they have not won.

Other consequences of these patrician restrictions on useful work are mere subsistence wages, as if the wage earner were no more than the substitute for the slave; morally, a swelling finickiness toward jobs linked with the shame of former slavery, vanity carried to sickly extremes, pedantry, self-sufficiency, the national cult of the hero who solves all situations without effort and without work, by craftiness, intrigue, calculation, astuteness.

Do you want to know the type capable of personifying the legion of good-for-nothing spongers the Empire bequeathed to the Republic? There is a stupendous example whose equal never has and probably never will be found. It is the hanger-on José Dias, in the novel *Dom Casmurro*, by Machado de Assis, the first complete historical symbol of the national *malandro*. Only that? No, much more, because José Dias is also the only integral, irrefutable, finished symbol of Brazilian culture. Caricatural and Rabelaisian symbol, if you will, but a symbol at all events.

To start with, he has the desire for quick riches and, naturally, a distaste for every kind of useful work. It may not be a desire for wealth as devouring as that in the two preceding centuries, the "sacred hunger" of the *bandeirantes*. It is still the desire one way or another to find a mine, or in the absence of a mine, at least to make a lucky strike that will allow him to do nothing. José Dias, when he first appears in Itaguaí, a place through which men passed in former days in quest of gold, is evidently wandering in search of adventure. A fever epidemic is laying waste the region. José Dias, who has with him a manual and a case of medicines, passing himself off for a homeopathic doctor, cures the overseer of a plantation and a slave woman, and will take no pay. This is a happy stroke. The grateful patriarch proposes that he stay there, with a small salary.

Soon José Dias has found his treasure. It is not much. But, lacking a mine—and mines have been scarce for a long time—it serves. At least he no longer needs to bother with a job, but only to defend his position in the house without working.

Everything goes just right for José Dias. But one day when another fever epidemic is raging in Itaguaí, the patriarch tells him to go to the plantation to look after the slaves. José Dias stands silent, sighs, and finally confesses he is no doctor.

He was not dismissed. The patriarch could no longer get along without him. The dependent had the gift of making himself agreeable and necessary. "His absence was felt as keenly as that of a member of the family."

José Dias had won his game, and had his "mine" all staked out and secure. So secure that when the patriarch died, the widow, very grateful for the grief that afflicts José Dias, will not let him give up his room. She insisted on his continuing as a family dependent.

We have here, therefore, very vividly, the two prime outlines of Brazil's development—the search for rapid wealth and the dislike for useful work—supplemented by the absence of professional preparation and a purely ornamental show of learning.

Brazilians maladjusted? Of course it was not to be expected, granted the very abnormal circumstances of their development, that they should have entirely purged the errors of the past. Unhappily, their nature has not yet been tamed, and the errors of the past are yet to be redeemed.

And what of Brazilian cordiality? Isn't cordiality a symptom of maturity? Strictly speaking, that cordiality does not exist to the extent it is proclaimed. What does exist is general acceptance as cordiality of what is no more than courtesy.

Blocked by the mountains of the coast, obliged to confront the insidious forest where dangers constantly lie in wait on land, on water, and in the air, having to adjust to a climate for which the white man never served an apprenticeship, it was practically impossible for him [the Portuguese] to conquer the tropics as the Anglo-Saxon conquered the temperate zones of the earth. He would, indeed, have to develop traits adequate to the new environment, among them sensibility and delicate courtesy.

While the Anglo-Saxon found in the New World natural conditions more or less similar to those of Europe, and problems long known to him and which he had long ago learned how to confront, the Portuguese in Brazil faced a completely strange world with very few similarities to his original habitat. The tropical heat with a high degree of humidity was unknown to him. The tropical forest of Brazil, the jungle that advances to the very edge of rivers like a veritable green wall, certainly would not inspire pantheistic ardors of immediate mastery. On the contrary, his dominant sentiment would be terror, the cosmic terror that persists in the Brazilian even in our day.

In Brazil, man would have to conquer nature by feeling his way, temporizing, detouring, distrusting, wriggling, tricking, biding his time, waiting for opportunities, developing subtleties that, in the end, by imitation, he would communicate to the social guest in the form of delicate courtesy. Hence the *jeito*, the famous Brazilian "way" (means, order, twist, skill, propensity, and so forth) of doing things—"Let's find a *jeito*," or "We have to find the *jeito*," the best way of getting something done. The foreigner never quite succeeds in comprehending it, a sign that the word *jeito*, with no exactly corresponding term in the principal Western tongues, fills a necessity of expression peculiar only to Brazilians and not to other peoples. Hence also, in part, their social manner, their politeness, their hesitations, their *jeito*, their *delicadeza* or courtesy, which is perhaps one of the characterological traits most peculiarly Brazilian.

Jeito and *delicadeza*, however, do not signify cordiality, and much less do they mean maturity. At times, actually, the contrary is true. Courtesy may be merely a means of defense for restraining aggressive impulses. There are neurotics who are terribly good at *jeito*. They are courteous almost by definition.

No confusing courtesy with cordiality, then. Cordiality is something else. And the Amazon will still have to spill a great deal of water into the Atlantic before Brazilians have attained fullness of cordiality and maturity. Furthermore, a phenomenon visible even to the eyes of the blind, and audible even to the ears of the deaf, is, unhappily, Brazilian psychic instability. From the most clear-cut cases of megalomania on the verge of schizophrenia, to the more benign cases of correctible maladjustments, everything in the Brazilian still betrays and confirms the existence of superficial cordiality and emotional immaturity. In turn, in the last analysis, these lead to other political and economic immaturities, if not psychological, social, spiritual, and cultural as well.

The maladjustment that most frequently generates immaturity and neuroses is the absence of a taste for useful work. It is intimately bound to the other main outlines of Brazilian culture, especially to the expectancy or hope of rapid fortune, and to the absence of a spirit of cooperation. The extremely Brazilian habit of leaving until tomorrow what can be done today is a habit that can, at the slightest pressure to get things done immediately, instantly let loose veritable states of panic and irritability.

Or can so-called Brazilian laziness have a biological and racial background? Can it be as biological and racial as so-called Brazilian melancholy? Much evidently is due to the tropical climate, because we cannot rightly expect man in hot climates to continuously produce as much as in temperate or cold climates, or maintain the same level of vitality as when he lives in more pleasant latitudes. Equal responsibility should be given to the Brazilian's state of chronic substandard nutrition, either through absolute lack of nourishment, or simply through not knowing how to eat properly.

But the great responsibility for Brazilian laziness, perhaps the greatest, lies at the door of the emotional prejudice against certain forms of activity.

The proof? Observe the half-breeds and *mazombos* [individuals born in Brazil of foreign parents, especially Portuguese] not reconciled to work in different jobs at the counter, in the workshop, in the office. All leave plenty to be desired in turning out work, and employers, above all foreign employers, will naturally conclude that nothing can be done about it, that laziness is congenital and racial in them.

Now let us take those same mulattoes and those same *mazombos* and put them on a football [soccer] team. We shall then witness great transfigurations. *Mazombos* and mulattoes who had no energy for work, whose indolence was taken as congenital, whose energy seemed nil, run for ninety minutes on the field, struggle together like wild men, do not spare themselves, and do not weaken for a second. Why the contrast? Because football is something they learned to love in childhood and in school—if they had any schooling—while useful labor has always been demeaned in their eyes. Because they have never been given heroes of constructive work to idolize, while the heroes of their football fields have filled their childhood dreams and reveries.

Historically, mestizos were likewise considered useless and turbulent fellows. Hardly adaptable to useful forms of labor, they ended by degenerating into human castoffs. And yet as woodland guides, *bandeirantes*, boatmen, guerrilla fighters, tamers of deserts, no one could surpass them.

Childhood dislike of work by *mazombos* and half-breeds was the initial nucleus of future maladjustment and neurotic indolence. Prejudiced against constructive labor, lacking any ideal of the symbols that dignify it, they reacted emotionally and neurotically, just as many other reactions attributed to racial indolence are neurotic and emotional in origin. To distaste for work add other ingredients—excessive love of the past, search for quick wealth, irreligiosity, and lack of concern with moral aspects of life—as well as geophysical and economic factors, and we will have torn away the veil that covers the mysteries of the neuroses afflicting Brazilians.

8 *Henry Koster* ◆ A Master-Slave Relationship

Henry Koster, a British traveler and businessman, was born in Portugal, and first came to Brazil in 1809. Years later he wrote that he felt "equally among my countrymen" whether in England, Portugal, or Brazil. He lived for the better part of eleven years in Northeast Brazil, dying there in 1820. His book is a full, balanced, and picturesque account of the realities of Brazilian life, including both the coast and backlands of the Northeast, in the years immediately preceding Independence. He was known by Brazilians as "the precise Koster." His observations deal with agriculture and trade as well as with military, religious, and social customs. Although he strongly condemns slavery, in this piece he nonetheless reflects the racial attitudes of his time.

That the general character of persons who are in a state of slavery should be amiable, and that goodness should predominate, is not to be expected. We ought rather to be surprised at the existence of that degree of virtue which is to be found among those who are reduced to a situation of so much misery. Slaves are much inclined to pilfer, and particularly toward their masters this is very frequent; indeed, many of them scarcely think that they are acting improperly in so doing. Drunkenness is common among them. A direct answer is not easily obtained from a slave, but the information which is required is learnt by means of four or five questions put in various ways. The Negroes show much attachment

From *Travels in Brazil* (1817, London; abridged ed., Carbondale: Southern Illinois University Press, 1966), 182, edited and with an introduction by C. Harvey Gardiner. Reprinted by permission of Southern Illinois University Press.

to their wives and children, to their other relations if they should chance to have any, and to their *malungos* or fellow passengers from Africa.

The respect which is paid to old age is extremely pleasing to witness. Superannuated Africans, upon the estates, are never suffered to want any comforts with which it is in the power of their fellow slaves to supply them. The old Negroes are addressed by the term of *pai* and *mãe*, father and mother. The masters likewise add this term to the name of their older slaves, when speaking to them. That the generality of the slaves should show great attachment to their masters is not to be expected; why should they? The connection between the two descriptions of persons is not one of love and harmony, of good producing gratitude, of esteem and respect; it is one of hatred and discord, of distrust and of continual suspicion; one of which the evil is so enormous that if any proper feelings exist in those who are supposed to benefit from it, and in those who suffer under it, they proceed from our nature, and not from the system.

9 *John Luccock* ◆ The Depraved Man

John Luccock, a British merchant and wool dealer, resided in Brazil from 1808 to 1818, an important period after the arrival of the king of Portugal and the royal court in Rio de Janeiro. Luccock traveled extensively throughout southern Brazil and kept a detailed journal in which he dealt broadly with the "ranks, employment, manners, and character" of the king, the court, and local residents. His observant eye recorded the behavior of doctors, lawyers, and shopkeepers; of masters and slaves; and of women and children. Also of interest are his comments on health, education, mealtime manners, buildings, furniture and furnishings, and vehicles. A cross-section of Luccock's impressions is reproduced here. As this selection demonstrates, some observers found only depravity among Brazilians.

Previous to the arrival of the Royal Family in Brazil, the country was governed by Vicereys, sent from Portugal, who enjoyed almost absolute authority. Hence those, who depended upon the great man's opinion, or were [in] any way connected with his Court, became disposed to pay

From *Notes on Rio de Janeiro and the Southern Parts of Brazil* (London: Samuel Leigh, 1820), 92–93, 106–7, 126, 133–35.

him even servile attention; and indemnified themselves, as well as they could, for the humiliation which they underwent, by exacting a like deference from everyone below them. In this way, servility pervaded all classes of society. When the representative of Royalty appeared in the streets, all who saw the distant shadow of his equipage, not only uncovered their heads, but bent one knee to the ground. No one thought himself entitled to pass a common soldier on duty, or to read a public notice stuck against the wall, without performing some act of homage. It is, no doubt, proper to pay the external and visible marks of respect to important officers and high characters; but in Brazil this principle is extended to a positive degradation of the manly character.

These modes of the country gave, however, to the Vicerey and his courtiers great facility in the distribution of graces and favours. A look, a smile, a bow—for a well-bred Portuguese never uses the familiar nod—but above all, a visit from him, were boons devoutly wished, and eagerly sought after. Such visits were bestowed with great condescension, and received with corresponding satisfaction. Among the higher classes, this led to frequent, extensive, and agreeable freedoms; for where the great man went, the lesser ones generally flocked, and the master of the house was as anxious to display the distinction with which he was honoured, as he was proud to receive it. He thus became habitually courteous and affable; the slightest acquaintance with the master was a sufficient introduction to the house, and gave authority to introduce also the friend of a friend's friend, to the tenth remove. The person, who now presided, did not forget that the next evening he should become a guest, and that then he would have to seek the notice, which he now dispensed. A habit of ease and urbanity was in this way introduced, which has been ill exchanged for more select parties and ceremonious behaviour.

None can more keenly feel, nor more sincerely lament, the change than the middle classes of Brazilians. The poor also partake of their regrets, for where the masters assembled, their dependants and slaves followed, and received and paid their humbler court with imitative ease and mimic politeness. Among their superiors, cards, music, and fruit filled up the evening; a fine climate, splendid moonlight or numerous lamps, good humour, and great gaiety of spirits, stole away the hours; and lateness alone dispersed the company.

But if the change of circumstances, occasioned by the emigration of the Royal Family and its followers, was thus painful to many of the Brazilians, they saw the newcomers in much more serious distress. None but those who were allowed a frequent and near approach to the court, can conceive the straits, to which it was reduced. . . .

~ All the Arts were practised in the most formal and tedious way. Every workman deemed himself initiated into some mystery, which none but his own fraternity could comprehend. Carpenters have expressed astonishment, when they have seen an Englishman take up a saw, and use it with no less dexterity, and with greater speed, than themselves. There was as little difficulty in rivalling the skill of many workmen, as their execution. So ignorant and stupid were they, that it was frequently necessary to form for them a rough model of the article which they were required to make, and to go from shop to shop before one could be found willing to undertake it. I have even been told, that what I wanted could not be executed by human ingenuity, although it was, perhaps, one of the most common instruments in domestic use. To this, white men, who were mechanics, added another folly; every one of them thought himself too much a gentleman to work in public, and that he would be degraded, if seen carrying the smallest burden, even the implements of his calling, along the streets. The silly pride, and formal self-importance, which pervaded all ranks of Brazilian society, were, in this class of men, singularly absurd and ridiculous. . . .

~ In the city persons retire, after dinner, to their own houses, to take their repose, and spend the evening as they please. Out of the city, particularly if the moon be nearly full, evening finds the remaining guests in full gaiety of spirits; sleep has dissipated the fumes of wine, if too much had been taken, the company is enlarged by an assemblage of the neighbourhood, the guitar strikes up, for everyone can touch it; the song succeeds, generally in soft and plaintive notes, and the dance is not forgotten. In this way the hours of evening pass . . . in free remarks and smart replies, in feats of agility and harmless frolics. The reserved character, which seldom fails to make itself conspicuous in the earlier part of the day, wears off, and not infrequently people run to the opposite extreme. The loose attire of the ladies is peculiarly favourable to the exertion of their limbs, and they engage with great hilarity in the rough, but innocent exercises of the other sex. Here and there a jealous old husband looks after his young and sprightly wife, and she deems it prudent to restrain her gaiety; but it makes little difference, and occasions no interruption of the general glee. . . .

~ Some highly disgusting features of the Brazilian character have been noticed; worse remain to be brought forward. In the delineation of them, all possible brevity may seem, on some accounts, to be desirable; but no one can comprehend the extent of depravity, among this people, without a short detail. The Cities . . . had joined, at the period when my acquaintance with the country began, to form the social order of Rio de Janeiro. The sacred precincts of truth, private property, and domestic virtue were violated in the most licentious way. Few were to be believed on their most solemn asseveration; fewer still to be trusted, even after some trial of their fidelity. Imposition and pilfering, of every description, where they could be attempted with the hope of safety, were so common as to excite only transient and inoperative feelings of resentment. Occasional thefts were bold and daring; but, in general, though accomplished with adroitness, so as seldom to fail of their object, they were skulking and dastardly. Assassination sometimes followed in their train; and sometimes was coolly practised for purposes of less moment than to make sure a booty, or prevent a discovery.

The life of an undistinguished individual was not worth two dollars; for a smaller sum, any Coward could hire a Bravo to take it away. When a body dropped in the street, though in broad daylight, the murderer walked on, and the people beheld him as if he had done nothing amiss, and even made way for his escape. Indeed, their own safety required such forbearance, for the Brazilians then wore, almost universally, wide-wrapping cloaks, under which they not only concealed the produce of their thievish industry, but also carried their never-failing companion, a knife. This, when they apprehended a pursuit, was openly displayed, firmly grasped, and held ready to strike the first person who should dare to interrupt their progress. . . .

That there were well-principled and honourable men among the inhabitants of Rio is readily allowed, and it would be uncharitable to question whether the mixture of good with evil qualities, which abounds everywhere else, was to be found there also. But in many of these mixed characters there was an unusual preponderance of the evil; and a much larger proportion than common seemed to be altogether depraved. Depravity, too, was not there redeemed by any national qualities of a solid, nor even of a shewy, kind; it was not, in general, thought necessary to maintain that shadow of virtue, hypocrisy. Vices, which elsewhere men are the most careful to hide, were seen stalking abroad as publicly and unblushingly as the most abandoned could desire. Not Negroes and the populace alone contemplated them with apathy; the moral taste and feeling of persons of a higher caste partook so much of the common taint that, when we mentioned with horror the worst of crimes, which we were obliged to witness, they often advanced something by way of defence, and really appeared as much surprized at our mode of thinking as if we had broached a new religion, or foisted into the old one some scrupulous fancies.

10 *Auguste de Saint-Hilaire* ◆ Self-Interest, Carried to Excess

Auguste de Saint-Hilaire, a French naturalist, arrived in Brazil at the age of thirty-seven with the duke of Luxembourg, French ambassador to Rio de Janeiro, and traveled extensively in the country between 1816 and 1822. The first of his nine books on Brazil was published in 1822 and the last in 1887, many years after his death. His observations are the most detailed, precise, and comprehensive of any foreigner about Brazilian flora and fauna, geography, history, politics, economy, and society at the end of the colonial period. Along with the preceding two selections, Saint-Hilaire's comments illustrate the European response to the people of the tropics. All three authors demonstrate their ability to look past reality, thus revealing more about their own culture than the one they describe.

~ *The Abandonment of Useful Enterprise* ~

Brazilians learn easily, they know how to make plans, but too often they start dreaming and do not measure obstacles or calculate undertakings in proportion to their resources. In carrying out projects they add fictitious obstacles to real ones. The spirit of envy and intrigue, more vehement here than anywhere else, gets in the way of everything that is done; obstacles are everywhere, wheeler-dealers are favored, and honest men are discouraged. No sooner is a useful enterprise begun than it is interrupted and abandoned. Sometimes a job ordered by the government that could be finished in a short time and with minimum expense never ends, although work continues on it forever. The undertaking almost becomes the birthright of a prominent man. How would he live if that possession was taken from him?

From *Livre du voyage que j'ai entrepris de faire de Rio de Janeiro à Villa-Rica et de Villa-Rica à St.-Paul* (Orléans, France: H. Herluison, Libraire, 1887). Translated into Portuguese by Vivaldi Moreira and published as *Segunda viagem do Rio de Janeiro a Minas Gerais e a São Paulo* (Belo Horizonte, Brazil: Editora Itatiaia, and São Paulo: Editora da Universidade de São Paulo, 1974), 19. Translated by G. Harvey Summ.

~ *Probity Is Rare* ~

When the supervisor is at the Hill, he keeps the workers encouraged by his activity; however, no sooner does he leave than everything stops. In a region where the heat invites one to laziness, where man has few needs, where work to a certain degree is considered shameful and seems to be something to be done by slaves, nothing is as hard as getting work done by free workers; for these reasons the administrator calculated that every month a thousand workdays were lost.

Every skilled worker, foundry worker, carpenter, sawyer, etc., has a list of his men and is supposed to keep track of those absent; however, the king, they told me, often pays for the labor of men nowhere near the foundry. Moreover, workers carry out tasks quite different from the ones that they are supposed to be engaged in.

If there is a country where the government should not undertake manufacturing on its own, it is Brazil. Laziness, and perhaps natural indulgence carried to excess, make supervision very lax if not based on personal self-interest. Even more, the loosening of social bonds resulting from the colonial system, the institution of slavery, the level of degradation into which the mother country has fallen, and finally, the bad example of the Europeans, have made probity even rarer among Brazilians than among many other peoples. As a result, the government is among those that are most likely to be fooled.

The indolence of the inhabitants of the backlands is perhaps greater than that of other residents of Minas Gerais. Their physical appearance reveals their nature, and the expression of this defect can be found in all the movements of the body. In fact, the heat in this climate tends to dispose men of this region to idleness. The cattle breeding in which they engage requires little activity and favors their tendency toward laziness, and the poor diet that they almost always have contributes still more to sap their energy.

Poverty is ordinarily the companion of laziness. Therefore, despite the advantages that the land offers, the inhabitants of the desert live in extreme poverty. Men born there, or in any other part of Brazil or Portugal, at times have founded considerable estates in the backlands, and they take advantage of the numerous resources that this region offers; however, their children are brought up in indolence, a defect that is always followed by vagrancy; they have no foresight; they dissipate their paternal heritage; the most beautiful plantations fall into ruin in a short time, and rarely are fortunes passed on to the third generation.

It is no surprise that men living in poverty and in isolation are ignorant and superstitious. Throughout the backlands there is great faith in magic, and these beliefs serve to enrich dealers whom the police would punish, if there were police there.

All of the above proves that even if backlanders do not commit great crimes and the heat unnerves and softens their customs, they gain little through civilization. The prostration which succeeds feverish agitation does not signify health. The people of the desert are good, hospitable, charitable, and peaceful, but these virtues are only the result of their temperament, which leads them, almost by instinct alone, to exert no effort. Foreign to elevated ideas and generous combinations, almost completely foreign even to the use of intellectual faculties, backlanders live an animal-like existence and do not rise out of their indifference other than to deliver themselves to grosser pleasures.

From *Voyages dans les Provinces de Rio de Janeiro et de Minas Geraes* (Paris: Grimbert et Dorez, Libraires, 1830). Translated into Portuguese by Vivaldi Moreira and published as *Viagem pelas Provincias do Rio de Janeiro e Minas Gerais* (Belo Horizonte, Brazil: Editora Itatiaia, and São Paulo: Editora da Universidade de São Paulo, 1975), 133–34, 308–9. Translated by G. Harvey Summ.

~ *No Society and Little Sociability* ~

There is absolutely no homogeneity among the inhabitants of Brazil. Nevertheless, one can say in general that they have peaceful habits, that they are good, generous, hospitable, even magnificent, and that in several provinces there are people who are notable for their lively spirits and their intelligence. But the colonial system had kept Brazilians in the most profound ignorance; the administration of slavery had made them familiar with the most abject vices; and, after the arrival of the Portuguese court in Rio de Janeiro, the habit of venality was introduced into all classes. A crowd of aristocratic patriarchs, divided among themselves by intrigue, puerile vanity, and petty interests, spread throughout Brazil, but in this country there was no society at all and only a few elements of sociability.

From *Voyage dans le District des Diamans et sur le Littoral du Brésil*, 2 vols. (Paris: publisher unknown, 1833). Translated into Portuguese by Leonam de Azeredo Penna and published as *Viagem pelo Distrito dos Diamantes do Brasil* (Belo Horizonte, Brazil: Editora Itatiaia, and São Paulo: Editora da Universidade de São Paulo, 1974), 1:216. Translated by G. Harvey Summm.

~ *In Rio Grande do Sul, Insensible Both to Favors and to Bad Treatment* ~

When I arrived in Porto Alegre, I asked Lieutenant-General Marques to discharge my two soldiers, which he very kindly did. However, he told me that in order to avoid my request becoming a pretext for other identical ones every day, he would only authorize the discharge on the eve of my departure.

During my whole trip I treated these men as well as possible. I never got angry at them and put up patiently with their gross behavior and their impertinence. I protected them for a month, although they were of no use to me at all. Yesterday morning I sent them their discharges, signed by the general; I gave them money and three horses, and received no thanks. They did not even say good-bye to me. I had regarded as extraordinary the fact that an Indian had left me after two weeks without thanking me for what I had paid him and without saying good-bye; I never imagined that I would have to relate an identical but much more notable case because it concerned men of our race.

They find it very hard to recognize favors received because they perceive such gestures as an admission of benefits conferred on them and they fear that this would show inferiority. The European would be ungrateful on purpose, but none of them, bad as he might be, would not express thanks for favors similar to those that I had given my soldiers. These two men are very different from Europeans and are like Indians; consequently, this is an example of the change that happens to our race in Brazil. I could cite several others.

In fact, in his ungratefulness the Brazilian is far from being as guilty as the European; in his country there is no reflected pride; if he is ungrateful, it is due to his lack of sensibility, to his ignorance of the value of a favor and because he does not foresee the consequences. What proves this assertion is the fact that my two soldiers showed no sign of joy, either to me or to my companions. It is known that the Guaranis are equally insensible both to favors and to bad treatment. In effect, that is their character, but white men are rather similar, depending on how they have been brought up; the life of rural people, the violent activities in which they engage, the lack of police with which they must live, and the habit of seeing blood flow and of mistreating animals, must smother the little sensibility that nature bestowed on them.

From *Voyage à Rio Grande do Sul, Brésil* (Orléans, France: publisher unknown, 1887), page unknown. Translated into Portuguese by Leonam de Azeredo Penna and published as *Viagem ao Rio Grande do Sul* (Belo Horizonte, Brazil: Editora Itatiaia, and São Paulo: Editora da Universidade de São Paulo, 1974), 186–87, 193, 199. Translated by G. Harvey Summ.

~ *Excessive Courtesy in São Paulo* ~

It would not be proper to conclude that men of the upper class in São Paulo are not well brought up. On the contrary, they are refined in their dealings, and their courtesy extends to the lower classes. Persons of position greet each other even when they are not acquainted, and individuals of the lower classes never fail to doff their hats to persons of a higher social class. However, such indications of deference are due less to the person than to the position he occupies. Everyone greeted me when I wore my uniform, but I was hailed less often in the streets when I wore civilian clothes. Nevertheless, courtesy that always forced me to uncover my head was excessive.

From *Viagem ao Provincia de São Paulo* (São Paulo: Livraria Martins, 1940), 186–87. Translated by G. Harvey Summ. Details of publication in original French version not available.

11 *Georg Wilhelm Freireyss* ◆ An Extremely Lively Imagination

Georg Wilhelm Freireyss, a German naturalist, arrived in Brazil in 1813 at the age of twenty-four. He collected and classified its flora and fauna, especially birds, mostly in Minas Gerais and Bahia. He included a great deal of detailed data on Indians. His writings, and this selection, touch on manners and customs, a topic he explored mainly for the purpose of encouraging German immigration to Brazil, on which he spent considerable effort. Freireyss died in Brazil in 1825.

As I have already shown elsewhere, a series of evils results from the diversity of colors. Among them, offended pride is one of the worst. The white is considered to be above all others, and the mulatto is judged better than the *caboclo*, the *cabra* [a mixture of black and mulatto], or the black; the *cabra*, in turn, wants to be more than a *cabra*, and, when born in Brazil, looks down on the recently arrived African.

The Portuguese, save for some insignificant changes, remains the same in Brazil; the Brazilian, however, is preferable. He is more alert, more ingenious, and in general has an extremely enterprising spirit, which, for lack of schools, is not properly developed.

The body of the Brazilian is beautiful, very resistant and strong, and his color often is not as dark as the Portuguese. The hair is usually black, but, as in Minas Gerais, blonds are not rare. The eyes are brown and the physical characteristics intelligent. Even though there are not beauties

From *Reisen in Brasilia* (Frankfurt, Germany: publisher unknown, 1824). Translated into Portuguese by A. Lofgren and published as *Viagem ao interior do Brasil* (Belo Horizonte, Brazil: Editora Itatiaia, and São Paulo: Editora da Universidade de São Paulo, 1982), 78–85. Translated by G. Harvey Summ.

among the women as in northern Europe, it cannot be denied that Brazilian women are noted for the beauty of their figure, their brilliant black hair, their fiery eye, and their great vivacity. Both sexes have a tendency toward corpulence, which certainly comes from their indolent character and love of comfort.

The Brazilian is not as suspicious as the Portuguese, is more cordial, and much less treacherous; he is proud, and more pleasant with foreigners, except when he considers one an enemy of his nation. For this reason, a German, a Swede, or a Russian is generally better received than a Spaniard, an Englishman, or a Frenchman. However, promises of Brazilians are excessive, and one should not believe everything they say, even after doing something for them; at the very least, one runs the risk of being considered unmannerly. And it is more out of courtesy than goodwill that the Brazilian offers his house and all he possesses to the foreigner, or when he says "Your servant" or "I am at your service forever." This excessive courtesy becomes ridiculous because he often seems to offer objects that do not belong to him.

In his way of life and even religion the Brazilian is much more tolerant than the Portuguese; however, there are many exceptions in the case of religion, especially in the towns and villages of the interior. There the foreigner would do well to follow the customs of the place. Superstition makes this necessary.

The extremely lively imagination of the Brazilian often leads him to exaggeration. Just as frequently he invents simple fantasy to explain something he does not know. Thus, for example, there are many birds whose voice he finds similar to his language. That is very exaggerated, although there are some grounds for it, because in fact there exist birds who "speak" some distinct words, in a way that makes it seem that Providence from the beginning destined the Portuguese to be the masters of Brazil. In particular, the *bem-te-vi* often gives rise to superstition, because it has the habit of making its cry heard when it sees someone. Thus it was often used in searching for runaway slaves, a fact interpreted as entirely supernatural.

There are two extremes in life in which there is little difference between men: happiness and pain, festivals and mourning. Among the festivals the Brazilian *batuque* dance should be mentioned. The dancers form a wheel and the dancer in the center moves to the beat of a viola. He advances and goes belly-to-belly with another person in the wheel, ordinarily of the other sex. In the beginning the beat of the music is slow; however, little by little it grows, and the dancer in the middle is replaced every time he bumps bellies. This lasts for many nights. A more lascivious dance than this cannot be imagined, as a result of which it has many enemies, especially among the priests.

The Brazilian is serious, and it is rare to see him happy; at night, however, at the sound of the guitar, men show their great talent for music, and women for song. Rarely, however, do the neighbors gather, and even in such cases that cordiality that so adorns our society is seldom seen.

The Brazilian is sober, even more in drinking than in eating, and in effect there may be no other country in which there are as few drunkards as in Brazil. Other vices, therefore, are more common.

12 *Karl Friedrich Philipp von Martius* ◆ A Worthy Subject for a Popular History

Karl Friedrich Philipp von Martius, a German botanist, arrived in Brazil in 1817 at the age of twenty-three. He was part of one of several European cultural and scientific expeditions that set out for Brazil shortly after the arrival of the Portuguese royal family there in 1808. Martius's mission, to conduct research in natural science, was sponsored jointly by the Austrian and Bavarian governments. He and other scientific collaborators eventually classified over ten thousand Brazilian botanical species.

Martius died in 1866. He had remained in touch with Brazil throughout his life and was highly admired by its people. He became a corresponding member of the Brazilian Historical and Geographical Institute, established in 1838. As the only foreign contributor to a special edition of the institute's journal to encourage the writing of a history of Brazil, Martius went far beyond the role of a naturalist. In this selection, in carefully couched language, he urges the historian to take into account Brazil's racial and geographic diversity, to avoid "pompous language" and "sterile citations," and to see the areas he writes about "with his own eyes" in order to stimulate the practice of "all the civic virtues" by the "politically immature population."

Anyone who undertakes to write the history of Brazil, a country which promises so much, should never lose sight of the elements which contributed to the development of man there. These diverse elements come

From "How the History of Brazil Should Be Written," in *Perspectives on Brazilian History*, edited by E. Bradford Burns (New York: Columbia University Press, 1967), 23–25, 38–41. The original Portuguese version appeared in *Revista do Instituto Histórico e Geográfico Brasileiro* 6 (Rio de Janeiro, 1844): 381–403.

from the three races, namely: the copper-colored, or American; the white, or Caucasian; and the black, or Ethiopian. Because of the reciprocal and changing relations of the three races, the present population consists of a novel mixture, whose history therefore has a very particular stamp.

Each human race competes, in a historical movement, according to its innate propensity and the circumstances under which it lives and develops. Therefore, we see a new people, born and developing from the union and contact of these very different races. I propose that its history will evolve according to a special law for these converging forces.

Each physical and moral peculiarity characterizing the different races offers a special force in this development of a new people. The more energy, number, and dignity that characterize the race, the more will be its influence on the common development. Thus, it necessarily follows that the Portuguese, as discoverers, conquerors, and masters, greatly influenced this development; and because the Portuguese created the conditions and the physical and moral guarantees for an independent kingdom, they emerge as the most powerful and vital force. However, it certainly would be a great error for the principles of a pragmatic historiography if we disregarded the force of the natives and the imported Negroes, who likewise contributed to the physical, moral, and civic development of the whole population. The natives as well as the Negroes resisted the dominant race.

I know very well that there will be whites who will charge that such a linking of these races disparages their ancestry. But, I am also certain they will not be found among those seeking to write a philosophic history of Brazil. On the contrary, the most enlightened people will discover from this investigation that the Indian and Ethiopian races have been and still are involved in the historic development of the Brazilian people. This investigation will be a new stimulus for the profound and humane historian.

The history of peoples, as much as that of individuals, shows us that the genius of world history, which leads mankind in directions whose wisdom we should always recognize, frequently resorts to mixing the races to obtain the world order's most sublime ends. Who can deny that the English nation owes its energy, resoluteness, and perseverance to the mixture of the Celtic, Danish, Roman, Anglo-Saxon, and Norman peoples?

Perhaps even more important, the genius of history proposes the blending of peoples of the same race with races so entirely different in their individualities, moral character, and physique in order to form a new and marvelously organized nation.

We will never be permitted to doubt that providential will predestined this mixture for Brazil. The powerful river of Portuguese blood ought to absorb the small tributaries of the Indian and Ethiopian races. This mixture has taken place in the lower classes. As in all countries, the upper class is developed from elements of the lower class, vitalized and strengthened by them. Thus, the highest class of the Brazilian population is made from this mixture. For centuries this mixture has had a powerful influence on the elevated classes and transmitted to them that historical activity for which the Brazilian Empire is noted.

I believe that the philosophic writer, comprehending the doctrines of true humanity and enlightened Christianity, will find nothing in this opinion that could offend the Brazilians' sensitivities. The current *conditio sine qua non* for the true historian is to appreciate man according to his true value, as the Creator's most sublime work, and to disassociate this from his color and background. This transcendent humanitarianism—which appreciates man in any situation in which he discovers him, as an instrument to work for and to serve—knows the infinity of the world's order and is the animating spirit of the true historian. Thus, I consider the Brazilians' personal relations, which allow the Negro and the Indian to influence the development of the Brazilian nationality, to be a benefit for the destiny of the country. I can contrast this with attitudes in other areas of the New World, where these two inferior races are excluded from the general development as unworthy by birth or because their small number in comparison to whites makes them of little importance.

The reflective historian's essential task should be to show that the conditions were established during Brazil's development for the improving of the three races, which are placed next to each other in a manner previously unknown in history, and that they should help each other in every way.

This reciprocity in the history of the development of the Brazilian people offers a picture of an organic life. The task of a truly human legislation will be the proper appreciation of this. The historian can judge the future from what has been done for the Negroes' and the Indians' moral and civic education so far. From this history, he can become a sibyl prophesying the future, and he can offer some useful projects, etc. The stronger his defense of the interests of these unprotected peoples, the greater will be the merit of his work. It will have the stamp of noble humanitarianism that our century requires of the historian. The historian who doubts the perfectibility of mankind allows the reader to suspect that he does not know how to rise above odious and partial opinions. . . .

The works published up until now on the separate provinces are of inestimable value. They abound with important facts and minutely examine many events. Nevertheless, they do not satisfy the requirements of real historiography, which demands more than mere chronicles. These historical works monotonously repeat many insignificant facts and certain information of slight historical importance. All this lessens the work's interest and bewilders the reader about the point of the work. What is gained by repeating each provincial governor's acts and omissions, or by relating unimportant facts about the administration of cities, or bishoprics, etc., or by a scrupulous list of citations and records of dubious historical authenticity? My opinion is that all this should be excluded.

The vast extent of Brazilian territory presents the historian with a difficult problem, for he is surrounded by an immensely varied natural setting and by a population composed of very different elements with different customs and practices. As Pará has an entirely different climate from Rio Grande do Sul, different soil, natural products, agriculture, industry, customs, and necessities, the same is true for Bahia, Pernambuco, and Minas. In one province the white descendants of the Portuguese predominate; in another an Indian mixture has the majority; in a third, the African race manifests its importance; and each of these exerts a special influence on the state of civilization in general. The author who does not see this broad interplay of forces risks the chance of writing, not a history of Brazil, but only a series of special histories of each province. Another historian who does not give these peculiarities the necessary attention runs the risk of not discovering the special local temperament that is indispensable when he is trying to rouse the reader's interest, to give vitality to his description, and to impress the reader with the ardor that we so much admire in the great historians.

In order to avoid these difficulties, it seems necessary to begin by describing the general state of the whole country in well-chosen epochs, including relevant relations with the mother country and the rest of the world. Passing on to those parts of Brazil that are basically different, only those provinces that have a real historical significance should be emphasized. By proceeding in this manner, it will not be necessary to start from the beginning in each province, and all the repetitious material can be omitted. Those parts of Brazil that are similar in physical conditions and belong with each other can be treated together. Thus, the histories of São Paulo, Minas, Goiás, and Mato Grosso converge into one; Maranhão and Pará can be treated as one; Ceará, Rio Grande do Norte, and Paraíba form a natural group influenced by Pernambuco; and finally, the histories of Sergipe, Alagoas, and Porto Seguro will be the same as Bahia's.

For such a work, it seems indispensable for the historian to visit these provincial areas and to penetrate the peculiarities of nature and population with his own eyes. Only in this manner will he be able to evaluate properly all the historical events that have taken place in whatever part of the empire, explain them by the particularities pertaining only to inhabitants of the place where they occurred, and connect them with other events in the area. How different Pará is from Minas! They possess divergent natural conditions, different men, different needs and passions, and consequently are influenced by different historical forces.

This diversity is not sufficiently recognized in Brazil. Because few Brazilians have visited all of the country, many erroneous ideas have been developed about local conditions. Without any doubt, this fact contributed to the length of time it took to extinguish the political turmoils in some provinces. Since the officials in Rio de Janeiro could not recognize the true causes of these vexing situations in the distant provinces, they did not administer the appropriate remedies. If the historian thoroughly acquaints himself with these local peculiarities, and presents them exactly, the administration will often ask him for his useful counsel.

If the reader is not acquainted with the details of the local natural setting, he will neither be interested in nor be able to develop an intimate knowledge of Brazil. Following the system of Herodotus, the "father of history," the historian will find many opportunities to include enchanting pictures of Nature. He will make his work attractive to the inhabitants of Brazil's different regions, for the reader will be able to recognize his own home in these descriptions and identify himself with the greater Brazilian scene. The European reader will be especially interested in such a rich and varied book.

In conclusion, I ought to add an observation about the position of a Brazilian historian toward his country. History is the master of the present and the future. It can spread noble patriotic sentiments among contemporaries. A history of Brazil ought to stimulate the love of country, courage, constancy, industry, fidelity, prudence—in a word, all the civic virtues—in its Brazilian readers. Brazil suffers from a politically immature population. There we see republicans of all complexions and of all types of ideologies. It is precisely among them that many people will be discovered with an interest in the history of their homeland. A book should be written just for them, to correctly convince them of the impracticability of their utopian plans, of the impropriety of licentious discussions about public business, of the undesirability of an unrestrained press, and of the necessity of a monarchy in a country where there is a large number of slaves.

Brazil has just begun to feel that it is united. Many provincial prejudices still prevail; they ought to be removed by judicious education. Each part of the empire should turn its face toward the others. They [all of Brazil's provinces] ought to attempt to prove that such a vast, rich country as Brazil with so many varied sources of good fortune and prosperity will attain its most favorable development when its inhabitants firmly support the monarchy and establish a wise organization of reciprocal relations among all the provinces. Often foreigners have tried to sow discord among the different parts of Brazil, and by the principle of "divide and rule" obtain an important influence in the state's affairs. The patriotic historian ought to take advantage of every occasion to show that the provinces belong together by organic law and that their progress can be guaranteed only by a closer union among them.

Brazil's greatness and power are based on its very vastness, the variety of its products, and also on its inhabitants, who are sons of the same land, with the same historical background and the same future aspirations. In order to render his fatherland a real service, the historian should write as a constitutional monarchist, a real unitarian in the purest sense of the word. His work should not exceed one sizable volume, written in a popular though noble style. It should satisfy the intelligence as well as the heart, not be written in a pompous language, nor be overburdened with a heap of sterile citations. It should avoid taking on the character of a mere chronicle or a dry, purely erudite historical investigation. As any history that deserves the name of history, it will be an epic! A really popular epic is written only when the people still believe in progressive development.

As Brazil is a country entering a phase that demands dynamic progress, it surely is a worthy subject for a popular history. Its author will find in the favorable development of the land a propitious stimulus to present in his work all his patriotic zeal and love, that poetic fire appropriate for youth, to which at the same time he can apply the depth of judgment and firmness of character belonging to a mature and virile age.

---

13 *Hermann Burmeister* ◆ Long-Standing Differences of Color, Position, and Wealth

Hermann Burmeister, born in 1807, was a professor of zoology and geology at the University of Halle, Germany. He visited the provinces of Rio de Janeiro and Minas Gerais in 1850 and 1851. After breaking a leg on his journey, he spent three months recuperating in a small town where he

From *Reise nach Brasilien, durch die Provinzen von Rio de Janeiro und Minas Geraís* (Berlin: Georg Reimer, 1853), 426–58. Translated into Portuguese by Manoel Salvaterra and Hubert Schoenfeldt and published as *Viagem ao Brasil, através das províncias do Rio de Janeiro e Minas Gerais* (São Paulo: Livraria Martins Editora, n.d.), 242–55. Translated by G. Harvey Summ.

had time to observe local customs at close hand. He later became director of the Museum of Buenos Aires. Burmeister died in Argentina in 1892. This selection deals with the importance of personal relationships, status, and race as well as with differences between the written law and actual practice.

My stay in Congonhas, which lasted more than three and a half months, allowed me to learn intimately about the life and customs of the Brazilians. I was able to observe them in various ways and I can permit myself to judge them up to a point. Almost all my observations, however, should be applied to the common people. The inhabitants of large cities all adapt themselves to identical life-styles and habits, so that one cannot speak of typical customs, nor is it worthwhile describing their habits. My observations about the *mineiros* and their life-style thus do not refer to that part of the Brazilian population.

In Minas, I found three classes of free people: whites, mulattoes, and blacks. I will not mention the slaves, whose condition is the same throughout Brazil.

The three above-mentioned groups of free persons are equal before the law, but both the differences in their circumstances and deeply rooted customs combine to create a law much more rigorous than the written law, which the Brazilians know how to ignore when it suits them. The population has little confidence in the judiciary, since everybody knows that good personal relationships and money succeed in overcoming even the greatest obstacles. This shortcoming can be blamed less on officials than on unpaid juries. Unjust decisions, which are an inveterate practice, mean that no one is any longer concerned with the law, but only with the conditions prevailing during deliberations. Thus, the richer man will always win out over the poorer one; the white man over the colored man; and, in case of a suit between whites, the one who has more prestige or social position will win. The same applies between mulattoes or between blacks.

There are no differences of color, position, or wealth before the law, but such differences do exist in fact, out of habits of long standing. In the annals of Brazilian justice, it is hard to find a case where a poor man will prevail over a rich man, or a mulatto receive justice with respect to a white man.

It is surprising to find racial differences within society and among various levels of the population. Large estates in the hands of colored people are exceptional. Land- and mine-owners are almost entirely white. It is rare to see a white man married to a colored woman, since each tries to maintain racial purity and avoids kinship with other races. Land planted and developed by whites almost always continues in their hands, and a black or a mulatto finds it very hard to become the owner of a farm or mine. A farmer may die without heirs and may leave his assets to his overseer, a capable black or mulatto, but it is rare for one of them to acquire a farm from a white who has been ruined by bad management. As a rule, we always find whites as landowners. Blacks' negligence and inclination toward their own pleasures contributes greatly to that situation: if a mulatto acquires some assets, you can be sure that his son or grandson will dissipate them; thus, everything ends up once again in the hands of whites, who place greater value on inheriting property than do men of other races.

Even though class differences are great and whites have little inclination to enter into close contact with colored people, in daily dealings one does not notice caste differences, except those between free men and slaves. Free men of all kinds treat each other with great deference when they meet in any public place, in church, at a party, or at a dance; a mulatto will never think of willingly behaving as an inferior toward whites, nor will the white put down the mulatto. All high-level officials or very rich people, even whites, display a kind of affection toward each other. Anyone who enters someone else's house is considered his equal; whoever does not desire this stays at home. A very rigorous etiquette, however, is observed with strangers. No mulatto will visit a white in his house, unless for business, and in such a case he will cross no farther than the threshold, after having made his presence known and having been invited to come in. He will not enter, even if the door is open, without permission of the resident of the house; it is the custom either to clap hands until someone invites him in or to shout, "Anyone home?" to attract the attention of the resident. Whoever enters a Brazilian house without being invited will get a cold reception and may even be thrown out, since no one puts up with such an offense to good manners without severe recrimination.

A few other characteristics [of the *mineiros*]. I can only praise their good nature. They are courteous and helpful to all; their hospitality is proverbial, and they have a lively interest in their fellowman. On various occasions and even after my accident, I observed that aspect of their character: they not only satisfied all my requests, but their desire to help was so manifest that I could not help but be touched. I received visitors, invitations, and presents, and everyone competed in their kindness and favors to me. In fact, I would have preferred less attention, but the *mineiro* is extremely communicative and sociable and is constantly with his fellows, in the streets and on corners. He likes to receive visitors, although he may not give parties at home, and is visited spontaneously by friends.

Farmers, who live a little remote from the world, always enjoyed welcoming visitors, and when the visitor was of some importance, they would redouble their attention. Well-off persons never accept payment for their hospitality; the poor ask for nothing but expect a present. However, it is the custom to pay for the forage of the animals. The guest is supposed to offer that payment, which generally is accepted. Foreigners, generally called "Englishmen," are considered very rich, and are welcomed and receive all kinds of attention from the population. Wealth is a fact of great importance to the *mineiro* and impresses him greatly. The greater the degree of ostentation, the greater the *mineiro*'s respect.

14 *Alfred Russel Wallace* ◆ This Universal Love of Trade

Alfred Russel Wallace, a British naturalist, originally came to Brazil at the age of twenty-five. He did field research in the Amazon from 1848 to 1852, first at Belem in the province of Pará at the mouth of the Amazon, and then in the western Amazon. He later spent eight years in similar research in the Malay Archipelago. A collaborator of Charles Darwin, Wallace made significant scientific contributions on the origin of species, natural selection, and the survival of the fittest. In this piece, first published in 1853, Wallace comments extensively on the "character and customs" of the Brazilians in Pará.

Before proceeding with my journey, I will note the few observations that occur to me on the character and customs of the inhabitants of this fine country. I of course speak solely of the province of Pará, and it is probable that to the rest of Brazil my remarks may not in the least apply; so different in every respect is this part of the Empire from the more southern and better-known portion. There is, perhaps, no country in the world so capable of yielding a large return for agricultural labour, and yet so little cultivated; none where the earth will produce such a variety of valuable productions, and where they are so totally neglected; none where the facilities for internal communication are so great, or where it is more difficult or tedious to get from place to place; none which so much

From *A Narrative of Travels on the Amazon and Rio Negro* (London: Ward, Lock and Company, 1890), 260–64.

possesses all the natural requisites for an immense trade with all the world, and where commerce is so limited and insignificant.

This may well excite some wonder, when we remember that the white inhabitants of this country are the Portuguese and their descendants—the nation which a few centuries ago took the lead in all great discoveries and commercial enterprises [and] which spread its colonies over the whole world, and exhibited the most chivalric spirit of enterprise in overcoming the dangers of navigation in unknown seas, and of opening a commercial intercourse with barbarous or uncivilised nations.

But yet, as far as I myself have been able to observe, their national character has not changed. The Portuguese, and their descendants, exhibit here the same perseverance, the same endurance of every hardship, and the same wandering spirit, which led and still leads them to penetrate into the most desolate and uncivilised regions in pursuit of commerce and in search of gold. But they exhibit also a distaste for agricultural and mechanical labour, which appears to have been ever a part of their national character, and which has caused them to sink to their present low condition in the scale of nations, in whatever part of the world they may be found. When their colonies were flourishing in every quarter of the globe, and their ships brought luxuries for the supply of half the civilised world, a great part of their population found occupation in trade, in the distribution of that wealth which set [out] in a constant stream from America, Asia, and Africa, to their shores; but now that this stream has been diverted into other channels by the energy of the Saxon races, the surplus population, averse from agriculture, and unable to find a support in the diminished trade of the country, swarm to Brazil, in the hope that wealth may be found there, in a manner more congenial to their tastes.

Thus, we find the province of Pará overrun with traders, the greater part of whom deserve no better name than pedlars, only they carry their goods in a canoe instead of upon their backs. As their distaste for agriculture, or perhaps rather their passionate love of trade, allows scarcely any of them to settle, or produce anything for others to trade in, their only resource is in the indigenous inhabitants of the country; and as these are also very little given to cultivation except to procure the mere necessaries of life, it results that the only articles of commerce are the natural productions of the country, to catch or collect which requires an irregular and wandering life, better suited to an Indian's habits than the settled and continued exertions of agriculture. These products are principally dried fish, and oil from turtles' eggs and cowfish, for the inland trade; and sarsaparilla, piassaba, india rubber, Brazil nuts, balsam of *capivi*, and cacao, for exports. Though the coffee plant and sugarcane grow everywhere almost spontaneously, yet coffee and sugar have to be imported from other parts of Brazil for home consumption. Beef is everywhere bad, principally because there are no good pastures near the towns where cattle brought from a distance can be fattened, and no one thinks of making them, though it might easily be done. Vegetables are also very scarce and dear, and so are all fruits, except such as the orange and banana, which once planted only require the produce to be gathered when ripe; fowls in Pará are 3*s.* [shillings], 6*d.* [pence] each, and sugar as dear as in England. And all this because nobody will make it his business to supply any one of these articles! There is a kind of gambling excitement in trade which outshines all the steady profits of labour, and regular mechanics are constantly leaving their business to get a few goods on credit and wander about the country trading. . . .

This universal love of trade . . . leads, I think, to three great vices very prevalent here—drinking, gambling, and lying—besides a whole host of trickeries, cheatings, and debaucheries of every description. The life of a river trader admits of little enjoyment to a man who has no intellectual resources; it is not therefore to be wondered at that the greater part of these men are more or less addicted to intoxication; and when they can supply themselves on credit with as much wine and spirits as they like, there is little inducement to break through the habit. A man who, if he had to pay ready money, would never think of drinking wine, when he can have it on credit takes twenty or thirty gallons with him in his canoe, which, as it has cost him nothing, is little valued, and he perhaps arrives at the end of his voyage without a drop. In the towns in the interior every shop sells spirits, and numbers of persons are all day drinking, taking a glass at every place they go to, and, by this constant dramming, ruining their health perhaps more than by complete intoxication at more distant intervals. Gambling is almost universal in a greater or lesser degree, and is to be traced to that same desire to gain money by some easier road than labour, which leads so many into commerce; and the great number of traders, who have to get a living out of an amount of business which would not be properly sufficient for one-third the number, leads to the general use of trickery and lying of every degree, as fair means to be employed to entrap a new customer or to ruin a rival trader. Truth, in fact, in matters of business is so seldom made use of, that a lie seems to be preferred even when it can serve no purpose whatever, and where the person addressed must be perfectly aware of the falsehood of every asseveration made; but Portuguese politeness does not permit him by word or look to throw any doubt on his friend's veracity. I have been often amused to hear two parties endeavouring to cheat each other, by assertions which each party knew to be perfectly false, and yet pretended to receive as undoubted fact.

15 *Henry Walter Bates* ◆ Lighthearted, Quick-Witted, Communicative, and Hospitable

Henry Walter Bates, a British naturalist, arrived in Brazil in 1848 at the age of twenty-three, together with Alfred Russel Wallace. He spent eleven years there, at first in the company of Wallace, and then on his own on the Solimões River in the western Amazon, where he collected eight thousand new insect species. His long residence in the tropics undermined his health, and his writing of The Naturalist on the River Amazons *might not have taken place without the encouragement of Charles Darwin, who wrote the introduction. Bates recorded his impressions, excerpted in this selection, of the Brazilians in the Amazon port of Belem, Pará, as well as upriver.*

I resided at Pará nearly a year and a half altogether, returning thither and making a stay of a few months after each of my shorter excursions into the interior, until the 6th of November, 1851, when I started on my long voyage to the Tapajós and the Upper Amazons, which occupied me seven years and a half. I became during this time tolerably familiar with the capital of the Amazons region, and its inhabitants. Compared with other Brazilian seaport towns, I was always told, Pará shone to great advantage. It was cleaner, the suburbs were fresher, more rural, and much pleasanter on account of their verdure, shade, and magnificent vegetation. The people were simpler, more peaceable and friendly in their manners and dispositions; and assassinations, which give the southern provinces so ill a reputation, were almost unknown.

At the same time, the Pará people were much inferior to southern Brazilians in energy and industry. Provisions and house rents being cheap and the wants of the people few—for they were content with food and lodging of a quality which would be spurned by paupers in England—they spent the greater part of their time in sensual indulgences and in amusements which the government and wealthier citizens provided for them gratis. The trade, wholesale and retail, was in the hands of the Portuguese, of whom there were about twenty-five hundred in the place. Many handicrafts were exercised by coloured people, mulattoes, *mamelucos* [mixtures of white and Indian], free Negroes, and Indians. The better sort

From *The Naturalist on the River Amazons* (1864; reprint ed., New York: Dover Publications, 1975), 21–22, 80, 83–84. Reprinted by permission of Dover Publications.

of Brazilians dislike the petty details of shopkeeping, and if they cannot be wholesale merchants, prefer the life of planters in the country, however small may be the estate and the gains. The Negroes constituted the class of field labourers and porters; Indians were universally the watermen, and formed the crews of the numberless canoes of all sizes and shapes which traded between Pará and the interior.

The educated Brazilians, not many of whom are of pure Caucasian descent—for the immigration of Portuguese, for many years, has been almost exclusively of the male sex—are courteous, lively, and intelligent people. They were gradually weaning themselves of the ignorant, bigoted notions which they inherited from their Portuguese ancestors, especially those entertained with regard to the treatment of women. Formerly the Portuguese would not allow their wives to go into society, or their daughters to learn reading and writing. In 1848, Brazilian ladies were only just beginning to emerge from this inferior position, and Brazilian fathers were opening their eyes to the advantages of education for their daughters. Reforms of this kind are slow. It is, perhaps, in part owing to the degrading position always held by women, that the relations between the sexes were and are still on so unsatisfactory a footing, and private morality at so low an ebb, in Brazil. In Pará, I believe that an improvement is now taking place, but formerly promiscuous intercourse seemed to be the general rule among all classes, and intrigues and lovemaking the serious business of the greater part of the population. That this state of things is a necessity depending on the climate and institutions I do not believe, as I have resided at small towns in the interior, where the habits, and the general standard of morality of the inhabitants, were as pure as they are in similar places in England. . . .

I will now give a short account of Cametá, the principal town on the banks of the Tocantins. . . . The most remarkable feature in the social aspect of the place is the hybrid nature of the whole population, the amalgamation of the white and Indian races being here complete. The aborigines were originally very numerous on the western bank of the Tocantins, the principal tribe having been the Camutás, from which the city takes its name. They were a superior nation, settled, and attached to agriculture, and received with open arms the white immigrants who were attracted to the district by its fertility, natural beauty, and the healthfulness of the climate. The Portuguese settlers were nearly all males, the Indian women were good-looking, and made excellent wives; so the natural result has been, in the course of two centuries, a complete blending of the two races. There is now, however, a considerable infusion of Negro blood in the mixture, several hundred African slaves having been introduced during the last seventy years. . . .

The people have a reputation all over the province for energy and perseverance; and it is often said that they are as keen in trade as the Portuguese. The lower classes are as indolent and sensual here as in other parts of the province, a moral condition not to be wondered at in a country where perpetual summer reigns, and where the necessaries of life are so easily obtained. But they are lighthearted, quick-witted, communicative, and hospitable.

16 *Louis and Elizabeth Agassiz* ◆ The Education of Men and Women

Louis Agassiz, born in Switzerland in 1807, was an ichthyologist who did his early scientific work on Brazilian materials collected by Karl Friedrich Philipp von Martius and Johann B. von Spix. He published his first studies on the fishes of Brazil in 1829. Agassiz then taught at the University of Neuchâtel until 1846. Famous for his hands-on teaching methods, Agassiz settled in the United States, where in 1848 he became a professor of zoology at Harvard University.

In 1865 and 1870–71, Professor Agassiz and his wife, Elizabeth Cabot Cary, traveled extensively in Brazil, almost entirely in the Amazon, except for relatively short visits to Rio de Janeiro and other coastal areas. His main task was collecting fish species, while his wife, a prominent Bostonian and later the first president of Radcliffe College, was primarily responsible for their joint book, A Journey in Brazil *(1868). Most of this work, an early American travel classic, comments on customs, people, and places rather than on ichthyology. This selection deals with Brazilian educational and intellectual life and reflects Elizabeth Agassiz's interest in the importance of education for women.*

We were received with a hospitality hardly to be equalled, I think, out of Brazil, for it asks neither who you are nor whence you come, but opens its doors to every wayfarer. On this occasion we were expected; but it is nevertheless true that at such a *fazenda*, where the dining room accommodates a hundred persons if necessary, all travellers passing through the country are free to stop for rest and refreshment. . . .

Of the public schools for girls not much can be said. The education of women is little regarded in Brazil, and the standard of instruction for girls in the public schools is low. Even in the private schools, where the

From *A Journey in Brazil* (Boston: Ticknor and Fields, 1868), 119, 478–81, 497–504, 516–17.

children of the better class are sent, it is the complaint of all teachers that they are taken away from school just at the time when their minds begin to develop. The majority of girls in Brazil who go to school at all are sent at about seven or eight years of age, and are considered to have finished their education at thirteen or fourteen. The next step in their life is marriage. Of course there are exceptions; some parents wisely leave their children at school, or direct their instruction at home, till they are seventeen or eighteen years of age, and others send their girls abroad. But usually, with the exception of one or two accomplishments, such as French or music, the education of women is neglected, and this neglect affects the whole tone of society. It does not change the general truth of this statement, that there are Brazilian ladies who would be recognized in the best society as women of the highest intelligence and culture. But they are the exceptions, as they inevitably must be under the present system of instruction, and they feel its influence upon their social position only the more bitterly.

Indeed, many of the women I have known most intimately here have spoken to me with deep regret of their limited, imprisoned existence. There is not a Brazilian *senhora*, who has ever thought about the subject at all, who is not aware that her life is one of repression and constraint. She cannot go out of her house, except under certain conditions, without awakening scandal. Her education leaves her wholly ignorant of the most common topics of a wider interest, though perhaps with a tolerable knowledge of French and music. The world of books is closed to her; for there is little Portuguese literature into which she is allowed to look, and that of other languages is still less at her command. She knows little of the history of her own country, almost nothing of that of others, and she is hardly aware that there is any religious faith except the uniform one of Brazil; she has probably never heard of the Reformation, nor does she dream that there is a sea of thought surging in the world outside, constantly developing new phases of national and individual life; indeed, of all but her own narrow domestic existence she is profoundly ignorant.

On one occasion, when staying at a *fazenda*, I took up a volume which was lying on the piano. A book is such a rare sight, in the rooms occupied by the family, that I was curious to see its contents. As I stood turning over the leaves (it proved to be a romance), the master of the house came up, and remarked that the book was not suitable reading for ladies, but that here (putting into my hand a small volume) was a work adapted to the use of women and children, which he had provided for the *senhoras* of his family. I opened it, and found it to be a sort of textbook of morals, filled with commonplace sentiments, copybook phrases, written in a tone of condescending indulgence for the feminine intellect. Women being, after all, the mothers of men, and understood to have some little influence on their education, I could hardly wonder, after seeing this specimen of their intellectual food, that the wife and daughters of our host were not greatly addicted to reading. Nothing strikes a stranger more than the absence of books in Brazilian houses. If the father is a professional man, he has his small library of medicine or law, but books are never seen scattered about as if in common use; they make no part of the daily life. I repeat, that there are exceptions. I well remember finding in the sitting room of a young girl, by whose family we had been most cordially received, a well-selected library of the best literary and historical works in German and French; but this is the only instance of the kind we met with during our year in Brazil. Even when the Brazilian women have received the ordinary advantages of education, there is something in their home life so restricted, so shut out from natural contact with external influences, that this in itself tends to cripple their development. Their amusements are as meagre and scanty as their means of instruction. . . .

In order to form a just estimate of the present condition of education in Brazil, and its future prospects, we must not consider it altogether from our own standpoint. The truth is that all steady progress in Brazil dates from her declaration of independence, and that is a very recent fact in her history. Since she has passed from colonial to national life her relations with other countries have enlarged, antiquated prejudices have been effaced, and with a more intense individual existence she has assumed also a more cosmopolitan breadth of ideas. But a political revolution is more rapidly accomplished than the remoulding of the nation which is its result—its consequence rather than its accompaniment. Even now, after half a century of independent existence, intellectual progress in Brazil is manifested rather as a tendency, a desire, so to speak, giving a progressive movement to society, than as a positive fact. The intellectual life of a nation when fully developed has its material existence in large and various institutions of learning, scattered throughout the country. Except in a very limited and local sense, this is not yet the case in Brazil.

I did not visit São Paulo, and I cannot therefore speak from personal observation of the Faculty which stands highest in general estimation; I can, however, testify to the sound learning and liberal culture of many of its graduates whom it has been my good fortune to know, and whose characters as gentlemen and as students bear testimony to the superior instruction they have received at the hands of their Alma Mater. I was told that the best schools, after those of São Paulo, were those of Bahia and Pernambuco. I did not visit them, as my time was too short; but I should think that the presence of the professional faculties established in both these cities would tend to raise the character of the lower grades of education. The regular faculties embrace only medical and legal studies. The instruction in both is thorough, though perhaps limited; at least I felt that, in the former, in which my own studies have prepared me to judge, those accessory branches which, after all, lie at the foundation of a superior medical education, are either wanting or are taught very imperfectly. Neither zoology, comparative anatomy, botany, physics, nor chemistry is allowed sufficient weight in the medical schools. The education is one rather of books than of facts. Indeed, as long as the prejudice against manual labor of all kinds exists in Brazil, practical instruction will be deficient; as long as students of nature think it unbecoming a gentleman to handle his own specimens, to carry his own geological hammer, to make his own scientific preparations, he will remain a mere dilettante in investigation. He may be very familiar with recorded facts, but he will make no original researches. On this account, and on account of their personal indolence, field studies are foreign to Brazilian habits. Surrounded as they are by a nature rich beyond comparison, their naturalists are theoretical rather than practical. They know more of the bibliography of foreign science than of the wonderful fauna and flora with which they are surrounded. . . .

Of the common schools I saw little. Of course, in a country where the population is sparsely scattered over very extensive districts, it must be difficult to gather the children in schools, outside of the large cities. Where such schools have been organized the instruction is gratuitous; but competent teachers are few, the education very limited, and the means of instruction scanty. Reading, writing, and ciphering, with the least possible smattering of geography, form the groundwork of all these schools. The teachers labor under great difficulties, because they have not the strong support of the community. There is little general appreciation of the importance of education as the basis without which all higher civilization is impossible. I have, however, noticed throughout Brazil a disposition to give a practical education, a training in some trade, to the poor children. Establishments of this kind exist in almost all the larger cities. This is a good sign; it shows that they attach a proper value to labor, at least for the lower classes, and aim at raising a working population. In these schools blacks and whites are, so to speak, industrially united. Indeed, there is no antipathy of race to be overcome in Brazil, either among the laboring people or in the higher walks of life. I was pleased to see pupils, without distinction of race or color, mingling in the exercises. . . .

I cannot close what I have to say of instruction in Brazil without adding that, in a country where only half the nation is educated, there can be no complete intellectual progress. Where the difference of education makes an intelligent sympathy between men and women almost impossible, so that their relation is necessarily limited to that of the domestic affections, never raised except in some very exceptional cases to that of cultivated companionship, the development of the people as a whole must remain imperfect and partial. I believe, however, that, especially in this direction, a rapid reform may be expected. I have heard so many intelligent Brazilians lament the want of suitable instruction for women in their schools, that I think the standard of education for girls will steadily be raised. Remembering the antecedents of the Brazilians, their inherited notions as to what is becoming in the privacy and restraint of a woman's life, we are not justified, however false these ideas may seem to us, in considering the present generation as responsible for them; they are also too deeply rooted to be changed in a day. . . .

The exaggerated appreciation of political employment prevailing everywhere is a misfortune. It throws into the shade all other occupations, and loads the government with a crowd of paid officials who uselessly encumber the public service and are a drain upon the public funds. Every man who has received an education seeks a political career, as at once the most aristocratic and the easiest way of gaining a livelihood. It is but recently that gentlemen have begun to engage in mercantile pursuits. . . .

Will my Brazilian friends who read this summary say that I have given but grudging praise to their public institutions, accompanied by an unkind criticism of their social condition? I hope not. I should do myself great wrong did I give the impression that I part from Brazil with any feeling but that of warm sympathy, a deep-rooted belief in her future progress and prosperity, and sincere personal gratitude toward her. I recognize in the Brazilians as a nation their susceptibility to lofty impulses and emotions, their love of theoretical liberty, their natural generosity, their aptness to learn, their ready eloquence; if also I miss among them something of the stronger and more persistent qualities of the Northern races, I do but recall a distinction which is as ancient as the tropical and temperate zones themselves.

17 *Herbert H. Smith* ◆ The Evils of Slavery

Herbert H. Smith was an American zoologist, based in New York, who first visited the Amazon as a student in 1870. He returned in 1874 and spent three additional years in Brazil, where he collected about one hun-

From *Brazil: The Amazons and the Coast* (London: Sampson Low, Marston, Searle, and Rivington, 1880), 465–68.

dred thousand animal specimens, mainly insects, in the Amazon. Invited by Scribner's Magazine *to write a series of articles on Brazil, he made two more trips there, studying economic and social conditions in addition to his own specialty. Smith later expanded the* Scribner's *series into* Brazil: The Amazons and the Coast, *which, particularly in the following excerpt, contains his observations on slavery in the years just before abolition.*

So we come to the fourth and lowest class in Brazil—the slaves. The class that originated in barbarism and selfishness—the class which Brazil, for very shame, is trying to get rid of, but whose influence will curse the children with the sins of their fathers for dreary years. I tell you, be they inspiration or revelation, or only bare philosophy, those words of Sinai are true with God's truth and justice; you cannot undo a wrong that is done; it must work itself out to the bitter ending, and you or yours, or blameless people on the other side of the world, will have to pay for your compact with Sin. We are paying ourselves for this hideous crime of slavery, as we paid for it during four years of hideous war; body and soul, we are all of us paying other people's debts. If there is no clearinghouse fiat ahead of us—there ought to be.

I came to Brazil with an honest desire to study this question of slavery in a spirit of fairness, without running to emotional extremes. Now, after four years, I am convinced that all other evils with which the country is cursed, taken together, will not compare with this one; I could almost say that all other evils have arisen from it, or been strengthened by it. And yet I cannot unduly blame men who have inherited the curse, and had no part in the making of it. I can honor masters who treat their slaves kindly, albeit they are owners of stolen property.

In mere animal matters, of food and clothing, no doubt many of the Negroes are better off than they were in Africa; no doubt, also, they have learned some lessons of peace and civility; even a groping outline of Christianity. But it would be hard to prove that the plantation slave, dependent, like a child, on his master, and utterly unused to thinking for himself, is better, mentally, than the savage who has his faculties sharpened by continual battling with the savage nature around him. Slavery is weakening to the brain; the slave is worse material for civilization than the savage is, and worse still with every generation of slavery.

That is not the main evil, however. The harm that slavery has done to the black race is as nothing to the evils it has heaped upon the white one, the masters. If every slave and free Negro could be carried away to Africa, if every drop of cursed mixed blood could be divided, the evils would be there yet, and go down to the children's children with a blight upon humanity.

Indolence and pride and sensuality and selfishness, these are the outgrowths of slavery that have enslaved the slavemakers and their children. Do you imagine that they are all rich men's sons, these daintily clad, delicate young men on the Ouvidor [a main street in Rio de Janeiro]? The most of them are poor, but they will lead their vegetable lives, God knows how, parasites on their friends, or on the government, or on the tailor and grocer, because they will not soil their hands with tools. "Laborers!" cries Brazil. "We must have labor!" and where will she get honest workmen, if honest work is a degradation? Slavery has made it so. For generations the upper classes had no work to do, and they came to look upon it as the part of an inferior race. So they have kept their hands folded, and the muscle has gone from their bones, and indolence has become a part of their nature. Still, they will be sham lords, if they cannot be real ones; so their money—what they have of it—goes for broadcloth coats and silk hats, and sensuality; a grade below that, they are yet shabby-genteel figures, with an eye to friendly invitations to dinner; and below that, they sink out of sight altogether, from mere inanition.

The rich men's sons are not parasites; sharp enough, many of them are, to keep the money they have, and double it. But from their cradle, the curse of slavery is on them. The black nurse is an inferior, and the child knows it, and tyrannizes over her as only a child can. The mother is an inferior, by her social station, and she does not often venture to thwart the child. The father, with whom authority rests, shirks it back on the irresponsible ones, who may not venture to lay sacrilegious hands on the heir of power. The amount of it is, that a child's training here consists in letting it have its own way as much as possible; and the small naughtinesses and prides develop into consuming vanity and haughtiness. It is characteristic of the Brazilians, this vanity; it may come out in snobbism, or overconfidence, or merely a fiery sensitiveness; but there it is plainly, in the best of them. Slavery is to blame for it—black slavery, and woman slavery that gives the mother no authority.

Of the sensuality that comes from slavery, the mixed races that overrun Brazil are a sufficient witness, as they are in our Southern States. But in Brazil, the proportion of these mixed races is vastly greater; I am safe in saying that not a third of the population is pure-blooded; social distinctions of color are never very finely drawn, though they are by no means abolished, as some writers would have us believe.

People who talk of "amalgamation," as a blessing to be hoped for, should study its effects here, where it is almost an accomplished fact. The mixed races are invariably bad; they seem to combine all the worst characteristics of the two parent stocks, with none of the good ones; and the evil is most apparent where the "amalgamation" is most complete. A light mulatto, or an almost black one, may be a very decent kind of a fellow; but the brown half-and-half is nearly always lazy and stupid and vain. So with the whites and Indians, or the Indians and blacks; the *mamelucos* [mixtures of white and Indian] are treacherous, and passionate, and indolent; the *mestiços* are worse yet; but a dash of mixed blood may not spoil the man that has it.

IV

The Republic (1889–1964): Movement toward Modernization

Brazil proclaimed itself a republic with almost no strife on November 15, 1889, the day after the emperor departed for exile in Portugal. A new 1891 constitution established a decentralized federation of twenty states, and provided for the election of a president to a four-year term and for two houses of Congress. The military took over the essence of the emperor's moderating power. Brazil continued to depend on agricultural exports and on foreign investment. Planters maintained their economic and political dominance. Some industrial leaders forced their way into the upper classes, and educated sons of immigrants became part of the urban middle class. Former slaves, suddenly emancipated and unprepared for freedom, formed a vast pool of unskilled labor, both on plantations and in the cities.

A coterie of tightly organized and corrupt political machines, under governors of large states—particularly Minas Gerais and São Paulo—and local political bosses (so-called colonels), ruled the country. The states had armed police forces that resembled small armies. Elections were manipulated, and fraud was used when necessary. Politicians dutifully paid rhetorical homage to elections, although only a tiny percentage of the population voted. The Brazilian elite viewed the lower classes as lazy, ignorant, and of weak character. Popular enthusiasm was whipped up for candidates, but between elections public opinion, largely ignored, turned indifferent. There were no national parties. Suffrage was restricted to literate adult male citizens. Educational opportunities were few; most rural districts had no schools. Of a population numbering fourteen million at the time the republic was proclaimed, between 80 and 90 percent were illiterate.

Although the transition from empire to republic eventually led to rapid urbanization and the rise of industry, the social structure of Brazil proved remarkably resistant to change. Those who governed under either system of government took little account of the mass of the population. The intellectual elite of the republic gave ground slowly because the concept of widespread social mobility ran counter to the country's traditional authoritarian and stratified heritage. Adapting to fashionable European "scientific" racist doctrines, Brazilians developed a "whitening" ideology aimed at bringing about "racial democracy." The "superior" white race would continue to dominate by amalgamating with other races. However, mulattoes in particular would be granted limited entry into higher social circles, depending on their appearance and degree of cultural "whiteness."

By the 1920s the republic had become the target of widespread criticism and ridicule from within. A new generation of "modernist" intellectual leaders, together with their political and military counterparts, rejected European (mainly French) orientation and the corrupt, cozy, and antiquated methods by which the small in-group of politicians retained power. Symbolic of the challenge to the old order was Modern Art Week, held in relatively cosmopolitan São Paulo during a 1922 centennial celebration. Nationalistic in tone, it featured daring new works of art and literature.

The worldwide 1929 depression hit Brazil particularly hard, especially its coffee export sector, and exacerbated domestic unrest. Dissatisfied military officers and dissident civilians, led by Getúlio Vargas, an opposition politician from the southern state of Rio Grande do Sul, overthrew the republican regime in 1930. Vargas became president and governed for fifteen years, first as provisional president until his election in 1934 and then, after putting down Fascist and Communist revolts, from 1937 onward with dictatorial powers under the Estado Novo, patterned after Antonio Salazar's Portugal and Benito Mussolini's Italy. He left a lasting mark on modern Brazil. A wily political opportunist, he was not averse to using authoritarian police-state methods where necessary, but he had no strong ideological bent.

Under Vargas, the upper class continued to draw its wealth primarily from coffee, but an industrial elite emerged under the leadership of the state, which took a central role in the economy and led Brazil's movement toward modernization. The Vargas administration stepped up industrialization. New homegrown manufacturing substituted for previously imported goods. A small middle sector developed in commerce and the professions, amounting to 30 percent of the population in some cities but to only about 10 to 15 percent of the total population (thirty million in 1930).

Electoral reforms provided for greater participation, including the vote for women, but the fraud and bribery common under the republic continued. The lower classes consisted of a large-scale peasantry eking out a meager living from the soil, a rural proletariat performing wage labor in the countryside, an urban working class, and migrants from the backlands. A new labor code created unions—from the top down—for the first time.

Although theoretically it provided broad protection for workers, the law was easily manipulated by the government.

At the outbreak of World War II, Vargas maintained neutrality, only entering the conflict, along with the United States, after the attack on Pearl Harbor in 1941. In return for American help in fostering industrialization and protecting its sea-lanes, Brazil furnished essential raw materials (for example, quartz and natural rubber) and air and naval bases to the Allied war effort, and it sent an expeditionary force to Italy. After taking part in a victorious coalition against fascism abroad, the military officers who returned to Brazil once again initiated a change in the political system, deposing the dictator in October 1945 and sending Vargas back to his ranch in his home state.

From 1946 to 1964 three parties—personalistic, opportunistic, and nonideological—were prominent in a democratic political system. Two of them, the Social Democratic Party and Brazilian Labor Party, were controlled by Vargas, who returned as elected president in 1951. Unable to govern as effectively as in his earlier presidency, he committed suicide in 1954 under pressure from the military and civilian opposition, prompted by scandals over corruption and fears that he might try to seize dictatorial powers again.

Vargas's successor was elected in 1955. Juscelino Kubitschek, a former governor of Minas Gerais whose slogan was "Fifty Years of Progress in Five," fostered rapid industrialization, particularly of automobiles and consumer durables, and built a boldly modernistic new capital. Brasília, completed in 1960, symbolized the beginning of a dramatic shift of the population and economy westward into the vast and largely unoccupied backlands.

Kubitschek's promising presidency gave way to an ill-starred and turbulent period in which much of the progress of the late 1950s was undone. The 1960 elections brought to office a populist politician named Janio Quadros, who resigned seven months after becoming president for reasons never satisfactorily explained. His campaign symbol had been a broom, to sweep away Brazil's corruption and inefficiency, but apparently he felt that he had insufficient powers to carry out his mandate. Congress refused to grant his demand for increased powers and instead accepted his resignation.

Vice President João Goulart, who succeeded Quadros, was also a populist and a political heir of Vargas. He was anathema to conservative military officers and prominent civilians, who only agreed to his taking office under a jerry-built constitutional compromise that lasted little more than one year: a hybrid parliamentary system that reduced his powers and observed constitutional niceties but proved unworkable. The odds were against Goulart on almost every count, but he made them worse with his inexperience, weakness, and indecision. His economic stabilization plan to deal with inflation and balance-of-payments deficits hurt workers, the social group to which he was most committed, and nationalists, who chafed at the harsh terms imposed by foreign lenders.

Government encouragement, financing, and logistical support under Goulart spurred radical nationalists, who began trying to organize—among others—enlisted men and rural workers. Their rhetoric and actions, at times revolutionary, raised suspicions among both the Brazilian military and other conservative groups. Since Goulart's opponents did not have the votes to impeach him, they began conspiring to overthrow him by a military coup. Initially, only a minority of officers was involved in the plotting, but a feverish atmosphere in early 1964, exacerbated by a navy petty officer mutiny, convinced centrist military officers to join the conspiracy. They started a revolt on March 31 that spread across the country. Within twenty-four hours Goulart had fled to Uruguay. Both his supporters and opponents were surprised at the speed and ease with which the government had collapsed.

18 *Gilberto Freyre* ◆ New World in the Tropics

Gilberto Freyre, born in 1900 to a traditional planter family in the northeastern state of Pernambuco, received his undergraduate degree from Baylor University in Texas and his doctorate in sociology from Columbia University, where he came under the influence of anthropologist Franz Boas. His long career as an author specializing in social history and race relations in Brazil began with his first book, Casa grande e senzala *(translated into English and published as* The Masters and the Slaves*) in 1933. The book explored African influences in Brazil and the racial and cultural adaptability of the Portuguese in the tropics. He went on to write a total of sixty-three books and countless articles, mainly on Brazilian cultural themes, especially race. Many of his books were written in or translated into English. Freyre died in 1987.*

Freyre's works epitomize Brazilian efforts at modernization during the republican period. The excerpts that follow, adapted from three of his works, illustrate how his basic concepts gradually evolved. He introduces the terms "Brazilian type of man and woman" and "racial democracy" in Sobrados e mucambos *(*The Mansions and the Shanties*). Later, in* New World in the Tropics*, he explores his concept of "Luso-tropical civilization." Finally, in an essay he wrote for a special issue of* The Annals of the American Academy of Political and Social Science*, he tries to define the Brazilian character.*

~ *A Brazilian Type of Man and Woman* ~

Schooling and book-learning developed in Brazil at the cost of the well-rounded development of the individual. The young men who in the reign of Pedro II assumed such importance in politics, letters, public administration, and law were characterized by an almost romantic note of delicate health.

It became almost as pleasant to die at twenty, or thirty, as to die an angel, before reaching seven. To die old was for the bourgeoisie, for the rich planters, for the obese vicars, for the favorite plantation slaves. "Geniuses" died young and, if possible, of tuberculosis. Health was not for them. Nor vigor, nor to be well-fleshed. And the "geniuses" collaborated in their own demise. They consumed quantities of brandy. They associated with prostitutes. They picked up syphilis in their cheap orgies. . . .

~ It was characteristic of the patriarchal regime for man to make of woman a being as different from himself as possible. He, the strong, she, the weak; he, the noble, she, the beautiful. But the beauty he prized was a somewhat morbid beauty. The delicate, almost sickly, girl. Or the plump, soft, domestic, motherly woman, ample of hips and buttocks. Without a trace of masculine vigor and agility, with the greatest possible differentiation in figure and dress between the two sexes.

The exploitation of woman by man justifies a double standard of morality, permitting man complete freedom in the pleasures of carnal love and only permitting the woman to go to bed with her husband when he feels like procreating. This double standard allows the man every opportunity for initiative, social intercourse, contacts of many sorts, while it limits those of the woman to domestic duties and activities, to contacts with her children, relatives, nurses, old women, slaves. And from time to time, in a Catholic society such as Brazil, with her confessor.

Members of the ruling class were subjective, weak, and mediocre in their approach, and lacked interest in concrete, immediate, and local problems. This almost total lack of objectivity may in part be attributed to the slight or nonexistent part played by women in artistic and political activity. By and large, women have a greater sense of practical reality than do men. Matters of general interest were dealt with in an almost exclusively masculine way.

In a repressive, oppressive, and overprotected society, Carnival served, as did the confessional on a higher level, as an outlet for repression suffered by men, women, children, slaves, Negroes, and Indians, which would otherwise have burdened many of them beyond endurance with resentments and phobias. Masked balls and street revelry provided psychic release and lowered social barriers for a part of the population barred by their daily routines from the noisy amusements and sensual dances they instinctively preferred.

The absence of woman as the collaborator of husband, son, brother, lover reveals itself in the aridity, the incompleteness, and even perversion in some of the most important men of patriarchal and semipatriarchal Brazil. Lack of a woman's intelligent collaboration or deep feminine sympathy for the work of these men seems to have led to a narcissism or monosexualism in intellectual and even personal aspects that bordered on the morbid.

We Brazilians liberated ourselves more quickly from racial prejudice than from that of sex. Sexual taboos were tenacious. "The inferiority of woman" took the place of "the inferiority of race." The weaker sex; the fair sex; the domestic sex; the sex kept in a completely artificial situation for the pleasure and convenience of men, the unchallenged master of this half-dead society.

The distance, social as well as psychic, between the white woman and the black slave was always greater in Brazil than between the white man and the black slave woman. As patriarchalism declined, however, the white woman of good family, responding to the physical attraction and the sexual allure of the mulatto—apparently stronger, more alert, more exotic, perhaps more ardent, than the white man—made possible the rise of the light mulatto or the poor university graduate or soldier to the highest ranks of Brazilian society. . . .

~ During three centuries of relative isolation of Brazil from non-Iberian Europe, a Brazilian type of man and woman had developed, or at least the outline had emerged. A type of master, another of slave. But there was a midpoint between the two: the mulatto, who little by little was budding out into university graduate, priest, doctor, with his academic diploma or his appointment as captain of militia serving him as a certificate of whiteness. The middle race comprised our middle class, which was so weak under our patriarchal system.

As the patriarchal system declined, particularistic or individualistic family, economic, and social organization began to develop. *Subjects* and then *citizens* began to emerge. The loyalty of the individual to his natural or social father—the patriarch, the guardian, the godfather, the head of the family—was transferred to the political father of all, the king, and later the emperor. He became the political father not only of patriarchs but of their sons, not only of whites but of colored men, not only of the rich but of the poor, not only of coastal inhabitants but of the backlands. At the close of the eighteenth, and above all in the nineteenth, century, ethnically and culturally mixed individuals developed alongside patriarchal families of Portuguese descent, which steadily became less powerful and less pure.

The Portuguese colonization of Brazil fundamentally emphasized religious status, not race; political status, not color. The civilized Christian colored man could be socially as Portuguese as any Portuguese, as Christian as any Christian. The priesthood and the military profession had long been open to Amerindians and, in exceptional cases, to descendants of Africans. Since that was the trend in our country since early times, Indians and Africans naturally behaved less like two races oppressed by the white man and more in accord with each individual's or family's status in society or in their region.

Regional factors modified the influence of race and class. In the richer plantation regions the Negro was a contemptible being in the eyes of the whites and of the natives. There was little social difference between ranchers and ranch hands on the numerous small ranches in the south, although on large ranches the Big Houses were the equivalent of plantation mansions. To be a plantation owner was, by and large, to occupy an honorable and ennobling position in patriarchal society. But the regional situation imposed restrictions on the owner. Owning a plantation that made brown sugar in Piauí was not the same as owning a manioc plantation in Santa Catarina. Owning a sugar plantation in Pernambuco was not the same as owning one in the Recôncavo of Bahia. The Bahian city dweller, in Salvador, took advantage of his city's being the capital of Brazil to overrate his origin or region, as though Salvador were the only civilized, urban, polite region of Brazil, and all the rest was backwoods.

The gaúcho reacted to this attitude in his own fashion, with contempt for any Brazilian of the North who could not ride a horse with the skill of those of the far South. He associated this limitation with being a Bahian. To be a Bahian was to ignore the manly art of riding. Therefore, the term "Bahian" became one of both praise and disdain. And the same was true of "gaúcho."

Brazilian values, life-styles, and culture contain characteristics or peculiarities of class, race, and region. Generalizations applicable to countries of greater ethnic purity or more clearly defined class structure lose their validity or strength in Brazil. We have not developed aristocratically in the sense of a single race, class, or region. Our history took essentially aristocratic forms, but with varying substance or content. It could proclaim itself noble or white, or native. It could glorify the planter or the city gentry. It might make the coastal dweller or the Paulista our hero. Sugar could be the basis of our economy, or this majestic role might be occupied by coffee.

We Brazilians are not really a Latin people. Even less are we strictly Christian. Catholicism was a powerful factor in integrating Brazil, but a Catholicism which acquired a dark or mulatto tinge in its contacts in the Iberian Peninsula with African forms of religion. It adapted to conditions of life in the tropics and to our people of hybrid origin.

Traits of the three races that have gone into our national composition persist. Reciprocity between cultures, and not domination of one by the other, is an active characteristic of the Brazilian social milieu. Psychological contours of race and class are not rigid.

Brazil is becoming more and more a racial democracy, characterized by an almost unique combination of diversity and unity. When Brazil was a slave economy, whites, almost exclusively Portuguese and Catholic in culture, had the best opportunities and held power. But as the patriarchal system gave way to a society that was mestizo, ethnically and culturally varied, and predominantly individualistic, the half-breed or the mulatto or—to put it more delicately—the dark-complexioned person fits better into the Brazilian milieu, and would seem to show more capacity for leadership than the white or near white.

From *Sobrados e mucambos* (Rio de Janeiro: Livraria José Olympio Editora, 1936). Translated by Harriet de Onis and published as *The Mansions and the Shanties: The Making of Modern Brazil* (New York: Alfred A. Knopf, 1963), 70–71, 73–74, 84–85, 88–90, 99–101, 204, 232–33, 244, 246–47, 253–54, 420, 422–23, 431. Reprinted by permission of Fundação Gilberto Freyre, Recife, Brazil. Adapted by G. Harvey Summ.

~ *Luso-Tropical Civilization* ~

The secret of Brazil's success in building a humane, Christian, and modern civilization in tropical America has been her genius for compromise in the cultural and social spheres. Ethnic democracy is the almost perfect opportunity for all men regardless of race or color. Not that there is no race or color prejudice mixed with class prejudice. There is. But no one would think of having churches only for whites. No one in Brazil would think of laws against interracial marriage. No one would think of barring colored people from theaters or residential sections of a town. A general spirit of human brotherhood is much stronger among Brazilians than race, color, class, or religious prejudice. The Brazilian solution of the racial question is certainly wiser, more promising, and, above all, more humane than any solution that operates through separation or segregation.

The sadness expressed in Brazilian folk music and guitar songs is explained by a trauma in the social past of a large part of the population: slavery. The slave, even when well treated, felt vaguely nostalgic, which made his song one of sadness, though his dance was often one of joy. From the Portuguese the Brazilians inherited the well-known nostalgia of the sailor, who is frequently far from his home—a feeling expressed in the Portuguese language by the word *saudade*.

Brazilians, already considerable pioneers in their history, are becoming pioneers of a new and even more exciting future. They are developing a modern civilization in the tropics whose predominant traits are European, but whose perspectives are extra-European. They found in tropical America an ideal space for expanding and developing their ethnically democratic civilization—aristocratic and even feudal in other aspects—which had begun to flourish in the African and Asiatic tropics.

In Brazil the tendency of national, subnational, or ethnic groups to fuse has been more decisive—and their tendency to remain monolithically apart has been less vigorous—than in the United States. Brazil's most important maladjustments and sharpest crises have been caused less by ethnic conflict than by conflict between regional cultures or groups. Interregional maladjustments are more critical and dramatic. They are caused by isolation and economic disorganization in tragically archaic regions, in contrast to more progressive regions which are technically and intellectually dominant. Geographically immense, Brazil lacks a dynamic interregional balance.

The lack of systematic and continuous African opposition to European dominance in Brazil seems to be explained by the fact that European dominance never became sharply exclusive. This dominance nonetheless existed, which explains why Brazil, in spite of its large non-European population, remains an area characterized by European and Christian civilization, preserved, carried on, and developed—with inevitable and desirable changes—not only by pure descendants of Europeans but also by pure descendants of non-Europeans and by a large number of intermediates, partly European, partly non-European.

This does not imply that Brazilians are only and passively an expression of a sub-European civilization. They are increasingly becoming ultra-European. They are renewing Western civilization in the American hemisphere. They are artificially preserving European values and cultural styles and adapting them to new surroundings in tropical America.

"Luso-tropical civilization" is an expression I have suggested to characterize what seems to me a particular form of behavior and a particular form of accomplishment of the Portuguese in the world: his tendency to prefer the tropics for his extra-European expansion and his ability to remain successfully in the tropics—successfully from a cultural as well as from an ecological point of view—an intermediary between European and tropical cultures.

The root of the matter lies in the patriarchal past of Brazil. Its civilization has been rather the efforts of a familistic organization than the achievement of state or church, of kings or military leaders. Hence its development as a civilization that has had at its core domestic, patriarchal, sedentary values: (1) the residential and agrarian buildings associated with a family economy, of a permanent, not a nomadic, character; (2) the cookery, always complementary to a family sedentary civilization like the Chinese in the East; and (3) the housewife, as an administrator of cookery and other important domestic activities.

From *New World in the Tropics: The Culture of Modern Brazil* (New York: Vintage Books, 1959), 7–9, 146–47, 149–54, 231. Reprinted by permission of Fundação Gilberto Freyre, Recife, Brazil. Adapted by G. Harvey Summ.

~ *A Synthesis of the Old and the New* ~

The Brazilian national character seems to remain conditioned by a sense of time that is distinctly Iberian. Is the rhythm of growth in some areas of Brazil—São Paulo, for instance—a significant departure from the Brazilian national character, the inclination of Brazilians not to rush, but to do things in a slow rhythm? Are phenomena such as the rapid material growth of São Paulo and the building of Brasília in four years to be considered anticipations of what is to happen in a few years to the Brazilian nation? Answers are not easy.

The Brazilian national character should not be considered, either on this point or on others, so static as to remain absolutely the same as it was a century and a half, a century, or half a century ago. It has changed. It is changing. In some aspects of their character and their behavior, Brazilians seem to be inclined to combine modernity with tradition. Hence the special pride of many Brazilians in the fact that Brazil was for some time a monarchy. Becoming politically independent, Brazilians never separated from their European sources in the same radical way that most of the Spanish people of America separated from Spain.

Brazilian national cuisine, though Portuguese in its basic traditional elements, has assimilated in an adventurous, experimental way Oriental, Amerindian, and African contributions and is now assimilating Italian, German, and Japanese elements. Brazilian invention is vividly present; this cuisine is a creative synthesis of the old and the new.

Some foreign critics are too severe with Brazilians when they see political developments in contemporary Brazil that do not seem to correspond to their ideas or ideals of democracy or some other complex. Such critics fail to understand a tendency—more pronounced in this century—toward bolder combinations of the old and the new, tradition and modernity, in finding Brazilian solutions to Brazilian problems, circumstances, and needs. The Brazilian national character inclines toward democratic solutions not only in social and racial matters, but in political matters as well. The history of the Brazilian national state—monarchy and republic—seems to confirm this interpretation. If so, some foreign observer may ask why Brazilians now seem to be reshaping their political system in such a way that authoritarian trends seem to be superseding the conventionally liberal-democratic ones.

For more than a century and a half Brazilians have tended to harmonize their idealism and even their adventurous romanticism with reality. The revolutionary movement of 1964 brought this trait into dramatic focus: Brazilian leaders tried to adapt their democratic political idealism to present-day reality—the reality of a world not exactly at peace. Not a few Brazilians are realistic enough to think of their country as too vast, physically and socially, to be left to an entirely free interplay of competition between partisan, political, and other groups.

The Brazilian national character in the twentieth century remains essentially the same as in the nineteenth century, though now as then adapting itself to new circumstances, national and international, technological and political, economic, social, and religious. Brazilians themselves are only now becoming fully conscious of their uniqueness, and bold enough to appear before the world as a people different in their music, architecture, and cuisine, and in their way of playing football [soccer], from more mature peoples.

Present-day Brazilians may still be weak in physical and natural science. Some of them, even when Roman Catholics, may continue to believe in astrology, spiritualism, and magic. However, planning is being undertaken by some of today's Brazilian leaders in financial and economic activities. Brazilian national character is changing, though not so much as to become adept at method and unqualifiedly receptive to planning. Brazil remains essentially plastic, flexible, and, in spite of the use of economic planning by some modern leaders of the country, "improbable," as Aldous Huxley would say. With all its contradictions, their style of behavior expresses their national character.

From "Brazilian National Character in the Twentieth Century," in *The Annals of the American Academy of Political and Social Science* 370 (March 1967): 59–62. Reprinted by permission of the publisher and Fundação Gilberto Freyre, Recife, Brazil. Adapted by G. Harvey Summ.

19 *Thomas E. Skidmore* ◆ The "Whitening" Ideal

Thomas E. Skidmore is Carlos Manuel de Cespedes Professor of Modern Latin American History and director of the Center for Luso-American Studies at Brown University. He previously had a long and distinguished career at the University of Wisconsin. Skidmore has written many books and articles on Brazilian political and racial history, including comprehensive works on politics in the Getúlio Vargas era and in the military period. He is also the author of interpretative histories on modern Latin America and was a general editor for the Cambridge Encyclopedia on Latin America and the Caribbean. *Among his many works is a history of Brazilian race relations, featured in this selection, in which Skidmore deals with the elite's ideology of "whitening," which reached its high point in the early years of the republican period.*

From *Black into White: Race and Nationality in Brazilian Thought* (New York: Oxford University Press, 1974), 38–40, 44, 46, 64–65, 77. Footnotes, table, and figure omitted.

As the more perceptive men of property had foreseen, abolition did not bring the economic and social transformation expected by the more naive abolitionists. Brazil was still a predominantly agrarian economy when abolition came. Its paternalistic system of social relations prevailed even in the urban areas. This system of social stratification gave the landowners (who were white—or occasionally light mulatto) a virtual monopoly of power—economic, social, and political. The lower strata, including poor whites as well as most free coloreds, were well accustomed to submission and deference. This hierarchy, in which social classification correlated highly with color, had developed as an integral part of the slave-based colonial economy. But by the time of final abolition it was *not* dependent upon slavery for its continuation. . . .

The majority of Brazilian planters, especially those in the prosperous coffee regions of Center-South Brazil, came to understand that abolition need not endanger their economic and social dominance. This analysis proved correct. The newly freed slaves moved into the paternalistic multiracial social structure that had long since taught free men of color the habits of deference in their relationships with employers and other social superiors. . . .

The half-million slaves who were freed in 1888 entered a complex social structure that included free men of color (of every shade). Skin color, hair texture, facial, and other visible physical characteristics were the determinants of the racial category into which a person would be placed by those he met. The apparent wealth or status of the person being observed, indicated by his clothes or his immediate social company, also influenced the observer's reaction, as indicated by the Brazilian adage "money whitens"—although the instances observed usually applied to light mulattoes. The sum total of physical characteristics (the "phenotype") was the determining factor, although perception of this might vary according to the region, area, and observer. Brazil had never, at least not since late colonial times, exhibited a rigidly biracial system. There was always a middle category (called mulatto or *mestiço*) of racial mixtures. The strict observation of color-based endogamy, which became sanctified by law during the 1890s in the United States, had never existed in Brazil.

The fact that Brazil had escaped the rigid application of the "descent rule"—by which ancestry, not physical appearance (unless one "passes" for white), determines racial classification—should not be overemphasized. Origin could still be thought important in Brazil. Upwardly mobile mixed bloods often took great pains to conceal their family background. And such behavior suggests that a mulatto, whose phenotypical features had given him his desired social access, felt insecure enough to believe his mobility would have been endangered by having his social status redefined because of his family origin. But the mulatto can be said to be the central figure in Brazil's "racial democracy," because he was granted entry—albeit limited—into the higher social establishment. The limits on his mobility depended upon his exact appearance (the more "Negroid," the less mobile) and the degree of cultural "whiteness" (education, manners, wealth) he was able to attain. The successful application of this multiracial system required Brazilians to develop an intense sensitivity to racial categories and the nuances of their application. Evidence of the tension engendered by the resulting shifting network of color lines can be found in the voluminous Brazilian folklore about the "untrustworthy" mulatto. . . .

The free colored played an important role long before total abolition in Brazil. Free coloreds had succeeded in gaining a considerable occupational mobility—entry into skilled occupations and even occasionally prominent positions as artists, politicians, and writers—while slavery was still dominant *throughout* the country. These economic and social opportunities enjoyed by free coloreds furnish proof that the multiracial pattern of racial categorization was well established before final abolition.

Although this pluralistic scale of social classification had given Brazil a flexibility notably lacking in some other ex-slave societies such as the United States, it is essential to realize that the multiracial society nevertheless rested on implicitly racist assumptions. The "caucasian" was considered to be the natural and inevitable summit of the social pyramid. . . . Brazilians generally regarded whiter as better, which led naturally to an ideal of "whitening," articulated in both elitist writings and popular folklore. . . .

We may assume that white males must have fathered many mixed bloods, thereby increasing the proportion of lighter-skinned offspring in the next generation. The ideal of whitening, as well as the traditionalistic social system, helped to prevent dark-skinned men from being such active progenitors because females, wherever possible, had powerful conditioning to choose lighter partners than themselves. In short, the system of sexual exploitation which gave upper-class (indeed, even lower-class) white men sexual license, helped to make the social reality conform increasingly to the ideal of whitening.

Brazilians found this apparent lightening of the population reassuring, and their racial ideology was thus reinforced. Since miscegenation had worked to promote the declared goal, white genes "must be" stronger. Furthermore, during the high period of racist thought—1880 to 1920—the whitening ideology gained scientific legitimacy, because racist doctrines came to be interpreted by Brazilians as supporting the view that the "superior" white race would prevail in the process of racial amalgamation. . . .

The whitening thesis was based on the assumption of white superiority—sometimes muted by leaving open the question of how "innate" the inferiority might be, and using the euphemisms "more advanced" and "less advanced" races. But to this assumption were added two more. First, the black population was becoming progressively less numerous than the white for reasons which included a supposedly lower birth rate, higher incidence of disease, and social disorganization. Second, miscegenation was "naturally" producing a lighter population, in part because whiter genes were stronger and in part because people chose partners lighter than themselves. (White immigration, of course, would reinforce the resulting white predominance.)

Obviously the optimistic conclusion to this racial analysis rested on another key assumption: that miscegenation did not inevitably produce "degenerates," but could forge a healthy mixed population growing steadily whiter, both culturally and physically. . . .

The whitening ideology squared with one of the most obvious facts of Brazilian social history—the existence of a large "middle caste," generally called "mulatto." Within this category there were enormous variations, ranging from socially prestigious figures who could be described only as mulatto in the most intimate circles, to underworld criminals. . . .

By any objective physical characteristic it was nonsense to refer to such a single category as mulatto. Yet the Brazilians consistently did so, and their belief in such a category was an essential part of their race thinking. Given the experience of their multiracial society, the whitening thesis offered Brazilians a rationale for what they believed was *already* happening.

20 *Euclides da Cunha* ◆ The Man of the Backlands

Euclides da Cunha, born in the state of Rio de Janeiro, originally planned a military career but turned to journalism at the age of twenty. In the

From *Os sertões* (Rio de Janeiro: Livraria Francisco Alves, 1902). Translated by Samuel Putnam and published as *Rebellion in the Backlands* (Chicago: Phoenix Books, 1944), 89–90. Reprinted by permission of the University of Chicago Press.

backlands of Northeast Brazil, in 1896–97, he covered the military campaigns at Canudos, which put down a rebellion rumored to be an attempt to reestablish the empire. Instead, da Cunha discovered—and grew to respect—a hidden lower-class culture in rural Brazil led by a mystic, Antonio Conselheiro, who was attempting to redress local grievances. Da Cunha later expanded his original articles into his classic Os sertões, *a literary masterpiece described as "the Bible of Brazilian nationality," which includes a section, reproduced here, that describes the transformation of the apparently indolent backwoodsman into "an amazingly different being" when the occasion demands it. Da Cunha's works also included reports on the Amazon and Brazilian-Peruvian border problems as well as a short political history of Brazil. He died in 1909 at the age of forty-three.*

The *sertanejo*, or man of the backlands, is above all else a strong individual. He does not exhibit the debilitating rachitic tendencies of the neurasthenic mestizos of the seaboard.

His appearance, it is true, at first glance, would lead one to think that this was not the case. He does not have the flawless features, the graceful bearing, the correct build of the athlete. He is ugly, awkward, stooped. Hercules-Quasimodo reflects in his bearing the typical unprepossessing attributes of the weak. His unsteady, slightly swaying, sinuous gait conveys the impression of loose-jointedness. His normally downtrodden mien is aggravated by a dour look which gives him an air of depressing humility. On foot, when not walking, he is invariably to be found leaning against the first doorpost or wall that he encounters; while on horseback, if he reins in his mount to exchange a couple of words with an acquaintance, he braces himself on one stirrup and rests his weight against the saddle. When walking, even at a rapid pace, he does not go forward steadily in a straight line but reels swiftly, as if he were following the geometric outlines of the meandering backland trails. And if in the course of his walk he pauses for the most commonplace of reasons, to roll a cigarro, strike a light, or chat with a friend, he falls—"falls" is the word—into a squatting position and will remain for a long time in this unstable state of equilibrium, with the entire weight of his body suspended on his great-toes, as he sits there on his heels with a simplicity that is at once ridiculous and delightful.

He is the man who is always tired. He displays this invincible sluggishness, this muscular atony, in everything that he does: in his slowness of speech, his forced gestures, his unsteady gait, the languorous cadence of his ditties—in brief, in his constant tendency to immobility and rest.

Yet all this apparent weariness is an illusion. Nothing is more surprising than to see the *sertanejo*'s listlessness disappear all of a sudden. In this weakened organism complete transformations are effected in a few seconds. All that is needed is some incident that demands the release of slumbering energies. The fellow is transfigured. He straightens up, becomes a new man, with new lines in his posture and bearing; his head held high now, above his massive shoulders; his gaze straightforward and unflinching. Through an instantaneous discharge of nervous energy, he at once corrects all the faults that come from the habitual relaxation of his organs; and the awkward rustic unexpectedly assumes the dominating aspect of a powerful, copper-hued Titan, an amazingly different being, capable of extraordinary feats of strength and agility.

This contrast becomes evident upon the most superficial examination. It is one that is revealed at every moment, in all the smallest details of backcountry life—marked always by an impressive alternation between the extremes of impulse and prolonged periods of apathy.

21 *Rudyard Kipling* ◆ A Mutual Accommodation from Highest to Humblest

Rudyard Kipling, the famous British poet, novelist, and short-story writer, was born in Bombay in 1865. He first became known for his short stories in India and was already famous in his mid-twenties when he settled in England, although he traveled often and lived for some years in the United States. A supreme storyteller, Kipling was noted for his remarkable freshness of invention, variety of character, vigor of narrative, raciness of dialogue, and magic of atmosphere. He won the Nobel Prize for literature in 1907. Among his longer works are Kim, Captains Courageous, *and* The Light That Failed.

When his doctor recommended a long sea voyage to help him recuperate from an illness, Kipling realized an old dream about which he had written in The Just-So Stories: *"And I'd like to roll to Rio/Some day before I'm old." In 1927, at the age of sixty-two, he visited Brazil, his first trip to the tropics in twenty years. Although much of his late work was*

From *Brazilian Sketches* (1940; reprint ed., New York: Doubleday, 1967), 101–6.

colored by ill health, in Brazilian Sketches *he wrote with all the gusto of forty years earlier. These excerpts are drawn from seven articles Kipling wrote for the* London Morning Post *in November and December 1927. They were originally published in book form in 1940.*

The Brazilians I met were interested in and entirely abreast of outside concerns, but these did not make their vital world. Their God—they jested—was a Brazilian. He gave them all they wanted and more at a pinch. For instance, once when their coffee crop exceeded bounds, He sent a frost at the right moment, which cut it down a quarter and comfortably steadied the markets. And the vast inland countries were full of everything that anyone wanted, all waiting to be used in due time. During the War, when they were driven in upon themselves for metals, fibres, and such, they would show a sample to an Indian and ask him: "Where does one find more of this?" Then he would lead them there. But, possessing these things, they gave one to understand, does not imply their immediate development by concessionaires. Brazil was a huge country, a half or third of which was still untapped. It would attend to itself in time. After a while, one fancied that, somewhere at the back of the scenes, there was the land-owning breed's dislike of the mere buyer and seller of commodities, which suggested an aristocratic foundation to the national fabric.

The elaborate rituals of greeting and parting among ordinary folk pointed the same way. Life being large, and the hours easy-winged, they expatiate in [the] ceremonial. On the other hand, widespread national courtesy is generally due to some cogent reason. I asked if that reason existed here. Oh, yes. Naturally. Their people resented above all things rudeness, lack of consideration, and injury to their "face." It annoyed them. Sometimes it made them see red. Then there would be trouble. Therefore, mutual accommodation from highest to humblest was the rule.

I had proof of this later at Carnival time, when the city of Rio went stark crazy. They dressed themselves in every sort of fancy-kit; they crowded into motors; they bought unlimited paper serpentines, which, properly thrown, unroll five fathoms at a flick; and for three days and three nights did nothing except circulate and congregate and bombard their neighbours with these papers and squirts of direful scent. . . . The pavements were blocked with foot-folk all bearing serpentines, and all wearing their fancy in clothes. City organisations and guilds assembled and poured out of their quarters in charge of huge floats and figures, which were guarded by amateur cavalry; and companies of Negro men and women fenced themselves inside a rope which all held, formed barbaric cohorts and platoons of red, green, and yellow, and so advanced, shaking earth and air with the stamp and boom of immemorial tunes as they Charlestoned through the crowds. It was Africa—essential and unabated. The forty-foot floats that cruised high above the raging sea dealt raw-handedly with matters that the Press might have been too shy to discuss—such as a certain State railway, which is said to be casual in its traffic. Hence it was represented by twin locomotives butting like rams. To all appearances, the populace was utterly in charge of everything, and one bored one's way, a yard at a time, into it, while it shouted whatever came into its well-informed head, and plastered everybody with confetti. The serpentines hung like wreckage after [a] flood on the branches of trees in the avenues; lay in rolls and fringes on the streets like seaweed on a beach; and were tangled and heaped over the bows of the cars till these resembled hay-carts of the operatic stage. But at no time, and in no place, was there anything approaching disorder, nor any smell of liquor. At two o'clock of the last night I saw a forty-foot avenue masked from kerb to kerb with serpentines and confetti. At five that same morning they were utterly gone—with the costumes and the revellers. There wasn't even a head-ache hanging over in the clean air! . . .

I had had the privilege of hearing an oration at their Academy in literary Portuguese, which carried the dignity, cadence, and clarity of age-old culture, as the tones of a musical glass carry the twin mysteries of fire and water. Later on, I listened to a popular ditty, sung at a gathering of friends by a girl with a mandoline. ("I think it comes from the North—from the Dry Country, where they sing to their cattle at night.") A warm rain was falling outside, heavy-scented from the gardens of Petropolis, and its half-tones exquisitely balanced the spirit of the old house, the shining ancient furniture, the priceless smooth silver, and, in some magic way, the ease and poise of the company. The girl's pale face was thrown up by reflected light; and three or four young men behind her strummed in and out of the tune with their mandolines as required. Every soul in the company knew the burden; and its dead-simple, heart-breaking wail did not need to be translated to a stranger. It was followed by a rattling, tear-ing Negro melody—no relation whatever to "coon-stuff"—evidently quite as well-known. (It came out of lordly, untouched Bahia, where, I fancy, the old heart of the land beats strongly.) One could hear the West Coast [of Africa] drums thudding behind the strings, while one watched the feet tapping the floor and the faces lit by the associations of the jingling words. (Most likely their *ayahs* had sung it to them when they were babies.) For just those few instants one felt nearer Brazil than one had ever been before.

22 *Ricardo Baeza* ◆ Affable, Solicitous, and Articulate

Ricardo Baeza, a Spanish journalist born in 1890, wrote for El Sol *of Madrid,* La Publicidad *of Barcelona, and other Spanish and Latin American publications. He traveled widely throughout Europe, lectured on Emile Zola, and wrote essays on Fyodor Dostoyevski, George Bernard Shaw, and H. G. Wells. He also translated works of Gabriele D'Annunzio, Joseph Conrad, John Galsworthy, Friedrich Nietzsche, Emil Ludwig, and Eugene O'Neill into Spanish. His book* Bajo el signo de Clio *(Under the sign of Clio), from which these light and ironic comments have been drawn, also contains essays on subjects as diverse as Woodrow Wilson, Charles A. Lindbergh, John Maynard Keynes, Roald Amundsen, a Pan-African congress, and the Soviet Union.*

Before going any further, I must state that the Brazilians are charming. I owe them this compliment, and I take pleasure in paying it to them and in thanking them publicly for the good times they have afforded me. Hospitable, affable, solicitous, incomparably articulate, the company of a Brazilian is the ideal company for an overworked neurasthenic for whom the doctor prescribed complete intellectual relaxation.

This admirable faculty of being able to speak interminably without ever saying anything, without one's having to demand to be included in a dialogue! The Brazilian is a conversationalist par excellence, the archetype of conversationalists, and whoever has not been in Brazil does not know how amiable a discussion with our peers can be. And in the Brazilian's case he should not be heard in Europe, where everything inhibits him, but here, surrounded by this overwhelming nature and under the sun that makes the blood boil.

How to describe a Brazilian chat, this kaleidoscopic small talk that flits from one theme to another without ever alighting on any, that in five minutes talks of a hundred things—such is its quickness of thought—that reduces our comment to a monosyllable—such is the generosity of the conversationalist—and that falls upon you like an irresistible shower, a shower that tastes of cane liquid and tropical nectar? The driest and stickiest matters flourish most unexpectedly and pleasantly on Brazilian lips. For everything the Brazilian will find the right word, the ingenious and smoothly ironic saying. Smilingly, he will speak to you of the crime com-

From *Bajo el signo de Clio: Reminiscencias del Brasil* (Madrid: Cia. Iberoamericana de Publicaciones, 1931), 305–8. Translated by G. Harvey Summ.

mitted last night—unless he brings his skill into play to horrify you, in which case you will not have enough hair to stand on end—and the problems of reparations or hunger in the Volga, which appeared terribly difficult to us, will lose all their gravity and momentarily take on a lighter hue.

Another rare virtue of the Brazilian conversationalist is not to require the slightest effort on your part. You will not have to torture your imagination to be at your interlocutor's level; the less you speak, the happier he will be. It won't even be necessary for you to make an effort to pay attention; your interlocutor cares little if you listen; like all true artists, he speaks for himself, out of pleasure and the need to speak.

Add to this a perfect discretion, and the most complete absence of curiosity or sinful thought. I personally had occasion to confirm this last virtue.

Just having arrived from Russia, from that arcane and legendary Soviet empire, closed for several years to almost every intrusion, I was already accustomed to being overwhelmed by questions and inquisitions everywhere. Brazil was to me a true oasis of relaxation. Hardly had my interlocutor found out that I had been in Russia, when his face would light up and he would begin to inform me what Russia and the Soviets were like. And in reality, what did my experience signify compared to his imagination? I am not a realistic author, and I am disposed to believe, with [Charles] Baudelaire, that imagination is the queen of faculties.

But there is something better in Brazil than the conversational art of the Brazilians. How far and how free we felt there from those annoying Western superstitions of seriousness, punctuality, formality, and so many other afflictions that spoil life! What utterly subtle happiness, which we had never enjoyed before, that of being able to arrive for an appointment two hours late, or not arrive at all, if we came across something more pleasant on the way; that of having tried thirty times to deal with a certain matter, and not having found an occasion to do so; that of being able to forget all one's commitments without scandalizing anyone or having a promise tersely thrown up to one! In Spain, we pretend that in this sense we are rather advanced; but how much we are still in diapers, if we compare ourselves to this country, the most fortunate of all! A free, enjoyable life, not tied down by convention, without the burden of ideas, dedicated happily to laughter, play, and the monologue!

From this old frowning Europe, concerned with obscure ideals, eaten up by vague aspirations, tormented by regret and envy, our memory goes irresistibly back to your golden shores, Brazil, new Arcady; toward your garrulous and laughing people, who do not yet know the poison of thought or the curse of work.

23 *Louis Mouralis* ◆ Liveliness of Spirit

Louis Mouralis, a French travel writer, visited northeastern and southern Brazil in 1930 and 1931. He was present during São Paulo's attempted secession in 1932. Mouralis was familiar with Brazilian, Portuguese, and other Latin American and Spanish literature. Brazilian journalist and essayist Alberto Rangel, who did considerable research in Paris on French observers of his country, described Mouralis as the "most likeable, independent, and profound" of the group.

In Un séjour aux États Unis du Brésil *(A stay in the United States of Brazil), Mouralis comments on Brazilian institutions, geography, history, race, culture, and literature. The book is a little gem, less encyclopedic than, but comparable in its insights to, travel books by John Gunther. The chapter included here contains penetrating remarks about "disharmony" in Brazilian life, and Mouralis distinguishes between the characteristics of the elite and the lower classes.*

A superficial impression is not necessarily the wrong one. A Frenchman arriving in Brazil has the feeling that he has hardly left his own country (but perhaps other people may note the difference immediately). Our language is spoken very widely. Our culture, assimilated unevenly but often well, is the object of people's concerns and conversations, and at the very least its presence is always felt. Even customs and everyday opinions about life appear similar to ours; they just have a more marked Iberian accent, but this does not make us feel like strangers.

Over a longer period one begins to notice the differences. The gap grows imperceptibly, and careful observations over a longer stay bring out basic differences that one had not felt during the first weeks.

One then realizes the profound disharmony that characterizes Brazilian life: the natural and irreducible contradiction between, on the one hand, a temperament that unhesitatingly follows the rules of its nature, and, on the other, a rich and wayward imagination that obstinately seeks ideals and purposes beyond itself and always looks to the highest levels.

Some live with perfect innocence on two planes: that of the imagination, of dreams and words, where they show themselves to be adroit, intelligent, even seductive; and that of action, where nothing prevails against

From *Un séjour aux États Unis du Brésil: Réflexions et impressions* (Paris: Presses Universitaires de France, 1934), 100–109. Reprinted by permission of Presses Universitaires de France. Translated by G. Harvey Summ.

hereditary instincts and habits. One would say that they suspect no connection between one and the other, but rather that human existence in their eyes normally comprises a dual reality: one exclusively material, where things order themselves according to their own laws, and usually rather badly; the other, where words create what they say merely by being said. This goes so far that one sometimes notes a truly mythological concept of words, as if words by themselves brought into being the thing described. Either spoken or written, words seem like a kind of incantation. That is why it is difficult for Europeans to understand and be understood.

Quite clearly it would be an unfair oversimplification to speak in this connection of lying and duplicity. Rather one can see there a highly exaggerated defect that other peoples have and that can be found in some parts of Europe itself.

As for the Brazilian temperament, which is burdened by too much inbreeding among races that are not all at the highest level, one must admit that it is not of rare quality. The Brazilian temperament contains a great deal of gentleness, makes social life very pleasant, and imparts extreme gentility, even tenderness, to superficial relationships and every form of intimate familiarity, to the point that the word, in some cases, could well be translated by complicity. But these are its principal virtues. One does not find often enough those virtues of generosity, lofty views, or self-mastery that the French term noblesse expresses. The Brazilian temperament allows itself to be absorbed unresistingly in matters of the immediate present and is as incapable of taking on a boring task as it is of tearing itself away from something pleasant. It has little interest in anything exact, rarely wants to perform a task for the sole pleasure of doing it well, and has an overwhelming aversion toward hard work. It has a frenetic taste for appearances only and, above all, an atavistic nonchalance, caused by weak nerves, against which a clear vision of its dangers is powerless. Overall, it has a kind of limited self-absorption that rarely judges things calmly, does not comprehend its own interest well, and does not know how to subordinate immediate advantage to greater long-term gain.

Too many people have in their blood that famous Indian lack of foresight that seems a capital offense in the eyes of Western societies, which are based on constant thought about the future. The uncertainty and indecision in which, as a consequence, many Brazilians live does not bother them. If they are struck by bad luck, they have not suffered in advance nor have they tried to do anything to avoid it. In Europe one is always concerned about what is going to happen. Here, no. That is why any improvement, whether it be of an individual, a family, or a generation, is only possible for a short time. What one sees is a series of happenings due to chance or to one's personal abilities. While the foreigner accumulates his fortune little by little, a Brazilian family that gets rich soon ruins itself. I have often heard a kind of proverb, uttered without regret, in fact, but rather with a certain admiration: "The father is rich, the son is ruined, the grandson remakes the fortune."

This explains quite well why the real prosperity that would permanently ensure the solidity of a well-balanced country is always precarious here and turns into misery as soon as credits are shut off and the proceeds no longer arrive at the expected time.

Certainly many Brazilians at times are aware of the disastrous course they are following. It is in Brazilian books that one finds the roughest and most virulent criticism of the Brazilian character, of Brazilian customs, of Brazilian vices and absurdities, compared to the character and customs of the great nations of Europe.

If character is sometimes weak, intelligence is not lacking in Brazil. On the contrary, it is widespread in all classes of society. The ordinary Brazilian impresses by his extreme liveliness of spirit, certainly superior to that of the Frenchman of the same level. Likewise, high-school students often reveal a powerful intuition, a capacity to adapt and assimilate that one would rarely find among their European counterparts. But this intelligence almost never appears in other than its passive form and is only used effectively in the domain of ideas and images. Everyone thinks that this intellectual brilliance is enough in itself, that to understand an idea is to carry it out, and that to understand something is the equivalent of having created it. But this error relegates its victim to the unenviable domain of imitation. What I mean by this is not the act of abandoning one's self to changing styles and snobberies, but something much deeper and sadder—the fact of depending strictly, in all aspects of life, on creative cultures and civilizations.

To make something out of nothing, so to speak, is a rare, unique accomplishment; however, to "understand" the ideas of others, to appropriate them as smoothly as one wishes, demands little more than imagination.

This latter form of understanding is condemned to inevitable inferiority. It remains necessarily incomplete, superficial, and visibly inadequate for its purpose and, when put to the test, engenders mediocre results if any complexity is involved. Brazilians, who give the impression of grasping everything quickly and following all kinds of reasoning, as long as it is not too abstractly scientific or philosophical, are generally incapable of perceiving cause-and-effect relationships. One is sometimes surprised to note that, although they have all the appearance of intelligence, their judgment is faulty.

Faced with failure, a strange notion appears, a kind of messianism that is a mixture of renunciation and hope. One no longer counts on human resources; one waits for a miracle, the unforeseen, the gratuitous but always possible event that will put things back on the right road. Generally this miracle does not arrive.

If there is one thing that one does not often encounter in Brazil, it is surely that intimate unity thanks to which man gives an impression of solidity, of depth, and of harmony. These people are not yet properly free (assuming that one day they will be) of the burden of three centuries of colonial life. If, despite their positive qualities and their charm, they can only hope for a mediocre place in the hierarchy of mankind, it is because they have so far invented nothing, they have not found within themselves a formula for life, and they have not found their proper personal style on this earth. Civilization and culture are not drawn from deep sources; they are always imported and always resent the trip. Moreover, one would say that on these plains of South America, the spirit is always affected by a strange sterility.

Among the lower classes, especially those that have not been spoiled by contact with large cities, one is very pleased to find a naturalness that may have great potential: much gentleness and goodwill; an extremely quick intelligence that grasps artistically the innate sense of things, a complete absence of vulgarity even in the deepest misery; certain ideas, like charming anachronisms, surviving from vanished aristocratic societies; a character harmonious thanks to its own weaknesses; and a stirring sense of rhythm in the broadest sense of that word, which applies initially to the way women walk and extends even to feelings and thoughts.

But things are different among the elite, that crowd of more or less educated people who doubtless have the same qualities as the common people, but blush to show them because they know, or think they know, other nations.

Something greatly diminishes the pleasure that one should find in contacts with them—that is, the general lack of originality and an often puerile affectation by which Brazilians do not fool themselves and only rarely fool the foreigner. The popular words *fita*, *tapeação*, when used in conversation, indicate rather well the national art of arranging things and words to have the air of, give the appearance of, give the impression of. The government itself does this. It spends amounts far beyond its means either for propaganda in which frantic optimism sometimes verges on lying, or for ostentation: maintaining outside the country useless agents and missions, mounting exhibitions, financing international meetings, receiving foreigners in splendor.

24 *Sérgio Buarque de Holanda* ◆ The Cordial Man

Sérgio Buarque de Holanda was a professor in the Faculty of Philosophy, Sciences, and Letters of the University of São Paulo. He was the general editor of the massive and authoritative História geral da civilização brasileira *(1960), which reached seven volumes under his supervision; the latest edition contains twelve volumes. Other books include* Monções *(1945) and* O extremo oeste *(1986, original edition 1976), both histories of colonial frontier expeditions in São Paulo and Mato Grosso states. Buarque de Holanda's career involved stints as a journalist, museum director, and librarian, and he translated into Portuguese books about Brazil by foreign observers.*

Raízes do Brasil, *from which this selection is taken, deals with early Portuguese colonization, Brazil's rural heritage, the empire, abolition of slavery, and the republican period.*

It has already been said, in a felicitous expression, that the Brazilian contribution to civilization will be that of cordiality—we will give the world the "cordial man." Delicacy of treatment, hospitality, generosity, virtues so praised by foreigners who visit us, are in effect a definite trait of the Brazilian character, at least to the extent that long-standing human relationships, formed in a rural and patriarchal environment, remain active and fertile. It would be a mistake to suppose that these virtues mean "good manners," civility. Above all they are legitimate expressions of extremely rich and overflowing basic emotions. There is something coercive in civility—it can be expressed in commands and sentences. Among the Japanese, where, as is known, politeness involves the most ordinary aspects of social conviviality, at times it reaches the point of religious reverence. Some have noted the significant fact that external forms of venerating the divinity in the Shinto ceremony are not essentially different from social ways of showing respect.

No people are further from that ritualistic notion of life than the Brazilian. Our usual form of social relations is basically just the opposite of politeness. It can be deceiving—and that is explained by the fact that politeness consists precisely in a kind of deliberate mimicry of the cordial man's spontaneous manifestations: it is a natural and live form changed

From *Raízes do Brasil*, 3d ed. (Rio de Janeiro: Livraria José Olympio Editora, 1956), 209–19. Translated by G. Harvey Summ.

to a formula. Beyond that, politeness is a kind of defense against society. It stops at the outer skin of an individual, serving as a means of resistance when necessary. It is equivalent to a disguise that allows a person to keep intact his sensibility and emotions.

Similarly, adopting external forms of cordiality, which do not have to be legitimate to be manifested, reveals a decisive triumph of one's spirit in life situations. Armed with this mask, the individual succeeds in maintaining supremacy over society. Politeness, in effect, also implies the continuous and sovereign presence of the individual.

In the cordial man, social life is to some extent true liberation from the panic that he feels from living with himself and from depending on himself under all circumstances of life. His way of revealing himself to others continually reduces the individual to the social and peripheral part of life, which in the Brazilian—as in a good American—tends to be what matters most. Above all, he lives through others. Nietzsche addressed this type of human being when he said: "Your inadequate love of yourselves turns isolation into captivity."

Brazilians generally find it difficult to feel prolonged reverence for a superior. This aversion is very significant because that social ritual often demands a strongly homogeneous and overall well-balanced personality. Our temperament even allows for a considerable degree of reverence, but almost entirely while a more familiar relationship is possible. Respect normally manifested by other peoples has its replica in Brazil in the desire to establish intimacy. And that is even more notable when one takes into account the fact that the Portuguese, so close to us in so many ways, frequently resort to titles and to signs of reverence.

In the realm of linguistics, to cite an example, that kind of behavior seems to be reflected in the accentuated tendency to use diminutives. The ending *-inho* added to words serves to bring us closer to people or objects and at the same time to pay more attention to them. It is a way of making them more accessible to our feelings and closer to our hearts.

The same surely applies to the tendency to omit family names in social relationships. As a rule the given, or baptismal, name prevails. That tendency, which among the Portuguese comes from a tradition with ancient roots—as is known, family names only began to predominate in Christian Europe in the twelfth century—became, oddly, even stronger among us. Perhaps that could be plausibly explained by the suggestion that using the simple first name implies abolishing certain psychological barriers because families are different and independent from one another. It fits the natural attitude of human groups that accept a considerable degree of closeness, of "concord," and which reject those based on abstract reasoning or which are not based on community of blood, place, or spirit.

Rejection of any form of relationship not based on an ethos of emotion is an aspect of Brazilian life that few foreigners succeed in understanding easily. And this custom is so characteristic among us that it does not even disappear in activities normally based on competition. A Philadelphia businessman was astonished to discover that in Brazil, as in Argentina, to win over a customer you have to make a friend of him.

Our old Catholicism, so characteristic, which permits us to treat saints with an almost disrespectful intimacy and which must seem strange to really religious souls, has the same explanation. The popularity of Saint Teresa de Lisieux—Saint Teresinha—is largely a result of the intimate character of those who believe in her, a kindly and almost fraternal worship that is uncomfortable with ceremony and eliminates distance. That also occurs with our Child Jesus, playtime companion of children, which makes one think less of the Jesus of the canonic gospels than of various versions of the Gospel of Childhood. Those who attend the festivals of Bom Jesus de Pirapora in São Paulo know the story of the Christ who comes down from the altar to dance the samba with the people.

A similar attitude characteristically transposes into the religious sphere that horror of distance that seems to constitute, at least so far, the most specific trait of the Brazilian spirit. Note that here we behave exactly opposite to the above-mentioned Japanese manner, where ritual invades the terrain of social behavior and gives it greater rigor. In Brazil it is precisely the rigor of the rite which is loosened and humanized.

This aversion to ritual does not fit well—as can easily be imagined—with truly deep and conscientious religious feeling. [Cardinal John Henry] Newman, in one of his Anglican sermons, expressed the "firm conviction" that the English nation would gain if its religion were more superstitious, more "bigoted" [in English in the original], if it were more accessible to the influence of the people, if it spoke more directly to the imagination and the heart. In Brazil, on the contrary, it was exactly our worship without obligation and without rigor, intimate and familiar, that, with some impropriety, could be called "democratic," a worship that exempted the faithful from all effort, all diligence, and all tyranny over themselves, and that fundamentally corrupted our religious sentiment.

A superficial religiosity, less attentive to the intimate meaning of the ceremonies than to the colorful and to external pomp, was almost carnal in its attachment to the concrete and in its rancorous lack of comprehension of all true spirituality. It was tolerant because it made agreement easier. No one would expect, certainly, that it be elevated enough to produce any powerful social moral. Religiosity was lost and confused in a formless world and for that reason did not have the power to impose order.

Our aversion to ritual is explicable to a point in this "remiss and somewhat melancholy land" of which the first European observers spoke, for the very reason that in the end ritual is not necessary for us. Normally our reaction to the environment in which we live is not defensive. The inner life of the Brazilian is neither cohesive enough nor disciplined enough to involve and dominate his whole personality and integrate it as a conscious part of society. He is free, then, to abandon himself to a broad repertory of ideas, gestures, and forms that he may encounter in his path and frequently assimilates them without great difficulty.

25 *Stefan Zweig* ◆ A Passion for the Lottery

Stefan Zweig, an Austrian author, wrote biographies of Erasmus, Marie Antoinette, Honoré de Balzac, and Mary, Queen of Scots as well as penetrating stories of European Jewish life. A refugee from Nazism, he first visited Brazil in 1936 and eventually emigrated there. He committed suicide in Petrópolis in 1942, presumably as a result of depression over prospects of returning to Europe. The favorable comments in Brazil: Land of the Future *took the intellectual community in that country by surprise, considering the repression of writers under the Getúlio Vargas dictatorship of Zweig's time.*

Zweig's book includes chapters on history, the economy, Rio de Janeiro, São Paulo, a coffee plantation, abandoned mining towns, and a visit to the Northeast. In "Culture," presented below, Zweig portrays the still unhurried society of almost sixty years earlier, in contrast to the more frenetic pace accompanying Brazil's rapid urbanization in the intervening years.

What characterizes the Brazilian physically and spiritually more than anything else is that he is more delicate than the European, the North American. Here the massive, strong-boned type is almost entirely absent. The same is the case in the spiritual sense, and it's a blessing to find this repeated a thousandfold within a nation: every form of brutality,

From *Brasilien: Ein Land der Zukunft* (Stockholm: Bermann-Fischer Verlag, 1941), 147–58. Translated into English by Andrew St. James and published as *Brazil: Land of the Future* (New York: Viking Press, 1941), 139–49.

loudness, rudeness, and arrogance is missing. The Brazilian is a quiet person, dreamy and sentimental, sometimes with a touch of melancholy. . . . Even in [his] personal behavior [his] manners are subdued. One seldom hears anyone talk loudly, and less often lose his temper. And particularly when crowds gather one notices more clearly this, to us, very striking quietness. . . . Even when they enjoy themselves in crowds the people here remain silent and discreet, and this absence of all roughness and brutality gives their pleasures a touching charm. To make a noise, to shout, to dance wildly, is entirely contrary to their habits; so much so, in fact, that whatever gaiety has been saved up is suddenly released during the four days of Carnival.

But even during these days of seemingly unrestricted joy the millions of people, in spite of their frenzied behavior, never run to excess, never become indecent or vulgar. The foreigner, even a lady, need have no fear in walking through these whirling streets. The Brazilian always preserves his innate gentleness and good manners. . . . Here courtesy is the basis of human relationship, accepting forms which we in Europe have long forgotten. . . . Anything brutal, cruel, or even slightly sadistic is foreign to the Brazilian character. He is kind, unsuspicious; and the people possess that warm, childlike quality native to the Southerner, but rather rare in so pronounced and general extent as it is here. . . .

For this extraordinary gentleness of the soul, this unprejudiced and unsuspicious amiability, this incapacity for brutality, the Brazilian pays with a strong—probably overly strong—sensibility. By temperament not only sentimental, but sensitive, every Brazilian has a very vulnerable sense of honor, a sense of honor of a very special kind. Just because he himself is so exceptionally and personally modest, he immediately takes even the most accidental impoliteness as an offense. Not that he would react violently. . . . On the contrary, he swallows the unintentional offense in silence.

One hears a certain story over and over again: There's a servant in a house (she can be black, white, or brown). She is kind and clean, giving not the slightest reason for complaint. One morning she is gone. The mistress of the house doesn't know why; nor will she ever know. Maybe yesterday she dropped a word of criticism, of displeasure; and with this one—possibly too loud—word, she has quite unwittingly but very deeply offended the maid. The maid says nothing; [she] neither complains nor attempts to discuss the matter. She simply packs her belongings in silence and leaves without a sound. It is not in these Brazilians to stand up for themselves, to demand justice, to complain, or to argue things out in a temper. They keep themselves to themselves. It is their natural defense; and this silent, mysterious, mute pride is to be found everywhere. If an invitation is refused, however politely, it will never be repeated. . . . And this secret pride, this sensitivity in regard to honor, is present even among the very poorest of the poor. . . .

This delicacy of feeling, this lack of vehemence, seems the most characteristic quality of the Brazilian. People here need no violent excitement, no visible or material successes, in order to find contentment. . . . People do not want too much; they are not impatient. It is sufficient pleasure for most of them between or after working hours to talk, drink coffee, go for a walk, or enjoy themselves in their homes and with their children. The lives of these people are led with less hatred between the classes and groups than in most countries, thanks to this inborn peacefulness and absence of envy.

This lack of impetus, absence of greed and impatience, which seems to be one of the greatest virtues of the Brazilian, might prove to be a certain drawback in the economic sense. . . . One cannot call this laziness. . . . It would be extremely unjust to call the Brazilian artisan or workman second-rate. . . . And thus it is by no means the ability or the readiness or the tempo which is deficient; what is lacking is this European or North American impatience to succeed doubly quick by increased effort, to "rise in the world," as the Germans say. It is more a lack of ambition which diminishes the general dynamic intensity. . . .

Here life itself is more important than time. . . . Whereas in a gray and monotonous country, work seems to be a man's only safeguard against the joylessness of existence, in such a climate as this, rich and abounding in fruit and beauty, life does not stimulate the desire to become rich as passionately and as wildly as at home. In the eyes of a Brazilian, wealth does not mean the piling up of money saved from countless working hours, or the result of hurried and nerve-destroying activity. Wealth is something one dreams about; it should fall from Heaven; and in Brazil the function of this Heaven is replaced by the lottery.

The lottery in Brazil is one of the few visible passions of an apparently quiet people—the daily hope shared by hundreds of thousands, even millions. The wheel of fortune rarely ever stops turning, and every day there is a new draw. Wherever one walks or stands about, in every shop, at street corners, on the boat and in the train, tickets are being offered, and every Brazilian—the barber, the shoe-shiner, the porters, the factory employee, and the soldier—all buy them with what is left over from their weekly earnings. At a certain hour in the afternoon large crowds gather round the drawing-booth; the radio is going full blast in every house and store; the expectancy of an entire city, or rather of a whole country, is in this moment concentrated on one single number. . . . The population here has invented a national game of their own, the *bicho*, the so-called animal game which, though strictly forbidden by the government, is being played incessantly despite all laws.

This *bicho*, this animal game, has a strange history, proving in itself how well this passion for luck suits the dreamy and naive character of these people. The director of a zoological garden had reason to complain of the public's lack of interest. Knowing his fellow-countrymen very well, he had the glorious idea of raffling according to a certain animal every day—a bear, a donkey, a parrot, or an elephant. He whose entrance ticket showed the number of the day's particular animal was paid twenty or twenty-five times the price of his admission. Success was immediate. For weeks the zoo was packed with people who came less to look at the animals than to win the prize. After a time, however, they found the zoo too far and too tiring to go to over and over again; so they began gambling among themselves, making bets in private on the animal to win each day. Behind bars and at street corners bookmaking establishments opened, which accepted the fees and paid out the winnings.

When the police finally forbade the game, it became attached to the lottery result in some mysterious way. For the Brazilian each number meant a certain animal. In order to avoid the police checking up on it they played on agreement. The bookmaker didn't supply his clients with tickets, but he has never been known not to pay up. Perhaps just because it was forbidden, this game has taken all classes of people by storm. Every child in Rio, even those barely able to count, knows which number corresponds to which animal; and it can recite the whole list better than it can the alphabet. All authority, all punishment, has proved useless. What was the good of a man dreaming at night, if in the morning he couldn't translate his dream into a number, into the animal-cum-lottery game? As usual, the law has proved powerless against the real passion of a people. Again and again the Brazilian will compensate for his lack of greed in this daily dream of sudden wealth.

There's no doubt about it, any more than there is about the earth itself, that the Brazilian people have not yet produced 100 percent of what their talent, their energy, and their resources are capable of. Seen as a whole, considering the climatic influence and the physical drawbacks, the result has been quite respectable; and in the light of our world experiences during recent years one hesitates to call a lack of impetus a fault. This is a question reaching far beyond the Brazilian problem: the question as to whether the peaceful self-contained life of nations and individuals is not more important than the overheated dynamism which drives people to compete against each other, and finally forces them into war; the question as to whether through the 100 percent utilization of all dynamic forces something in the spiritual domain of humanity does not dry up and wither when exposed to this perpetual "doping," this artificial stimulation. Commercial statistics, the dry numbers of the trade balance, are faced with something invisible as the true gain: a well-balanced, unviolated humanity, and a peaceful contentment.

26 *Tullio Ascarelli* ◆ Courtesy Mixed with Distrust

Tullio Ascarelli was an Italian jurist who wrote books on Italian, Portuguese, Spanish, Brazilian, and Mexican commercial and financial law in the 1930s and 1940s. His Sguardo sul Brasile *(Glance at Brazil) was designed to provide background for foreign intellectuals and businessmen on historical, political, economic, social, and cultural themes, and is apparently the only book he wrote on other than legal subjects. This selection reflects the considerable time that Ascarelli spent in southern Brazil, where—probably because of the presence of large numbers of Italian immigrants—he noted greater egalitarian tendencies.*

The immensity of the country and the sensation that there is always land for whoever wants to work it and that any individual can always count on unexpected fortune and on a special providence perhaps contribute to the atmosphere of courtesy characteristic of life in Brazil.

Courtesy is naturally linked to a certain formalism, the consequence perhaps of a certain Iberian courtliness that harks back to the colonial period, but much more, I believe, to the profound if unconscious conviction of the need to shape into a common mold the diverse elements that make up the country: the unity of form is the first step on the road to real unity.

All this explains why Brazilians are often a little irritated, and are strongly shocked, even to the point of reacting violently, by lack of courtesy and manners. And since manners in Brazil are not always the same as in Europe or in the United States, the foreigner can happen to violate social norms without knowing it, and commit faux pas. For example, the foreigner is often surprised at the Brazilian official's reaction when the foreigner insists on pointing to the law; that insistence, implying the official's lack of intent to carry out the law, indicates a lack of consideration by the foreigner. That undeniably offends the official.

From *Sguardo sul Brasile* (Milan: Dott. A. Giuffre, 1949), 129–33, 137, 144, 152. Translated into Portuguese by Olinto de Castro and published as *Apresentação do Brasil* (São Paulo: Edições SAL, 1952), 126–30, 133, 139–40, 146–47. Translated by G. Harvey Summ.

Brazilians are constantly inspired by the principle of live and let live; they are basically convinced that on the complex road of history everything may have its justification, and the daily difficulties of life can always be worked out with a little patience and agility, with *jeito*, as it is commonly called.

The political and economic struggle is therefore inspired, in Brazil, by a great spirit of tolerance. This atmosphere of acceptance and blandness is constant and is a lot more than the consequence of climatic conditions, as some say. It is the result of the deep conviction that in such a vast country there is room for all.

A certain physical boldness is really typical of the Brazilian, easily driven by sudden impulses to violent actions. Despite this, the view of life accepted by all Brazilians is dominated by the philosophy that everything and everybody has the right to a place in the sun.

The Brazilians are, as a rule, psychologically simple, even when they consider themselves very complicated. They are essentially moved by a few elementary sentiments, and get enthusiastic easily. But their sense of humor is extremely lively, and a spirited phrase comes easily.

Popular songs improvised by folk poets in the backlands generally express a simple, clearly religious, psychology and good-natured humor. All the small incidents of daily life that would exasperate a European or a North American—a train delay, waiting in line, an incident in the streetcar—in general only provoke good-humored phrases, sometimes very apt, among Brazilians.

Although melancholy, Brazilians are not sentimental and their view of life is as a rule realistic, keen, and—not rarely—positively cynical. Brazilians always, in fact, criticize themselves very severely. They often do not tolerate criticism by foreigners, however, either because they consider it tactless or because they have a certain diffuse sense of inferiority, a fear that they may be considered a colonial and backward people.

~ The confidence of Brazilians in the importance of personal relationships and equitable judgments results precisely from the view that in the end men are more important than laws. They also believe that in such a vast and diverse country rigid norms are impractical to apply, either because they often result inevitably from a legislative approach imported from abroad or are not well thought out or are based on isolated examples. The foreigner who comes to Brazil tends to consider all problems on the basis of law. The Brazilian, however, often considers the same problems in terms of equity. He approaches them from the standpoint of a humane philosophy, he is inclined to allow for exceptions, or he is more fearful of scandal. For those reasons he places the person above the legal norm.

A poor society—and life in Brazil . . . is, especially in the north, very harsh for the great majority of the population—does not allow for a psychology of absolute trust. "To trust while distrusting" is a common saying in Brazil. Behind government actions and public opinion one often finds a spirit of mistrust, in contrast to the mark of cordiality of daily life. Consequently, a certain sharpness is common in Brazil, and some forms of illicit acts (like those connected to land invasions and the manufacture of nonexistent titles to property) are related to this cunning, often in a legal sense.

Brazil's own literary tradition and colonial disdain for manual labor, and perhaps a certain tradition of Jesuitic moral relativism, create an atmosphere of admiration for intellectual sharpness on the basis of which a considerable degree of moral flabbiness is condoned.

~ The south of Brazil, like in other immigrant countries in the Americas, is a community of hope. What links, and really links, people is an awareness of the future, a common hope, despite differences in origin and in their pasts, a hope that unites diverse traditions. This common hope, which naturally is translated into a strong sense of social egalitarianism, gives a profoundly democratic tone to the countries of the Americas that always impresses the European. And this psychology of "hope" leads to a rather widespread optimism, tolerance, or even lack of foresight—the conviction that the country is blessed by God and destined to sure progress, a psychology that for the same reasons always takes a positive attitude regarding the future. This psychology of hope gives life in the Americas a continuing character of tolerance and cordiality.

This American psychology of hope is in Brazil more accentuated in the states of the south, where the fusion of immigrants took place and where the rhythm of economic progress is intense. However, it can be found in the whole country. Although to a much smaller degree, immigration is not unusual in the north; the north has the glory of having overcome racial differences; the north produced and brought to fruition the ideas that led to the abolition of slavery. The unitary character of Brazil, despite the profound economic differences that affect its psychology, is also shown in this fundamental psychological predisposition toward hope, tolerance, and cordiality in human relations.

The lack of racial differences (since colonial times), republican ideals, and, in the south, immigration and the fast-paced rhythm of economic change, as well as rapid change in the economic conditions of individuals, have given Brazilian life, especially in the south, a sense of social egalitarianism that is nourished by industrial development and immigration into the cities.

This tone is widespread in urban daily life. The boss, when he arrives at the office, is the first to greet his employees; it is discourteous to make an employee remain standing when the boss calls him in; in encounters outside the office, boss and employee feel at the same level; in social relationships, despite differences in pay and in level, dealings on both sides are effectively and sincerely egalitarian; each treats the other as an equal, and servility on the part of the inferior is as rare as vain haughtiness on the part of the superior.

27 *James B. Watson* ◆ The Quiet, Simple, Self-Reliant *Caboclo*

James B. Watson is professor emeritus of anthropology at the University of Washington. During most of his career, he specialized in the study of New Guinea. He was associate editor of the American Anthropologist, *president of the Central States Anthropological Society, a senior specialist of the East-West Center, and a consultant to the United Nations Fund for the Development of West Irian.*

Watson taught at Washington University, St. Louis, Missouri, from 1947 to 1955, the period during which he published the paper from which this selection is drawn. He deals with the way of life of the "simple and self-reliant" Brazilian caboclo, *or peasant. Watson described the* caboclo *as being at a level of development (toward Westernization) equivalent to occupying a way station or "half-way house."*

The *caboclo* is the Brazilian approximation of the mestizo of certain parts of Spanish America, a lower-class country person, a peasant, or rural subsistence producer. It is almost tiresomely commonplace to find the *caboclo*'s low estate deplored by foreign travelers and native writers. . . . A good many general things have been asserted of Brazil's illiterate rural classes, but some of these views appear to have been taken from a distance, some have gathered strength and acceptance simply from repetition, and not a few are seen from the superior altitude of a library armchair.

From "Way Station of Westernization: The Brazilian *Caboclo*," in *Papers Presented in the Institute for Brazilian Studies* (Nashville, TN: Vanderbilt University Press, 1953), 9–12, 16–18, 23–24, 26–28, 30–31, 39, 49–50. Adapted by G. Harvey Summ. Footnotes omitted.

Caboclos are nonliterate and relatively isolated descendants of more or less assimilated Indians mixed, in varying degrees, with Europeans and (in certain areas) Africans. They inhabit the rural areas between the coastal belt and the westernmost point of settlement, from Rio Grande do Sul to Amazonas.

Caboclo horizons are narrow. They [*caboclos*] are provincial, have a very low economic status, typically a scattered settlement pattern, and a high degree of economic self-sufficiency. They have little resort to money exchange. Their production is preponderantly noncommercial in purpose and usually for short-run, direct consumption. Illiteracy, both functional and technical, is very high among Brazil's *caboclos*. This in turn effectively excludes them as a group from organized political functions.

The type of culture and society represented by the Brazilian *caboclo* is a way station in the slow Westernization of a mode of life that emerged early in colonial Brazil in local and special terms. This mode of life, which to an important extent still endures, developed in most of its major outlines through the adjustment of Europeans to the new environment and through their contact with the native Indians of the Brazilian colony. This way station has been occupied by relatively many people in Brazil for nearly four hundred years.

The tradition of unremitting hard work is not of the *caboclo*. His work week is frequently truncated to four days or less. The *caboclo* does not work so much by the day as by some designated job or work. His isolated farmstead manner of dwelling is supposed to militate against a marked development of community institutions. However, he does have work groups composed of friends and neighbors, and there are certain other forms of helpfulness and some of cooperation on a kinship and locality basis.

The *caboclo* family is monogamous. The basic unit is the nuclear or elementary family, parents and children. Other relatives are not typically a part of the domestic unit. A large percentage of unions is on a common-law basis. There are opinions both ways on the stability of the *caboclo* union. We are not utterly without evidence of family stability.

Although illegitimacy, generally high in Brazil, may be particularly high in rural areas, the statistics do not automatically warrant the conclusion that *caboclos* are immoral and conform less frequently to their sexual and marital norms than others. The probability is to the contrary.

The *caboclo* economy is basically a subsistence economy. Production is not for commerce but essentially for their own consumption. In the absence of the regular use of money for the majority of goods and services, the *caboclo* is practically prevented from developing certain common Western ideas as part of his economic thinking or as goals that motivate him. The economy is only to a limited degree harmonized with the expansive Western economy; it is relatively static in growth while the Western form of commercialism has been—and certainly tends to be in modern Brazil—dynamically expansive.

A price for, and attachment of money value to, a wide range of objects, time, effort, skills, prestige, influence, knowledge, power, and other "commodities" are not considered in similar fashion among *caboclos*. This is in harmony with the thoroughly *caboclo* institution of the *mutirão*, or joint-work group. The *mutirão* involves calling together a number of one's friends, neighbors, or relatives to help perform some task, such as raising a house, or clearing ground for planting, and similar work undertakings. The reigning motives for the "host" of a *mutirão* and for the participants are not commercial and money-oriented but are rather social conviviality, helpfulness, and reciprocity, making for local social solidarity. Eating, drinking, music, and dancing usually climax the *mutirão*. Even the work with its zestful and good-natured banter and rivalry is pleasurable. Yet the production which the *mutirão* has as its object is usually at the very heart of the *caboclo*'s sustenance.

The Indian origin of the *mutirão* coincides clearly with the historical derivation of much of *caboclo* culture in Brazil. However, the functional character of the *mutirão* marks it as a feature or "symptom" of a "folk" culture. Other such features are: the slight division of labor, the low level of exchange of goods and services, the small amount of money exchange, the limited concept of money price, and the high level of individual and familial economic self-sufficiency. The overall folk nature of *caboclo* culture marks a significant gulf between *caboclos* and many other Brazilians. The gulf is all too easily ignored because *caboclos* speak Portuguese, although with marked and even stereotyped dialectic differences. Even while jokes and stories are legion of *caboclo* faux pas and economic mishaps in the city, even though "the hoodwinked *caboclo*" is a standard theme of Brazilian humor and a common item of news reportage, these are not always seen as evidence of actual cultural differences, both deep-seated and of some magnitude.

If we consider the *caboclo* "worldview," a deep-seated characteristic distinct from the more Westernized parts of Brazilian society comes into focus. Thus, the peculiar idea of time as a dimension measuring progress is either rudimentary or lacking among most *caboclos*. The idea of losing time if one lets it flow past without achieving a sense of movement—that is, achieving a fuller realization of certain quantifiable values—is largely alien to him. The variety of material goods, the acquisition and accumulation of which constitute one of the easiest measures of progress-time, simply are not and have not been a part of the *caboclo* world. The wants and corresponding goods that the *caboclo* culturally recognizes are nearly all cyclic, like his concept of time; they are not cumulative and superannual. This means food for today, and shelter and clothing for the present. He has neither the idea nor in most cases the possibility of saving or investing money or accumulating anything else toward a distant future.

In emphasizing his non-Western cultural tendencies and the *caboclo*'s low degree of participation in the commercial economy of the nation, it would be a mistake to give the impression that the *caboclo* has stood apart from Brazilian history; nothing could be further from the facts. Though exaggerated, the familiar notion of the *caboclo* as the "real Brazilian" is at least closer to the truth. The *caboclo*'s historic role has been that of *desbravador*, or civilizer. At first this appears to be paradoxical, since the *caboclo* himself is now regarded by the progress-minded as being in need of civilizing. He is a civilizer, nevertheless, in having developed a workable ecological adaptation of some Western traits to the country he [the European] invaded. And he is even more so in the sense of furthering the type of social organization which, though now itself at odds with "progress," was necessary before civilization could penetrate into the interior.

For good or for ill, the *caboclo* has a viable if limited way of life, developed by trial and error and thoroughly proven for nearly four centuries. This represents considerably more survival value than commercial Brazil's evanescent forms of production. In the tropical rain forest this point is especially cogent. His mode of living may not impress us as rich or ennobling, but the likelihood is great that it measures up to the expectations that *caboclos* hold. What better prospect for them as non-*caboclos* does the future hold? It is much too easy simply to say, "Anything would be better." Perhaps the urban *favela* or *cortiço* is not appreciably "better."

For those who hope that the *caboclo* will always remain a *caboclo*, the quiet, simple, self-reliant, and sometimes romanticized "real Brazilian," the problem may certainly be hopeless. For those with visions of healthy, energetic, progress-minded country people who will convert the rural face of Brazil along the best school-of-agronomy lines, the prospect is equally hopeless—at least for a long time. What many hope for we have called Westernization, and the *caboclos*, though some are moving in that direction, have long been at a way station perhaps equivalent to a half-way house.

28 *William Lytle Schurz* ◆ Subjective, Unpredictable, and Capricious

William Lytle Schurz received his undergraduate degree from Oberlin College and did graduate work at the University of California. He spent two years in research at the Archivo de las Indias in Seville, Spain. He wrote on Latin America for the New York Herald Tribune, *taught history at the University of Michigan, and was on the faculty of the American Institute for Foreign Trade in Phoenix, Arizona. Schurz lived in Latin America for sixteen years; he served in the U.S. Department of State, as a cultural affairs officer in the Latin America Bureau, and as the commercial attaché, stationed in Rio de Janeiro, in the 1920s. He later traveled extensively in Brazil.*

Schurz wrote several books and reports on Brazilian commercial problems; his works on other topics include Latin America: A Descriptive Survey *(1959);* American Foreign Affairs: A Guide to International Affairs *(1959);* The Social Security Act in Operation: A Practical Guide to the Federal and Federal-State Social Security Programs *(1937); and* The Manila Galleon: The Romantic History of the Spanish Galleons Trading between Manila and Acapulco *(1959).* This New World, *his work dealing with intellectual and cultural aspects of Latin American history, provides the material for the first excerpt that follows. The second, from his survey* Brazil: The Infinite Country, *examines the people as "unconventional individualists."*

~ *The Predominance of Feeling over Intelligence* ~

What the Brazilians call *sensibilidade* is the key to their national character. It is neither "sensibility" nor "sensibleness," but rather it is sentimentalism, and in motivation implies the predominance of feeling over intelligence. In other words, where the prospect of some action is concerned, the Brazilian tends to think with his heart, more than with his head. Thinking and attitudes are likely to be subjective rather than objective, for life is a highly personal matter, made up of relations between individuals. General concepts like "duty" or "morality" are philosophic catchalls, and in serious conversation may be useful as rallying points for lesser ideas, but they are difficult to convert into practical terms where it is a matter of one's own private actions or interests. People are either *simpático* or *antipático*; if they are *simpático*, you like them, but if not, you dislike them. *Amizade* or friendship assumes an importance unknown among the cooler temperaments of northern peoples, and people may be classified as *amigos* or *inimigos*.

The dominion of affective or emotional considerations complicates the conduct of serious affairs, and makes it hard to settle a question on its merits. It has a marked effect on the functioning of the will, and . . . people are liable to act on impulse, according to their emotional reflexes. These internal promptings or motivations may be very violent in their intensity, even if short-lived. Thus, crimes are generally passionate actions, committed on the spur of the moment and without plan or premeditation.

The unpredictability, and what to a more calculating people is capriciousness, that are implicit in so subjective an atmosphere, are further aggravated by an irregular rhythm of effort. . . . Like the buildup of atmospheric pressures in a storm area to the explosive point, these may be relatively long preliminaries of preparation for action. The indolence generated in the process is congenial to the Brazilian nature, even though the actual circumstances of life may be unfavorable to indulgence. The enjoyment of idleness is evidence of superiority over economic pressures, just as white and uncalloused hands are a mark of social category. Over much of the country, it is also a defensive reaction against the climate, and so represents an economy of forces, rather than downright laziness or flabbiness of character. On the other hand, there exists no cult of hard work. . . . More interested in the present than in the distant future, the Brazilians seem, by our standards, an improvident people. On the way to whatever fate the future may hold in store for them, they wish to take time to enjoy the little pleasures and satisfactions by the road.

In the meantime, nobody expects or desires to become rich by hard work. So pleasing an eventuality must depend on either luck or some superior prowess of the individual. Brazilians have much faith in *sorte* or chance. A race of inveterate gamblers or speculators, they are always hoping to win the big prize in the lottery or in the *bicho*, Rio's equivalent of the "numbers" game, in which one bets on some familiar animal or *bicho* (bug). "The *Bicho*" has resisted all the occasional frantic efforts of government to suppress it, and manages to keep the lower classes of Rio in a chronic state of expectation and insolvency. In default of luck and its caprices, one must lean on himself, as it were, and win wealth by some stroke of shrewdness. Thus, business is not business, but a game. The predilection for the brilliant stroke explains the "gimmick" or trick which one is expected to look for in a Brazilian deal. Perhaps no conscious dishonesty is implied, but rather a challenge to a battle of wits. For . . . the Brazilian's standards of personal honesty are probably as high as those of other peoples in a comparable state of evolution.

The possible "antisocial" consequences of the Brazilians' emphasis on sentiment are tempered by the presence of certain other qualities in the national character. One of these is *bondade* or goodness of heart. There is a deep humanity in the people that is Christian in its essence. They are sensitive to the sufferings of others, and are disposed to be open-handed and generous to those in their own circle who are in need of help. If . . . they tend to be indifferent to the miseries of those whom they do not know, it is not from any hardness of heart, but because they are aware of the limits of their capacity to play the good Samaritan. . . .

There is, too, a certain indifferentism in the Brazilian's nature which may prevent him from taking anything too seriously, so long as it does not immediately menace the satisfying rhythms of his life. It is a devil-may-care attitude that nothing matters very much provided one can go on enjoying the things that make for his happiness. It tends to make it easier to pardon small offenses and to shorten the life of grudges. There are few expressions that one hears so often in Brazil as, "Não faz mal" or "Não importa" ("It doesn't matter"). A variation of this easygoing fatalism or resignation is found in another expression which goes, "Leave it as it is, so that one can see how it turns out" ("Deixa-o como está para ver como fica").

The Brazilian mind is a sharp instrument. It can cut easily and clearly, though when it would dig deeply into the mountains of thought, it may quickly become tired or bored. Its workings are characterized by facility and grace. But it is a two-dimensional mind, and tends to lack depth and persistence, and a feeling for exactness and precision. It emphasizes mental agility and brilliance, and it is likely to put a higher value on the fruits of inspiration and intuition than on the substantial products of plodding and plugging. The Brazilian, particularly the Nordestino [Northeasterner], often has a tropical luxuriance of imagination that gives wings to his brain, though they may be the wings of the swallow rather than of the wild goose. . . .

The tolerant spirit and deep humanity of the Brazilian people; the general attitude of live and let live, even though a passive sentiment, grounded in indifference; an extraordinary mellowness and warmth in the closer personal relationships; a general distaste for extreme solutions; the old tradition of an easygoing patriarchal regime in the backcountry—all these traits of national character ease the normal tensions of community living and provide . . . a propitious setting for the building of the eventual Brazilian society. In the slow process of assimilating the ingredients of a composite civilization, there is a disposition to accept differences of outlook and opinion and not to insist on uniformity, so long as the essentials which distinguish Brazilians from other peoples are observed.

From *This New World: The Civilization of Latin America* (New York: E. P. Dutton and Company, 1954), 397–99, 401–2, 412–13. Footnotes omitted.

~ *Unconventional Individualists* ~

While certain qualities are common to the majority of Brazilians wherever they live, the local variables remain striking and important. The Nordestino, or man of the old north-coast country, best exemplified by the Bahiano on its southern fringe, is warm-hearted and sentimental, given to fluid speech and endowed with a lyric imagination. The *sertanejo* [backwoodsman], who lives inland to the west of him, is austere and laconic, nomadic and physically hardy. The Mineiro, a true mountaineer, is . . . conservative and cautious, sober and prudent, reserved and undemonstrative, and with a deep fund of common sense and passive strength. The Carioca of Rio is volatile and voluble, irreverent and cynical, sybaritic and devil-may-care. The Paulista is practical-minded and dynamic, adventurous and energetic. The gaúcho of Rio Grande do Sul is frank and unemotional, a rugged horseman with a yen for the open spaces. . . .

The family names of most Brazilians are conventional enough. . . . But their first or Christian names are probably the most unconventional on earth. The result is that except for a myriad of Joãos and Josés, or Johns and Joes, a Brazilian is liable to be known by his first name. Families often try to find so unusual a name for a newborn child that there is little likelihood of its being duplicated in the city. A man is frequently listed in the telephone book according to his Christian name. For example, President Vargas, the famous Brazilian dictator, was universally known as "O Getúlio," or "The Getúlio." Brazilians ransack the classics and the Bible and history and the dictionary for distinctive names for their children. They even resort to numerals, as the prominent Rosado family in Maranhão did, to designate their twenty-one offspring. In this case the numerals were French and not Portuguese, and the children were called Un, Deux, Trois, Quatre, Cinq, and so on up to Vingt-un. Number Eighteen, or Dix-huit, was elected to the National Congress, and one day a Rio newspaper carried the headline, "Dix-huit was met at the airport by his brother, Vingt." One Mineiro mother hopefully christened her child Ultimo (the last), and lived to see him a member of the Chamber of Deputies in Rio. In 1959 among the 326 members of that body were the following: Epílogo (Epilogue) de Campos, Expedito Machado, Bonaparte Maia, Philadelpho Garcia, and Ferro (Iron) Costa, besides a sprinkling of such un-Portuguese names as Yukishigue Tamura, Rachid Named, Wilson Fadul, Antonio Baby, and Alberto Hoffmann.

The variety of Christian names of the large Oliveira clan in Rio, as listed in the local telephone directory, is probably typical. Besides a Sétimo, or Seventh, and Treze, or Thirteen, thirteen of them bear classical Greek names that range from Alcibiades to Pericles, and include, among others, an Amphilophio, an Apollinario, a Diogenes, and a Euripides. Four of them are named Caesar, Cicero, Tacitus, and Diocletian. Six of the local Oliveiras are named Gladstone, Jefferson, Milton, Nelson, Newton, and Washington. Among others are a cosmopolitan assortment which includes namesakes of Atahualpa and Napoleon; Hammurabi, the Babylonian king, and Kropotkin, a princely Russian anarchist; and out of the Dark Ages, a Carloman and a Dagobert. There are also a Bonanza and a Rockefeller Chrysóstomo. The biblical influence in Brazil is further represented by Ananias Matta in Rio and Methuselah Wanderley in Recife.

Contrary to the usual impression, by no means all Brazilian women are named Maria. The diversity of feminine names is illustrated by women of the large Silva family in the Rio telephone directory. They are generally melodious names, sometimes derived from Indian legend, and include Alzira, Aurea (Golden), Ayrosa, Beleza (Beauty), Dulce (Sweet) and Dulcina, Belmira, Djalma, and Iracy. Among the Oliveiras, Greek mythology was drawn on for the names of Eurydice and Mnemosyne.

The salutations used in addressing persons in Brazil depend on such considerations as age, social position, education, [and] occupation, but mostly on the degree of intimacy in the relationship. Brazilians dislike formulas where people are involved, and things like forms of address are likely to be subjective. Foreigners learn only by trial and faux pas the correct thing to say. For example, a married woman who has reached matronage may be hailed by her first name, preceded by "*Dona*," as [in] "*Dona* Elena." If she is a servant, the "*Dona*" is omitted. There is no equivalent for the Spanish "*Don*," and the term "*Dom*" is applied only to certain members of the clergy. The nearest approach to the Spanish "*usted*" or formal "you" is "*O senhor*," which means literally "the mister." The next step toward complete informality is the use of the word "*você*." Friends and members of the family address one another by their first name and use the familiar "*tu*" in conversation. Brazilians are much given to the use of diminutives which are composed by affixing an *-nho* or *-nha* to the person's name or appellation, as "Mariozinho." They are an expression of endearment or familiarity, as when a child addresses its grandmother as "*avozinha*."

Since the doctorate is the mark of the educated man in Brazil, Brazilians are liable to take no chances of offending one who wears an air of learning and so address him as "*doutor*." If the one addressed is not a doctor, he is pleased by the compliment anyway, so that nothing is lost by the error and some goodwill may be gained. The degree is rather liberally dispensed, so that more realistic, though well-informed, natives do not take it very seriously. Thus a cartoonist shows a Carioca saluting a doctoral friend from a taxi on the Avenida Rio Branco as every face on the block turns about to answer the greeting. One with no claim to intellectual distinction, but with "status" in the community, may become a "colonel" by acclamation, as in Kentucky. Most of the honorary colonels in Brazilian life seem to come from the state of Minas. It is still possible to hear the old-fashioned and courtly form of address, "*vossa Excelência*," applied to important personages, but well below the level of presidency. Also, a judge may be addressed by the ponderous Portugueseism, "*Desembargador*," and a lawyer as "*Licenciado*," or "licensed one.". . .

The basic quality of Brazilians is humanity. This takes the various forms of respect for the lives and personalities of others. It is expressed in the Brazilian's strong aversion to violence, whether between nations or individuals. The crime rate in the cities is probably "normal," but little of it [the crime] is calculated or premeditated. Murders are generally prompted by sudden outbursts of passion, except among the *caboclos* of the *sertão*, where the vendetta is common. . . .

The law runs thin in the backlands, as it always does in an open frontier. And much of Brazil is still frontier. When it is present, authority is liable to be capricious, exercised by some local chieftain, ignorant or contemptuous of codes and courts. Where the formal panoply of authority and the restraints of civilized society are absent, each man tends to be a law unto himself, restrained only by individual conscience or whatever elemental concepts of justice and mercy he may harbor—or by the primitive fear of personal vengeance. So men may kill for greed or because their blood runs hot in them.

In the rest of the country there are accepted rules that govern personal relationships and mitigate the clashes of personality. These rules are dictated by good taste or good sense. For example, one does not mix in another's affairs. A foreigner, traveling at night along a dark street in Rio, comes upon a man beating a woman, who is presumably his wife. He goes to the woman's rescue, only to have both turn on him for interfering in something that was not his concern, and he learns quickly that there is no place for would-be Galahads in Brazil. Two open streetcars or *bondes* meet at a switch on the line. The motormen, obviously enemies, alight and begin to belabor each other with their iron switch rods. Meanwhile, the Brazilian passengers remain outwardly unconcerned, though a woman faints. But when a foreigner makes a move as if to break up the fight, his neighbor seizes his coattail and pulls him back into his seat.

In their dealings with others, Brazilians would rather please than hurt, but the formalized courtesy that marks relationships is more sincere than otherwise. At least it very seldom is a cover for ill will. In the structure of human relations, there are four distinct levels. The first, and closest, is the sector of the family, within which the ordinary guards of privacy are down and the heart has full play. The second is the privileged area of friendship. The third is that of regular acquaintances, with whom no sentimental ties are involved. The fourth is that of the stranger, toward whom there are certain impersonal responsibilities. Thus the manner of address and the degree of warmth in communication are determined by a code of natural good breeding that may have little to do with social position.

From *Brazil: The Infinite Country* (New York: E. P. Dutton and Company, 1961), 117, 119–22, 134–36.

29 *Marvin Harris* ◆ In the Backlands, Dreaming of the City

Marvin Harris, a prominent anthropologist formerly at Columbia University and now at the University of Florida, is the author of Cows, Pigs, Wars, and Witches: The Riddles of Culture *(1974);* Cannibals and Kings: The Origins of Culture *(1977);* Cultural Materialism: The Struggle for a Science of Culture *(1979); and* Our Kind: Who We Are, Where We Came From, Where We Are Going *(1989). Minas Velhas, in the state of Bahia, is the name that he gave to the mining community where in 1950 and 1951 he did the fieldwork required for his doctoral dissertation, later published as* Town and Country in Brazil. *The rapid Brazilian exodus from rural areas is partially explained by Harris's description, presented below, of the townspeople as despising farming and the work of the peasant; their community "stands like a deserted fort in the wilderness."*

In the central and northern portions of the Eastern Brazilian Highlands, there are many communities of less than two thousand people, strikingly isolated from the nation's metropolitan centers, with a retarded level of technological development and a worldview which is essentially nonscientific, but which nonetheless present a large number of conspicuously

From *Town and Country in Brazil* (New York: Columbia University Press, 1956), 4–5, 288–89.

urban features. . . . The inhabitants of these towns feel themselves to be profoundly different from their country neighbors who live nearby in villages and on farms.

The Eastern Highlands were the first portions of the Brazilian interior to be settled by any substantial number of people. The discovery of gold and diamonds early in the eighteenth century provided the reason for the bulk of this settlement. With respect to the settlement of the interior of the three important states of São Paulo, Minas Gerais, and Bahia, the early founding of a number of sophisticated, nonagricultural urban centers based upon mining is of paramount importance. . . .

If Brazil is to be best understood as a rural nation, many of its rural areas cannot be understood at all except in relation to hundreds of deeply entrenched urban nuclei which, like Minas Velhas, got their start in the halcyon days of the mining boom.

These urban centers were on the whole premature. If one considers the agricultural potential and the population density of the surrounding countryside, they were like an abundance of leaven amid a shortage of flour. Flung westward on a wave of prosperity that quickly retreated and left them stranded in the most unlikely places, they have waited for two centuries for the new Brazilian frontier to catch up with them. . . .

Having pushed on far too quickly, the Brazilian frontiersman in the mining region has been as much the sophisticated, conservative city dweller looking back to the comforts of the east as the rough and ready man with the ax seeking to carve out a new empire in the west. . . .

The strength of urban culture traits, especially of the urban ethos, in the town subcultures of Brazil must be taken into consideration by those who are interested in improving living conditions in the Brazilian interior. The people of Minas Velhas are ready to accept radical cultural changes, especially as these pertain to technological innovations. Far from presenting any ideological resistance to technological progress, they desperately desire it in all forms, from automobiles and electric power, to modern housing and miracle drugs. Modernity is well-nigh a passion with them and the new is valued over the old in almost all situations where the townspeople are presented with a choice. This is true despite the fact that Minas Velhas enjoys a local reputation for being a "traditional" and conservative community.

Yet wishes alone are clearly not enough to bring about the changes which the townspeople so greatly desire, and in many respects the very intensity of the urban complex is the greatest obstacle to the development of improved standards of living and of technology. The townspeople have adopted for their own, prestige standards derived from urban life, which cannot effectively be supported under the given techno-environmental condition of the town and its hinterland. The level of agricultural and industrial productivity is simply not high enough to support the intense individualism, competition, and conspicuous consumption which the urban model demands. By facing toward the coast, lured by the truly stupendous achievements represented by cities like São Paulo and Rio de Janeiro, the townspeople have in effect turned their backs on what is ultimately their only possible source of future betterment. They refuse to admit that they are of the country and hence the wilderness all but engulfs them. They despise the work of the peasant and see in him the destroyer rather than the creator of civilization. They take from the soil and give nothing back, not even their labor. When fortune comes, they desert the interior and take their skills and money to the coast. . . .

The townspeople are the logical media for organizing and improving agricultural production. They have capital to invest; they have bureaucratic ability suitable for organizing and directing cooperatives; they go to school and are literate and could easily be taught scientific principles of soil management and crop production; they are ready to use machines and believe in progress. Yet there is not a teacher in Minas Velhas who knows the rudiments of agriculture or who does not despise farming as a profession. Agricultural interests are represented in the town by absentee landlords who desire from their land what their sharecroppers are able to produce for them, i.e., enough so that *they* need not touch the hoe. But the town is not really there in the backlands. It stands like a deserted fort in the wilderness. Its people are away, dreaming of the city.

30 *Elizabeth Bishop* ◆ The Usual Moderation

Brought up in New England and educated at Vassar College, Elizabeth Bishop, author of many works of poetry and prose, won the Pulitzer Prize in 1956 for poetry. She also won the National Book Award in 1970 and the National Book Critics Circle Award in 1977. American poet Robert Lowell, one of her closest friends, predicted that "she will be recognized as not only one of the best but also one of the most prolific writers of our century."

An inveterate traveler, Bishop made her home in Brazil from 1951, when she was forty, until 1974. She died in 1979. Much of her poetry and prose dealt with themes connected to Brazil.

Brazilians poke fun at their usually bloodless revolutions: "No one fought in that revolution—it was the rainy season." Like the Portuguese form of bullfighting in which there is no killing, Brazilian revolutions or *golpes* (coups) sometimes seem to be little more than political and rhetorical maneuvering. A man's speeches, his moral and physical courage, are admired, but actual violence is going too far. Duels are still fought in Argentina, but they are out of style in Brazil. Brazil has not fought a major war for almost a century. It has rarely wanted more land, already having more than it knows what to do with.

Jokes tell even more. There is an old favorite, perhaps not even Brazilian originally, about a man walking down a street with a friend. He is grossly insulted by a stranger, and says nothing. The friend tries to rouse his fighting instincts, "Didn't you hear what he called you? Are you going to take that? Are you a man, or aren't you?" The man replies, "Yes, I'm a man. But not *fanatically*." This is the true Brazilian temper. . . .

The ordinary, average Brazilians are a wonderful people, cheerful, sweet-tempered, witty, and patient—incredibly patient. To see them standing in line for hours, literally for hours, in lines folded back on themselves two or three times the length of a city block, only to get aboard a broken-down, recklessly driven bus and return to their tiny suburban houses, where like as not these days the street has not been repaired, nor the garbage collected, and there may even be no water—to see this is to marvel at their patience. Other people undergoing the same trials would surely stage a revolution every month or so. There may still be more than one *golpe*, or coup, in the offing to change the course of government—because there is certainly a growing determination among Brazilians to achieve a better government. But if this determination brings troubles, let us hope they can be solved with the usual Brazilian moderation. Brazilians have never had the government they should have; there is no knowing how long it will be before they get it.

31 *Peter Kellemen* ◆ Find a Way Around

Peter Kellemen was a Hungarian doctor who emigrated to Brazil after World War II and was later deported for running a confidence game and other dubious artifices. His Brasil para principiantes: Venturas e

From *Brasil para principiantes: Venturas e desaventuras de um brasileiro naturalizado* (Rio de Janeiro: Editora Civilização Brasileira, 1962), 9–12. Translated by G. Harvey Summ.

desaventuras de um brasileiro naturalizado *(Brazil for beginners: Adventures and misadventures of a naturalized Brazilian) is an amusing and insightful series; as of 1962, five editions had already been published. The story that follows, which leads off the book, is apparently drawn from Kellemen's own experience in applying for a visa.*

Name?

—Paul Kenedy.

—Profession?

—Doctor.

—Age?

—25.

—Recently finished your studies?

—Yes. Eight months ago.

—Do you intend to practice your profession in Brazil?

—I don't know . . . perhaps in time. I don't know the language.

—Then, instead of doctor, let's put down: agronomist. That way I can give you the visa immediately. You know how these things are, don't you? Quotas for professions, confidential instructions from the immigration department, silly rules . . . unimportant. In any case, this way it will remain 100 percent within the rules.

The Brazilian consul spoke clear and understandable English and smiled at me as if I were a high-school student who, in complicity with a friend, had just fooled the professor.

—Thank you. But I would like to avoid a false declaration that in the future might tend to incriminate me. I know nothing about agronomy. . . . It might turn out badly. I will not know how to explain to the authorities. . . . To be frank, I do not find this a recommendable solution.

As I talked, there paraded through my mind all my previous experiences with high officials of several countries and governments, including those of my own country.

"Well, this man is provoking me. He wants to get me to make a false declaration. . . . Who knows why? He wants to observe my reaction. . . ."

I redoubled my efforts to face that man, apparently so sincere, but in reality a true *agent provocateur.*

However, he paid little attention to me. He came quite close to me.

—My son, the agronomist matter will not be a problem. As soon as you arrive, when you are in Brazil . . . in Brazil.

He stopped. I understood that he was looking for the right word. He spoke a heavily accented but fluent English. He thought for a few moments and then turned to his assistant:

—Castro! How do you say in English, "There in Brazil you will *dar um jeito* (find a way around)?"

Castro seemed to be about fifty or fifty-five. Fat, he wore heavy glasses and was completely bald. He turned to me:

—Mr. Paul, I speak English well, but I prefer German. I can even consider German my second language, since I was born in southern Brazil, where German settlement was widespread. My father was the son of Germans and I went to schools where some of the exams were given in that language. But I cannot translate *dar um jeito* into German . . . nor into English.

He patted me on the shoulder, took me over to a sofa, and sat down at my side.

—Listen carefully. Let's see if I can translate. You are a doctor, aren't you?

—Yes.

—You are going to declare that you are an agronomist?

—Yes.

—You think that this will be a false declaration or, let us say, an unsupported statement?

—More or less.

—My dear Paul, that is absolutely not the question. We only want to find a way for you to travel without any more delay. The only result will be that we will avoid your wasting your time and you can leave soon. Your visa will be ready this afternoon.

I then understood that it was not a matter of a provocation, but I still did not know if I had just spoken with two representatives of a nation where the laws are reinterpreted, where the regulations and central instructions of the government are enacted in advance with prior calculation of the percentage to which they will be carried out, where the people are a great filter of laws, and where officials, small or powerful, create their own jurisprudence. Even if this jurisprudence does not coincide with the original laws, it meets general approval, or is dictated by good sense.

The consul, José de Magalhães e Albuquerque, is one of those individuals who, in accordance with his own convictions, modifies or simply ignores the paragraphs that do not coincide with his particular opinion.

He did not suggest the change from doctor to agronomist out of a concern for earning money or a gift. He was a third-generation millionaire, a consul for sport or as a hobby. And he did not order the visa given immediately to get rid of me: he had more than thirty employees to kick me out, chat with me, discourage me—that is, to send me on my way.

The consul general of the United States of Brazil gave an order to find a way around. Despite immigration laws, quotas, and professional preferences, he knew that in that year there would enter Brazil, through the old, proven, and uncontrollable system of natural birth, more than two million beings, without consulting councils, consuls, or ambassadors, but also that these two million "newly arrived" would not have a recommendable profession, money, or immediate capacity to produce and . . . would not even know how to speak.

My consul may have been thinking of the problem of the constant increase in population. But he was not inclined to bargain with a thousand or five thousand souls, whether they might become doctors, agronomists, or night watchmen. For him the problem did not exist, at least in those petty dimensions, and he was ready to assume before the world the responsibility for his liberal attitude. He also knew that he would not run great risks, since there will never exist a Brazilian, including the very legislator of immigration laws, who does not understand and support this consular "way around."

V

The Military Period and After (1964–Present): Another Boom-and-Bust Cycle

On April 1, 1964, the military, led by moderate Marshal Humberto Castelo Branco, took over the government. Although, after the empire, it had exercised the "moderating power" and intervened in politics several times, on this occasion the military was not satisfied with merely participating in behind-the-scenes civilian coalitions or scheduling new elections and then stepping down from power. Hard-liners argued that since self-seeking and subversive politicians had corrupted Brazilian democracy, the military would have to remain in power long enough to bring about economic development and cleanse the country of subversion. Moderate officers originally balked at such an outright assumption of power, but events favored the hard-liners.

The military ran Brazil for twenty-one years, at first purging legislators and suppressing direct elections. Then technocrats under its supervision instituted austerity measures to bring inflation under control and improve the balance of payments. When short-term results were disappointing, the opposition, encouraged by relatively tolerant attitudes of the ruling group, mobilized protests and mass demonstrations.

In 1968 the government put down strikes strongly, setting a dictatorial pattern in which it kept wages low, repressed labor unions, and recruited foreign investment. The following year a small cadre of revolutionary activists—often members of the middle class—turned to guerrilla warfare, principally in the cities. They kidnapped foreign diplomats and businessmen, robbed banks, and engaged in other terrorist tactics. The military government struck back harshly, with assassinations, torture, imprisonment, and exile, and easily vanquished the guerrillas. The opposition's challenges, however poorly organized, had given the hard-line regime the rationale it needed to maintain a police-state apparatus well into the 1970s.

The repressive period closely paralleled spectacular economic growth. From 1968 to 1974, during the so-called Economic Miracle, the growth rate averaged 10 percent. Under five military presidents and their civilian successors, Brazil became a modern industrial nation. Newly established state-owned enterprises led the expansion. Computers and arms were among the new industries established, exports grew impressively, São Paulo became the engine of both industrial and agricultural growth, and the country's population swelled to almost 150 million. Educational opportunities, particularly at higher levels, multiplied many times over, and chances for women increased.

For a time some Brazilian leaders were convinced that their country was on the verge of taking its place on the world stage as a great power. International events in the 1970s, however, led to another of Brazil's boom-and-bust cycles. The 1973 oil shock quadrupled the price of the oil imports on which the economy was highly dependent. Government energy policies attempted to increase domestic oil production and to develop alternate energy sources, with varying success, through giant hydroelectric projects and the use of nuclear power and ethanol. On the financial side, government policy called for continuing rapid growth for the rest of the decade, mainly by borrowing petrodollars at variable interest rates; inflation was kept tolerable by a broad-based system of indexation.

The quadrupling of oil prices once again in 1979 led to an inflation rate of over 100 percent in Brazil in 1980 and a serious balance-of-payments problem. During the 1980s, often referred to as the Lost Decade, per capita income stagnated at about $2,000 per year. Foreign debt mounted and industrial production sagged. Unemployment spread, and emigration—a new phenomenon for Brazil—grew, particularly among the middle class. Labor staged a series of strikes, dramatizing the disproportionate share of sacrifice that workers had borne during the Miracle. A world recession depressed the value of Brazilian exports, and high interest rates kept the cost of servicing the foreign debt at a crippling level; by the end of 1982 the foreign debt was the largest in the world.

Brazil's social structure, in which a small, homogeneous, and self-perpetuating elite governs a vast majority, in many ways has not changed fundamentally compared to earlier eras. Local political bosses in the more backward regions are the modern equivalent of the captains of colonial times. The "haves" are still a minority, although no longer the exclusive minority they were in the colonial, imperial, or early republican periods. Some of the underprivileged have been able to claw or worm their way into a small middle sector. Yet disparities in wealth and income—among the most glaring of any country in the world—widened even further, except for a short prosperous period in the early 1970s when most classes benefited to some extent.

New intellectual currents have made more Brazilians aware—and even proud—of their extensive African heritage. However, functional illiterates, a disproportionate number of whom are black, make up at least half the population and have little opportunity to become productive citizens in a rapidly industrializing economy. Measures that might reduce social inequities, such as agrarian reform and improvements in basic education, hardly have been tried or have failed. Neglect and oppression of the poor have grown.

Some Brazilians have described their country as "Belindia," a small developed country—Belgium—inside an enormous poverty-stricken area with conditions resembling those in India. More accurately, southern Brazil resembles a poor developed country, while the misery in parts of northern and northeastern Brazil is comparable to that in the worst of the Third World. By 1990 the proportion of the population living in cities was in the neighborhood of 80 percent, as opposed to about 25 percent in 1920. A new nationwide road network opened the Amazon for development, with mixed results. The native Indian population, down to about two hundred thousand, has been under increased pressures from new settlement, ranching, and prospecting activities, and worldwide reaction to Amazon deforestation has led to a growing Brazilian environmental consciousness.

The dictatorship's human rights violations have also garnered public attention, particularly from the Catholic Church, which is the leader of a peaceful opposition movement. The progressive clergy, a significant faction that emerged after Vatican II (an ecumenical council held from 1962 to 1965 with a goal of spiritual renewal and reconsideration of the Church's role in the modern world), broke away from the Church's long alliance with the elite and supported grass-roots reform movements aimed at bettering conditions for the poor. Meanwhile, traditional Church tolerance for other forms of religious worship, including Afro-Brazilian practices, in the world's largest Catholic country, has been sorely tested by the recent phenomenal growth of Protestant fundamentalist sects.

In 1974 the military began to extricate itself from politics and return to the barracks. At first the pace, in a controlled "political opening" toward democracy, was gradual, to avoid provoking a hard-line reaction, but it was stepped up as economic conditions worsened. The military created new political parties, allowed limited free elections, lifted censorship, dismantled the government's repressive apparatus, and permitted leading opposition politicians to return from exile. An amnesty—Brazilian style—pardoned both revolutionaries and overzealous government supporters for excesses in the early years of military rule. In elections held in 1982 for almost all national offices except the presidency, the opposition won convincingly, particularly in Brazil's more developed south, despite government attempts to manipulate the elections.

In 1984 opposition groups failed, despite widespread demonstrations, to amend the constitution to permit direct election of the president. Nevertheless, in indirect elections the next year, a widely respected opposition candidate, Tancredo Neves, won an overwhelming victory through a combination of his own appeal and the inability of the military government to control the succession. When Neves became ill and died without taking office, his vice president-elect, José Sarney, a civilian politician with close ties to the military, became president of the so-called New Republic on April 22, 1985.

Sarney preserved civil liberties but was ineffectual in dealing with Brazil's economic problems. In 1986 his first austerity plan, which froze prices, made him extremely popular for a few months and led to smashing majorities later that year in Congress and in state and local offices for parties in his coalition. However, his lifting of price controls a few days after those elections destroyed his credibility, which he never regained. Inflation grew from an annual rate of 250 percent to over 1,700 percent. Sarney presided over a twenty-month process that resulted in the 1988 constitution, Brazil's eighth. It was extremely progressive on paper, if not in practice. To gain the political support from Congress that he thought he needed for a full five-year presidential term, Sarney spread political patronage around widely; corruption was rampant.

Brazil returned to full democracy in November 1989, when the first direct elections for president since 1960 were held. The victor, Fernando Collor de Melo, governor of the small northeastern state of Alagoas, was another civilian politician first appointed to political office by the military. Collor and Luis Inácio ("Lula") da Silva, leader of the relatively new Workers' Party, were the two candidates who made it to the second round (twenty-two candidates were on the original ballot).

Collor won the runoff in December with about 53 percent of the votes. Age forty, telegenic, and from an elite family, he benefited from the prominent role that television played in the campaign. Under the new constitution, illiterates and young people age sixteen and over were eligible to vote. True to Brazilian tradition, Collor drew the votes of many of the underprivileged, who voted for whom they saw as one of their betters rather than Lula, one of their own.

Collor started out his five-year presidential term in March 1990 with a dramatic series of austerity and free-market measures designed to break the back of runaway inflation, but he had only middling success. He also deftly downgraded the military's role in politics. His lack of party support in Congress, however, made his task of governing more difficult. He resigned the presidency at the end of 1992, after impeachment on charges of corruption, ironically an issue at the center of his own presidential campaign. He was succeeded by his lackluster but honest vice president, Itamar Franco. The October 1994 elections ended the last vestiges of the military regime, and Fernando Henrique Cardoso, the victor in those elections, assumed the presidency in January 1995.

32 *Roberto da Matta* ◆ Do You Know Who You're Talking To?!

Brazilian anthropologist Roberto da Matta is professor of anthropology at the University of Notre Dame. He received his doctorate from Harvard University and has taught at the National Museum, Rio de Janeiro. In addition to the work from which these extracts are taken, his other books include Universo do Carnaval: Imagens e reflexões *(1981);* Universo do futebol: Esporte e sociedade brasileira *(1982);* O que fazo brasil, Brasil? *(1986); and* A casa e a rua: Espaço, cidadania, mulher, e morte no Brasil *(1987).*

While writing about contemporary phenomena such as Carnival and soccer, da Matta touches on traditional characteristics that go as far back as the colonial period. Thus, the first excerpt, from his book Carnavals, malandros e heróis *(Carnivals, Rogues, and Heroes), points up the discomfort that Brazilians feel at the contradiction between their authoritarian and hierarchical tendencies and their desire for affability and cordiality.*

Exploited, plundered, assaulted, and unknown—especially unknown, this anonymous mass is called *o povo* (the people). And who does not speak for it in Brazil? It is like a God without priests and theology, a truly Brazilian God of *umbanda* [an Afro-Brazilian spirit cult] in which the mysticism born of political dissatisfaction is enough to engender a morality ensuring a mystical relationship between the great powers up above and the mortals suffering affliction.

By studying our carnivals, rogues, and renouncers (our heroes), I also attempt to approach the Brazilian people in terms of their hopes and perplexities. For I have always been deeply struck by the connection between a people so impressed by, and a system of personal relationships so preoccupied with, personalities and sentiments; between a multitude so faceless and voiceless, and an elite so loud in calling for its prerogatives and rights; between an intellectual life so preoccupied with the heart of Brazil, on the one hand, and so attuned to the latest French book, on the

From *Carnavals, malandros e heróis*, 4th ed. (Rio de Janeiro: Zahar Editores, 1978). Translated by John Drury and published as *Carnivals, Rogues, and Heroes: Toward a Sociology of the Brazilian Dilemma* (Notre Dame, IN: University of Notre Dame Press, 1991), 2–4, 24, 137–39, 218–19. Adapted by G. Harvey Summ. Footnotes omitted.

other; between domestic servants who go unnoticed, and employers who are so egocentric; in short, between a society that is so rich in inventing modern rational laws and decrees and one that is nevertheless looking for the return of its Don Sebastian I, the old Portuguese father of all the renouncers and messiahs. Indeed, Don Sebastian seems to be such a perfect model of renunciation that he has decided, paradoxically enough, never to return, as if he foresaw his inevitable demystification and routinization by the very same people who claim to love him and wait for him so patiently. These people, the Brazilian people, intrigue me with their generosity, wisdom, and, above all, their unfailing hope.

In a word, the aim is to learn what makes "brazil" Brazil. In other words, like so many other scholars I am trying to explore the tendencies that make Brazilian society different and unique even though it, like other systems, is subject to certain common factors of a social, political, and economic nature. We, unlike the people of the United States, never say "separate but equal"; instead we say "different but united," which is the golden rule of a hierarchical and relational universe such as ours.

I think it is truly trite to say that Carnival reproduces a class society, something which I already know well, or the birth of urban social awareness, something which I doubt. I think it is far more important to pay attention to what everyone says but which does not seem to be taken seriously by sociologists: that at Carnival we Brazilians leave aside our hierarchized, repressive society and try to live freely and more individually. That, I think, allows us to embrace with a single theory not only the class conflicts (which are, indeed, functionally compensated for and mitigated at Carnival) but also the invention of a special moment that still retains a highly significant and politically charged relationship with everyday Brazilian life. The alarming thing is to recall that a nation of millions, an industrialized, capitalist nation at this point in time, allows "the poor" to become "rich" for four days of the year. Is that a banal fact, as some observers of the Brazilian scene would have it? Or is it what helps to make brazil Brazil? My approach is to consider ritual as a dramatization of certain elements, values, ideologies, and relationships in a society. I apply this perspective to a few basic rituals of Brazilian society with the presupposition that we are much closer to the participant when we look at Carnival in terms of what it suggests, presents, and offers by way of attraction.

I now wish to examine a little Brazilian ritual embodied in the use of the familiar Brazilian expression, "Do you know who you're talking to?!" This commonly used expression implies a separation, radical and authoritarian in nature, between two objectively or conceptually different social positions in classifying Brazilian culture. This form of addressing someone, which is very popular among Brazilians, is systematically left out of both superficial and serious works that attempt to describe the essential traits of our "character" as a people or nation. It is not something we are proud of, given its unpleasant overtones of authority, hostility, and arrogance. Thus we leave it out of our self-image, since we see it as an undesirable way of being a Brazilian, because it reveals our formalistic and our veiled—or even hypocritical—way of expressing extreme sorts of prejudice.

The ritual embodied in the use of "Do you know who you're talking to?!" puts us on the side of hierarchical ranks and authoritarian figures. We systematically try to hide that, or—what comes to the same thing—feel no need to demonstrate or prove it, because "everyone should know his place." We prefer to see ourselves on the side of free, modern, spontaneous, affable associations related to drinking beer on the beach, dancing the samba, and partying at Carnival.

Every Brazilian knows that this question is a ritualized and dramatic expression of a division in society that sets us miles apart from the positive image of the *malandro* (rogue) and his usual means of social survival. For the expression rudely denies and rejects cordiality, the *jeitinho* (clever dodge or bypass), and *malandragem* (roguery), traits that have always been used to define our way of life. Indeed, by virtue of its intensive and extensive use by all social segments and classes, in newspapers, books, popular histories, reviews, and anecdotal pieces, this ritual expression reveals an interaction rooted in the heart of our culture, alongside Carnival, the lottery, soccer, and roguery.

The expression has two important features. The first is the hidden or latent nature of learning and using it, since it is almost always regarded as an illegitimate and inadmissible recourse available to members of Brazilian society. In other words, we teach soccer and the samba and we talk about sunny beaches and love, about our informal and open ways, as signs of our truly "democratic vocation"; but we never voice our nasty question, "Do you know who you're talking to?!" in front of children and foreigners. On the contrary, we try to forbid its use as undesirable, even if we then use the accursed formula the first time an opportunity presents itself the next day. We consider the expression to be a part of the "real world" and of the "harsh reality of life." It is a tool we learn and use in the domain of the *street*, that cruel world we keep separate and far away from our hearth and house. We choose not to incorporate it into the pleasant, nonroutinized picture of the social universe we prefer to construct for ourselves. And so the expression is not examined seriously at either the scholarly or common-sense level, just as it is not employed in the lyrics of samba music.

The second feature of the ritual expression is its connection with a disturbing aspect of Brazilian culture. This "authoritarian ritual" always expresses conflict, and Brazilian society seems to be inimical to conflict. Needless to say, that does not eliminate conflict. Like every other dependent, colonial society, Brazil has an intimidating number of conflicts and crises, but there is a long way between the existence of a crisis and its recognition. Whereas some societies try to confront crises promptly, regarding them as part and parcel of the very structures of sociopolitical life, other societies seem to be unable to acknowledge conflict and crisis. For one society crises may indicate the need to correct something, while in another they represent the end of an era, the portent of catastrophe. Everything suggests that we Brazilians see conflicts as omens of the end of the world, as signs of unbearable failure that make it difficult for us to accept them as part of our history, especially as part of the official versions of that history, with its idealized and understandable emphasis on our solidarity. This is why we always prefer to put more stress on our universalist and cosmopolitan tendencies, in the process sidestepping a more penetrating and accurate look at our problems.

It might be more accurate to say that the dominant, triumphant sectors of any society always read its history and social structure as a narrative of solidarity, whereas the dissident and dominated sectors systematically reveal the role of conflict, violence, and crisis in the system. Losing sight of the dialectical character of social life and assuming that only one of these positions represents the correct view of our social reality would be an obvious mistake.

~ In the stories of Pedro Malasartes [Peter Badarts, a character in Brazilian folklore] we are struck by the looseness of the narrative style, in which countless independent episodes are combined as the narrator sees fit. These accounts—which define the character of the hero and the society in which he operates—depict Pedro deceiving or outwitting people in social positions of power and prestige, even selling feces to a very rich man. Others depict much more ambiguous situations where the distance between shrewdness and social offense is muddied—for example, inducing a powerful plantation owner to murder, the use of a corpse to make money, and the conscious, deliberate destruction of goods of production and consumption owned by a large proprietor.

Here we have a "hero without any character." To put it better, we are dealing with a personage who characteristically knows how to transform every disadvantage into an advantage, an ability which is the sign of any good rogue and all good roguery. Thus, Pedro Malasartes shows us how to turn death and a corpse into something positive and alive, deriving gain and money from his own sorrow and loss. He also teaches us to accept the relationship between "crap and money," to learn the profound equation that money (and its corresponding social position) is rotten and disposable, like the feces he sells to a rich and conceited fool. In the modern language of Brazil, Pedro Malasartes is not only a hero without any character but also a "subversive." Persecuting the powerful, he always administers the dose of vengeance and destruction that points up the absence of a more just social relationship between the rich and the poor. He thereby reveals the moral code that should guide the relationship between the weak and the strong, a code grounded mainly on social involvement and moral respect between rich and poor.

33 *John F. Santos* ◆ Bypassing the System

John F. Santos is professor of psychology at the University of Notre Dame. He has also taught at Tulane University, was a social science research associate at the University of Texas, and served as codirector of the Perceptual Learning Project and the Program in Reality Testing of the Menninger Foundation. During his years in Brazil, he was visiting professor of experimental psychology at the Institute of Experimental Psychology, Catholic University of São Paulo. He also served as a coinvestigator for a research program of a Peace Corps project on the São Francisco Valley in Northeast Brazil. In this selection, Santos highlights a number of Brazilian characteristics, including lack of confidence, casualness about work, a tendency toward circumvention, and joy in relationships with family and friends.

Any attempt to "explain" a group of people as varied and complex as Brazilians poses the very practical problem of where to begin and which characteristics to discuss. Since all of the important characteristics cannot be covered, only the more obvious ones that usually impress the foreigner and are probably most responsible for his attitudes and opinions about Brazil and Brazilians will be considered.

The comments, observations, and analyses that follow do not intend to evaluate Brazilian characteristics as good or bad, superior or inferior,

From "A Psychologist Reflects on Brazil and Brazilians," in *New Perspectives of Brazil*, edited by Eric N. Baklanoff (Nashville, TN: Vanderbilt University Press, 1966), 234–40, 242–43, 248–51. Adapted by G. Harvey Summ. Footnotes omitted.

nor to indulge in point-by-point comparisons of Brazilian behavioral characteristics with those found in the United States or other Latin American countries. On the other hand, there was no great compulsion to avoid comparisons which might be useful or interesting, and admittedly some biases have probably crept in inadvertently.

More critical opinions about Brazil were voiced by Brazilians to the writer than appear here, and stronger opinions about Americans were expressed than the writer has ventured here about Brazilians. At any rate, to imply that we are invariably right, effective, and superior and that they are invariably wrong, ineffective, and inferior is just as rigid and unrealistic as the opposite point of view. It might be said more realistically that they are more adept in coping with certain types of problems and that we are more successful in dealing with others. At least a partial explanation for the difference in effectiveness of the two groups may well be found in their characteristic perceptual and cognitive "styles," in their systems of attitudes and beliefs, and in their methods of coping with problems.

A Way of Life

The realities of life in Brazil certainly do not encourage confidence. They seem more likely to inspire a sense of helplessness. For the Brazilian, it becomes a necessary mode of adaptation to play the game, to accept the frustration and ambiguity of the system, and to hope for the best. Confronted as they were by the awesome obstacles of mountains, jungles, and vast distances, the dominant reaction of Brazilians was that of terror—a cosmic terror that has been passed down through generations and persists today. The tortuously slow progress—all that was possible against this awesome nature—certainly did not inspire any feelings of pantheistic order or immediate mastery; it was conducive, rather, to the acceptance of inevitable reversals and detours, and it encouraged general vigilance, distrust, and opportunism. The *jeito* and the emphasis upon skills in the ways of life and the intricacies of the system may thus be explained as a carryover from adaptation patterns developed in the past to cope with the physical environment.

Perhaps the most important characteristic of the *jeito* is the subtle bypassing of the system through the mechanism of mere "formal" satisfaction of rules and regulations. The behavior that first arises from the need to deal with the system may, however, become self-reinforcing and undergo further development and elaboration at least partially independent of past or present needs. Mastery of the system and the satisfaction of accomplishment do not, therefore, ordinarily seem to necessitate dealing with the system directly or bringing about changes in its structure or function. The real problems may remain untouched, unchanged, and forgotten.

The longer one copes with the demands of life in Brazil, the more one becomes aware of the rules of the game, and what first seems to be lost motion and unnecessary gestures eventually becomes a natural way of getting things done. In developing skill in the art of the *jeito*, the adept foreigner often begins to feel a certain amount of appreciation for, and even pleasure in, its execution. But foreigners are almost inevitably amazed and confused by the number and complexity of rituals that must be fulfilled before even relatively simple things can be accomplished. While Brazilians are quite helpful and eager to lead the way through the morass of rituals, they also seem to take more than a little delight and satisfaction in remaining calm while the foreigner fumes and despairs in the process.

There are, however, undeniable limits to the Brazilian's great tolerance for frustration. Careful observation of his reactions in a variety of situations suggests that a great deal of the frustration is discharged in such behavior as aggressive driving and the mass emotional orgies of Carnival and the football [soccer] games. It is not at all strange that the latter two are so important to so many Brazilians, and it is probably well that they continue to provide the occasions for such outlets.

Involvement in the Self, the Community, and the Country

There is a casualness about work, responsibility, and ambition and a joy in personal contact and good fellowship, but there is also an obvious determination to take care of one's self because no one else will. The constant threat to financial security created by inflation, combined with the lack of social agencies, may be largely responsible. This does not imply that Brazilians are devoid of cooperativeness and social consciousness, but in adjusting to difficult and unstable conditions they have become necessarily accustomed to depending upon few people and have become hardened to misfortune and poverty. Interestingly enough, they often use social agencies for the poor and needy in the United States as examples of the impersonal American way of life. Brazilians prefer to give personally. This attitude is probably somewhat related to the lack of effective programs of aid for the mentally and physically ill, orphans, and illiterates. The Northeasterners that flood into São Paulo day after day have created tremendous problems for the city, the police, and the few social agencies that do exist, but so far as it is possible to tell, relatively little has been done to help these people now or to plan for future solutions. Again, a circumvention of problems is suggested along with a lack of involvement in the difficulties of others. Implied is the hope that God and his favorite children, the Brazilians, will find a way, without need for excessive effort and sacrifice.

The Brazilian is principally concerned with his own and his family's happiness and well-being. The Brazilian realizes that he cannot solve all of the problems, so he doesn't expend any appreciable amount of energy trying to do so. He accepts the reality of the situation as he sees it and goes about taking care of himself as best he can, while he overlooks, deemphasizes, or forgets the problems of others. The Brazilian often appears overwhelmed at the magnitude of the problem. He decides, without trying and without guilt feelings, that it can't be solved.

Everything said thus far might indicate that Brazilians are not self-critical people. This is not the case. Brazilians are most critical of themselves, their products, their government, and just about anything Brazilian. This is a very self-defeating attitude, and even in proclaiming national pride Brazilians' boasts are not always convincing. Foreign goods and foreign lands are obviously preferred, as indicated by the buying habits of Brazilians and their eagerness to visit foreign countries. The preference for foreign goods often causes them to overlook national products comparable in quality and workmanship. Much of this attitude has developed because products newly on the market have understandably been poor in quality and have not always improved as rapidly as they should have. But, for better or for worse, the opinion has been formed, and being strong and definite in their likes and dislikes, Brazilians tend to stick by their opinions regardless of changes or improvements. Probably because they had access to so little power or pressure to use on government or producers, they have had to express their feelings of frustration and hostility solely through verbal criticisms, stylistic noninvolvement, and ritualistic distance.

The reluctance of Brazilians to invest financially in the future of their country might well be related to their limited range of involvement and concern and to their lack of confidence in the country and its destiny. Perhaps the lack of confidence is fostered by too much knowledge of the system and its difficulties and a fatalism toward the chances of doing anything with it.

The Interpersonal Reality

The friendliness of Brazilians is somewhat comparable to that of Southerners in the United States. It is at first extremely difficult to know just how deep it goes. There are also great regional variations. Certainly the friendliness encountered in Rio, where much time and effort are devoted to good fellowship, is different from the relatively brusque treatment characteristic of the busy, bustling city of São Paulo. The description of Brazilians as joyous, happy, smiling souls is more appropriate to Rio during Carnival than to Lapa during the Festa of Bom Jesus or to Porto Alegre. There is warm friendliness in the interior, to be sure, but superimposed upon it is a shyness not immediately penetrable. Foreigners who have lived for some time in the interior almost invariably find friendliness and courtesy, even in the poorest homes, once the initial shyness has been overcome. Certainly better treatment and consideration can be expected in the outlying areas where foreigners are a novelty than in the large cities where they are not. Any indications of prestige will usually bring invitations that are difficult, if not impossible, to refuse from the local officials and other persons of importance.

With some regional variations, interpersonal contact is generally easy and warm. Beyond the initial contact, however, some difficulty is encountered in developing a close relationship with individuals—more so with whole families. The family is a very tightly knit unit, especially in the interior, and the center of activities, including entertainment. Having a close friendship with a member of a family is one thing; being invited into family activities and accepted therein is quite another thing. But while gaining entrance into the family group is certainly not easy, once the breach has been made and the circle has been entered, the warmth and acceptance found there are truly gratifying.

More than a fear of thieves probably prompts Brazilians to build high walls around their homes. The walls are indications of a strong desire to protect privacy and to maintain the separateness of family units. Much of Brazilian life takes place within those walls, and for the most part only the family knows about it. There is very much of the "I-you, we-they" attitude. In a very real sense, the extension of the self is narrowly confined, extending primarily to the immediate family and a core of close friends but dropping off sharply beyond this restricted range. There is a sharp decrement in the investment of energy, emotion, and concern beyond the self, the family, and the close circle of friends.

A discussion of human relations leads appropriately to a consideration of promises and their function in the interpersonal situation. In Brazil the promise is a quick, natural, and easy gesture. It is often made in the fervor or stress of the moment, in an eagerness to say the right thing at the right time; but these promises so easily made are just as easily forgotten. To say that the gesture is insincere or meaningless would do an injustice to the personal involvement that Brazilians experience in interpersonal contact. It is the gesture that is important, the warmth and friendliness generated in the interpersonal encounter, the joy and satisfaction derived by both of the parties playing the "let's-be-friends" game. The details of what is said, and their projection into the future, place the emphasis where it should not be and detract from an appreciation of the experience of the contact. Undoubtedly a sense of embarrassment in not being able to help and an unwillingness to admit this are also involved. The promise thus serves to protect the self as well as the other person because it preserves the cordiality of the situation.

The naive foreigner who accepts the promise with the expectation of future action is usually disappointed. He may also lose considerable time and often his faith in the sincerity of Brazilians. However, just at the point when he concludes that they cannot be expected to keep a promise, they may do so and retain a consistent course of unpredictability. There are undoubtedly certain principles which govern this behavior, but to the uninitiated they seem very vague and ambiguous and present difficult problems in adapting to the culture and in coping with reality in the Brazilian context.

Attitudes toward Work

Attitudes toward work have often been considered as providing some important clues about people and their way of life. For Brazilians, careful and systematic planning and attention to dull details and organization seem to detract from the full appreciation of the moment and from the spontaneity of life itself. It places the emphasis on the wrong thing at the wrong time.

The importance of work in Brazilian life thus presents a contrast to the American tradition. Americans impress Brazilians as being overly compulsive about work—getting the job done—and as emphasizing efficiency too often as an end in itself. The American in turn often perceives the Brazilians as lacking in these "essential" qualities and predictably attributes many of their problems and misfortunes to this and nothing more.

There are considerable individual and regional variations in attitudes toward work in Brazil. Persons may be found who hold down several jobs and work hard at each, while others specialize in doing nothing. The latter behavior does not seem to be regarded as undesirable and is even appreciated as an indication of "talent" and perhaps a form of industriousness in itself. Such "deals" are not easily arranged, and their successful execution is certainly prized as accomplishment, which in fact it is. The degree of industriousness found in São Paulo, where there are more opportunities for work and a greater probability that hard work might lead to a better life, is an exception. The cities of Curitiba, Caxias do Sul, and Porto Alegre to the south also seem to have an unusual atmosphere of industriousness, possibly because of German and other European influences, the climate, or a combination of these and other factors. In Rio, on the other hand, the attitude toward work is certainly not one of enthusiasm.

To the north, in the coastal cities of Vitória and Salvador, the pace is noticeably slow. Activity may not decrease from Salvador to the interior, but it certainly does not increase. In the interior, however, this is greatly complicated by a number of factors, including the scarcity of job opportunities and potential rewards, even for a considerable expenditure of effort. Possibilities for advancement and gain, for luxuries and comfort, for education and prestige, are so minimal as to create a situation in which work has practically a negative reward value.

A great deal is summarized in the opinions and attitudes of a number of young Brazilians about work. Their comments generally indicate that the most desirable state of affairs is to have a well-paying job or jobs with minimal obligations in actual work or effort. They seem to feel little or no guilt about such an arrangement, because it is not their problem that they are allowed to do little or nothing. Responsibility for the work that is done is seen as the concern of the employer, not the employee. The fewer demands a job makes in time and energy, the freer one is to enjoy life and the pursuit of happiness. The situation is similar in the interior, but the opportunities to operate in this manner are considerably fewer. Throughout Brazil, the hard-working, conscientious, ambitious person apparently receives little support and encouragement from the economic and social systems and from family and friends. Such characteristics are more likely to be viewed with puzzlement and concern. Only strong-headed, strong-willed individuals could be expected to prevail against such rousing disinterest.

34 *Charles Wagley* ◆ A Most Personal People

Charles Wagley, who died in 1991, was an American anthropologist and professor at Columbia University and the University of Florida. He was president of the American Anthropological Association and an esteemed Latin Americanist. Wagley's close involvement with Brazil dated from the 1940s, and he worked actively as an author, a teacher, and a mentor to two generations of Brazilianist scholars. Moreover, he was instrumental in the formation of the University of Florida's strong program on the Amazon. In addition to the two books from which these excerpts are taken, he wrote Amazon Town: A Study of Man in the Tropics *(1953); with Marvin Harris,* Minorities in the New World: Six Case Studies *(1958);* Welcome of Tears: The Tapirapé Indians of Central Brazil *(1977); and many other books and articles on Brazilian and Latin American society.*

The first excerpt examines the importance of kinship. In the second, Wagley discusses the strengths and weaknesses of society, including attitudes on race and politics, and the people's sense of humor, all from the vantage point of an imagined Brazilian.

~ *Strong Bonds of Kinship* ~

The persistence of the widely extended *parentela* [kinship group] in Brazil must be considered as the reflection of deep-seated Luso-Brazilian values. The patriarchal family system of the plantation era may have disappeared, yet the strong bonds of kinship have been re-formed in terms of contemporary conditions of life. The traditional emphasis on the family and the *parentela* provides a model for human relations that is an aspiration for even those segments of the society that cannot live in this way. The predominance of kinship in ordering social life explains the relative absence in Brazil of such voluntary associations as parent-teacher groups, garden clubs, civic clubs, and the like. People give greater value to kinship relations than to relations based on common interest or even occupation. . . .

The persistence of kinship in Brazilian society, or in any Latin American society, should be viewed not as a social or cultural lag but rather as the continuation of a fundamental cultural value. There is a growing body of evidence that kinship relations and awareness of kinship need not disappear with industrialization and urbanization. . . . There is every reason to believe that, especially in those cultures where the tradition of familism has been strong, such as Brazil and other countries of Latin America, kinship will continue to play an important role in ordering social relations. A true comparative sociology cannot be based on the United States and northern Europe alone; it must consider the different cultural traditions of the "new" countries.

From *The Latin American Tradition: Essays on the Unity and Diversity of Latin American Culture* (New York: Columbia University Press, 1968), 192–93. Reprinted by permission of Conrad P. Kottack.

~ *If I Were a Brazilian* ~

In seeking the unity of a society and national culture so complex as that of modern Brazil, I realize that certain things cannot be stated scientifically, with full substantiation. Much of the unity of Brazil comes from just being a Brazilian—from feeling and acting like a Brazilian. These implicit, almost intuitive, aspects of a culture are difficult to make explicit and to define, even for the native observer, although they are expressed every day in books, newspapers, and movies, and in the common understandings which the members of a culture share. Sometimes the foreign visitor who has come to know a people sees them with a freshness and objectivity which helps them understand themselves. . . .

I have often daydreamed about what I might do or be if I were a Brazilian. Sometimes I have thought that I would be a revolutionary attempting to break rapidly and drastically through the lethargy of an archaic class system. Yet, if I were a Brazilian, I would, of course, almost certainly want to be of the upper class. I would not want to be one of the unfortunate 49 percent who cannot read or write, and I would want to be one of the small minority who somehow achieve a university education. I would want to travel abroad to Europe, to the United States, and perhaps even beyond the Iron Curtain to compare my own country and society with that of others. If my Brazilian friends will forgive me, I shall indulge this fancy for a while and write subjectively, as if I were a Brazilian, seeking to describe the pros and cons, the strengths and weaknesses, the unity and disunity of Brazilian society.

~ We Brazilians have suffered for a long time from what many of us call a national inferiority complex. Our fathers and grandfathers looked toward France as a country of superior culture and traveled there if they could afford it. They learned French early and read French books throughout their lives. They valued all things French—art, wine, and women. Until the last generation, we of the upper class depended almost entirely on foreign things and ideas. Butter was often imported from Europe in cans and our clothes were made of imported linens and woolens. Of course, we attended the Brazilian theater, sang Brazilian Carnival songs, and danced the samba; but these were not valued so highly as visiting French players, a French crooner, or the fox trot. Brazilian wines were commonly said to damage the liver. There was a disdain for anything made or produced in Brazil.

We must admit that some of this national feeling of inferiority derived from the fact that we are a racially mixed people. . . . Anxiety about miscegenation was shared by many Brazilians; many of us suspected, or feared, that the theories of the racists of the early twentieth century might be correct and that we were doomed to be an inferior people. . . . There was a feeling that the Negroes of Brazil somehow detracted from the image of ourselves as a white, European people living in the New World.

Then, almost imperceptibly, the world of my generation in Brazil began to change. This change in perspective on the world and on Brazil had been in the making many years before World War II, but it was only after the war that it reached most Brazilians. . . .

Alongside those who felt that they must apologize for Brazil, we have always had many strong nationalists, almost blindly proud of our country. . . . Quietly, Brazilians had harbored a national pride for centuries, but after World War II it appeared with new strength. Many of us became more articulately nationalistic, proud of our country and countrymen and jealous of those who would interfere with our national destiny.

This new nationalism took many forms. Sports became a matter of national interest. . . . *Futebol* [soccer] came to be a symbol of the nation and of national unity. . . . National pride takes other forms. . . . Each year there are local, then state, and finally national contests to select Miss Brazil. The newspapers, magazines, and newsreels give these contests full coverage, and Miss Brazil becomes a figure of national pride and renown. . . .

In less than three years we built Brasília, a new city in a wilderness. We often discuss far into the night whether this effort and expense should have been undertaken, but most of us agree that Brasília stands as a symbol of national achievement, and we are proud of its international fame as a planned city. . . . Our interest has turned inward, toward the grandeur of our own country. . . .

Thus we have in this generation overcome to a large extent the national inferiority complex from which we suffered so long. We believe in the strength and future of our own country. . . .

We Brazilians are very political. When we are not talking about soccer, we are discussing politics, endlessly speculating on the tortuous twists and turns of political figures and parties. . . . When someone asks, "O que há de novo?" ("What's new?"), as often as not he is asking for the latest political gossip. This is not just our favorite indoor sport, it is serious business. We are patriotic and want the best possible government for our country; but (as we often say to each other) look what we get, a bunch of dishonest demagogues whose astronomic expenditures in their campaigns make it a sure bet that they will recoup their finances when they win. We are highly critical of our politicians . . . and rather cynical about their motivations. This is one reason for our close attention to politics, but not the only one.

Politics is very close to home for most upper- and middle-class Brazilians. Of course, I have a government job in addition to my private activities, and so do most of the people I know. If I did not have a position with the municipality, the state, or the federal government, then almost certainly my brother, sister, uncle, first cousin, or *compadre* would have. One of my first cousins has a high appointive office in the present government. I have never called upon him for a favor, but it gives me a feeling of security to know that I could, if and when I should need to. Each of us has a *panelinha* (little pot)—a group of friends, associates, relatives, and supporters who are related to the political sources of power. When a minister resigns, a new governor takes office, or the leadership of a political party changes, we are directly affected. My first cousin who works for the Ministry of Labor does not get a needed promotion, and my sister-in-law who is anxious to get a teaching position in a public high school loses out. . . .

You know little about us as yet. You had better take us more seriously, for we are certainly at present the most important South American nation and what we intend to do in our ambivalent and contradictory fashion is to become far more important. If you want to know us, then you must know us personally, because we are a most personal people. We try to be objective, but it is the individual who really interests us. . . .

There is another Brazilian trait that gives us a common national understanding and which you North Americans would understand if you understood our language, namely, a strange and objective sense of humor about ourselves. We are appalled at the seriousness with which most Spanish-Americans view themselves. They have a sense of "face" and dignity that works against them. We take life more lightly. We say that you can live in Brazil only with a sense of humor. . . .

We also create and relate stories about ourselves each day, and we have traditional sayings that reveal our humorous self-criticism. "God is a Brazilian" indicates both some confidence in ourselves and a worry as to what would happen to our country if He were not. We also say, in the same vein, "At night, God corrects the errors that Brazilians make during the day." We exchange sly political stories and jokes. Not too long ago, the hippopotamus in the São Paulo Zoo was elected to public office. Some citizens collected enough signatures to put him on the ballot. His opposition was rather weak, so theoretically he was elected. Since he could not speak Portuguese, he never took office, but he is a famous hippo. I could tell you story after story, for we, especially the Cariocas of Rio de Janeiro, invent one every day, but not many of them can be easily translated into your language. An old one concerns a politician of national prominence whose honesty was doubted. A bishop or archbishop had died, and our politician joined the line at the church to pay his respects to the corpse. The body lay with the jewels of office prominently displayed. As our politician knelt at the bier, the corpse moved slowly, covering the jewels with his hands. Our sly sense of humor extends into our music, our daily press, our literature, and our lives. It is an important factor of our national unity. . . .

~ I have looked in this book for the unity of the Brazilian people and for Brazil's unity as a nation. I have not fully answered my own query as to how Brazilians achieved and maintained their identity. But I did learn, at least for myself, that for all their diversity they are a people and form a nation distinct from all others.

From *An Introduction to Brazil* (New York: Columbia University Press, 1971), 267–70, 272–75, 287–88, 291, 294–97.

35 *David Maybury-Lewis* ♦ The Persistent Patronage System

David Maybury-Lewis has been professor of anthropology at Harvard University since 1960. He has made field expeditions to the Indian peoples of Central Brazil, carried out research on social change and development in Brazil, and helped launch programs in anthropology at universities in that country. He founded and is president of Cultural Survival, an organization that defends rights of indigenous societies worldwide. His books include Akwe-Shavante Society: A Study of Indians in Central Brazil *(1967);* In the Path of Polonoroeste: Endangered Peoples of Western Brazil *(1981);* The Attraction of Opposites: Thought and Society in the Dualistic Mode *(1989); and* Millennium: Tribal Wisdom and the Modern World. *(The latter is a companion volume to a ten-part television series of the same name, hosted by Maybury-Lewis and shown on public television in 1992.) This selection seeks to explain modern Brazilian phenomena such as the lack of community spirit, political factiousness, the patron-client relationship, the rootlessness of the rural Brazilian, and rural-urban migration in terms of historical patterns, be they "colonial or imperial or republican."*

The lack of "community spirit" has been noted again and again by students of the Brazilian interior and has occasionally been presented as something of a paradox; but it is paradoxical only if one starts from a

From "Growth and Change in Brazil since 1930: An Anthropological View," in *Portugal and Brazil in Transition*, ed. Raymond S. Sayers (St. Paul: University of Minnesota Press, 1968), 161–69. Footnotes omitted.

presupposition about the nature of rural communities in general. Still, paradoxical or not, it does call for some explanation.

Experienced observers of the Brazilian scene suggest that the answer lies in politics. Politics is the prototypical urban activity, the enduring passion of the small town of the interior, where factionalism is carried to such lengths that partisans patronize different shops, different bars, even . . . different airports. . . . Politics everywhere entails patronage but in the Brazilian interior it involves little else. Elections pit personalities against one another, and the defeat of an incumbent usually means that members of his party lose their jobs. But since political activity and the dispensation of patronage are universals, it is only the vehemence and the divisive effects of partisanship which are peculiar to the Brazilian interior, where they are part and parcel of an ancient tradition.

The tradition dates to the beginning of Brazilian history. The central government, whether colonial or imperial or republican, was never strong enough to impose its authority throughout its vast domains. It was therefore obliged to sanction, or at least permit, considerable local autonomy. Sometimes local leaders were appointed by the central government and acted in its name, if not always in accordance with its wishes. At others, powerful families exercised de facto control over localities where the central administration hesitated to challenge them. And when this control was threatened by other families, then each clan would arm its retainers (sometimes even its slaves) and fight it out. . . .

Traditionally, then, Brazilian politics has been factious in the extreme. Since the society was dominated by a small landed upper class, this meant that the average citizen had either to become a client of one of the local strong men or leave the region or be forced into virtual outlawry, which came to the same thing. . . .

Brute force was only one of the means by which a *coronel* [colonel] could get what he wanted. Almost as important was the patronage at his disposal. . . . The oligarchies discovered that they could protect their interests more subtly by manipulating their still considerable economic powers and by ensuring that the right people were elected to state and federal offices. Nor were they particularly hampered in this by the emergence of party politics: the electorate, especially in the more backward states where the *coronéis* were strongest, was small, since illiterates could not vote. It could be easily influenced, and, as a last resort, there were numerous possibilities of fraud at the polls to be exploited. Moreover, the parties themselves were no more than local vote-getting arrangements and thus perfect instruments for the local bosses. . . .

Indeed, I should suggest not only that Brazilian society before 1930 could best be understood as a complex patronage system, but that this still serves as the most useful model for understanding the Brazilian social process in the period 1930–1964. This emphasis on patronage might seem excessive, but it does offer the most economical interpretation of certain aspects of Brazilian society. Take, for example, the phenomenon from which this discussion started, the extraordinary factionalism to be found in small towns in the interior. This results from a combination of factors. Weak central government went with powerful local leaders. Powerful and personal local leadership in a society dominated by a landed elite led to a tradition of patron-client relations which became the very warp of Brazilian social life. The inhabitants of small towns were therefore either clients of the local patron, in which case there was less likely to be political factionalism in the community, or caught up in the rivalry between patrons. There was also a third and increasingly frequent possibility—that no patron existed in the area anymore. In such a case, the town might either generate its own "lion" (which was extremely difficult) or look to the city to supply the patronage it needed; in the latter case, prominent members of the township were likely to seek different sources of urban patronage and thus recreate division in their community.

Note that there is a perpetual search for vertical, patron-client relations. In a society where upward mobility is difficult and restricted and where the conditions of life enjoyed by the majority are wretched, these vertical ties provide the surest, sometimes even the only, form of security and advancement.

This helps to explain another aspect of Brazilian rural society which has puzzled some observers: the apparent atomization of the peasantry. It is understandable that the urban-oriented small towns should be caught up in the vortex of politics, but how about the mass of people living in the country outside the townships? For them there are two major patterns of settlement, the isolated homestead pattern and the *fazenda* or estate pattern. The "communities" of the homesteaders are often so amorphous that they are hard to perceive. This is, of course, characteristic of homestead communities. . . . But . . . the Brazilians are again and again reported to have little sense of community participation. They feel themselves to be outsiders in the town which acts as their service center. At the most they come together in work parties of the *mutirão* variety or feel a common bond with cocelebrants of the festival of a patron saint. This is because there is little tradition of cooperation among equals in the countryside—the important ties that a family must maintain are vertical ones. Even ritual godparenthood in this stratum of society is usually manipulated so that the child acquires a godparent who can act as his patron.

On the big estates this was taken to its logical conclusion. The traditional *fazenda* was a closed community, completely self-sufficient and providing for all the needs of its inhabitants, who, in turn, were a group of people united in their mutual dependence on the owner, the *fazendeiro*. The *fazendeiro* thus combined the roles of employer, patron, and often godfather as well. Not only was the dependence of the inhabitants on the paternalistic patron encouraged, but any show of independence on their part was actively opposed. Workers on many *fazendas* were forbidden to improve their houses or their private garden plots in case they should begin to feel that they had rights independent of the patronage extended to them. They were especially forbidden to cultivate cash crops. Their gardens were for subsistence only, and they were held at the discretion of the *fazendeiro*. Finally, any attempt at cooperative activity on their part was vigorously opposed. . . .

The effects of the circumscribed, microcosmic world of the *fazenda* on the lives and attitudes of the people virtually confined to it are difficult to exaggerate. It accounts in large measure for the "apathy" of the peasantry in the Northeast and their comparative slowness in taking advantage of the changing circumstances of the times. . . . Landowners have tended to leave their estates and move to the cities, leaving their properties to be administered by overseers, who cannot function as patrons. Worse still, some *fazendas* in the 1950s were bought up and maintained as supply units by factories that, for example, milled cane. In such cases the boss was not only distant, but he was a factory owner, and his interest in the *fazenda* was purely commercial. The workers usually saw this withdrawal of patronage as a major disaster, and it led predictably to an increase in their mobility. But where could they go and what could they do? Many of them had been reared in the *fazenda* system, prevented from acquiring any but the most rudimentary agricultural skills, and trained to be dependent. Large numbers of them joined the mass of migratory, unskilled workers that eddies constantly about the interior of Brazil.

This rootlessness of the rural Brazilian has so impressed observers that some of them, unable to account for it by any other means, have fallen back on a postulated "migratory instinct" to explain it. This, I suggest, is because they sought an explanation primarily in terms of ecological or economic factors. From a social anthropological point of view, these wanderings do not seem so puzzling. There are basically two kinds of migration at issue here—namely, movement from country to town and movement from one part of the country to another. The first is easier to understand. In Brazil, as just about everywhere else in the world, the lure of a better livelihood to be gained under less arduous conditions attracts people from the countryside into the cities. The reasons for the current tremendous upsurge of rural-urban migration in Brazil have to do with the still miserable conditions in the country and with the pace of industrialization and consequent expansion of the urban labor market, together with improved communications so that people are more likely to learn about the attractions of the city and better able to make their way there.

Yet the romantic stereotype of the rural migrant commonly held both in Brazil and elsewhere is only partly accurate. According to this notion, the rural migrant is typically a poverty-stricken peasant who decides one day that he cannot stand it anymore, sells his few possessions for the fare to a big city, and, taking his family with him if he can, sets off to face a new life, even if it is the slums that await him at his destination. Often this decision is prompted by a severe drought in the Northeast which goads his restlessness with [the] spur of famine. Yet, though the famous "parrot perch" (*pau de arara*) trucks do roll into São Paulo with their dusty and bewildered cargo of northeastern peasants, studies have shown that the majority of immigrants to the big cities do not come so dramatically, direct from the farm. Instead, rural-urban migration proceeds in the more familiar fashion of a steady seepage from the countryside to the small towns, from the small towns to the bigger ones, and thence to the cities. . . .

A large proportion of the migrants to the cities are the semiskilled people from the interior, anxious to get ahead, rather than the unskilled agricultural laborers who are understandably nervous about taking such a drastic step. When unskilled people move, they are likely to try their luck elsewhere in the interior. But why do they move? The droughts of the Northeast are too facile an explanation. For one thing, this wanderlust also affects the peasants in other regions of the country, and for another, it is a constant factor in the Northeast, augmented but not instigated by the droughts.

No, these people move on again and again in a constant effort to better their lot, to escape from the constraints of a miserable existence. They are not tied to the land. Even if they started out as homesteaders rather than as workers for someone else, they are unlikely to have owned the land they cultivated. Titles to land are unclear throughout Brazil, and it is a difficult matter to establish legal ownership in most states—so difficult that in many parts of the interior there are men who make a practice of first waiting until some unsuspecting squatter has worked and improved a piece of land for a year or two and then going into town to obtain a legal title to it. In any case, the traditional outlook of rural Brazilians is far removed from that usually associated with peasantry. To value land for its own sake, to develop it, and to hope to prosper on it has always been an upper-class pattern, or, one might say, privilege.

Yet even the rural upper class has regarded the land as something to be exploited rather than tended. Land produced cash crops much as it might produce valuable minerals, and all too often the outlook of its owner was essentially extractive. So the economy was characterized by a transient boom in this followed by an equally ephemeral boom in that. Sugar, gold, diamonds, rubber, cacao, and coffee have all had their ups and downs, attracting migrants during the boom periods and carrying on beyond rationality in the ensuing slumps.

If the owners of the land thought in these terms, it is not surprising that the landless laborers have perennially sought their fortunes in whatever seemed to offer the chance of a short-term profit. . . . The rural migrants have learned that they will not prosper by staying where they are. Their only chance is to move on in the hope that, by some lucky fluke, they might escape from poverty. At the very least, even if they do not profit from some boom harvest or make a lucky strike at a mining camp, they may find a good and generous patron. Yet it has been noted that even when rural migrants do happen on comparatively good conditions of work, this does not necessarily make them any less footloose. They seem to suffer from what might be termed an acute lack of confidence in their own society—good things, they feel, do not last, and therefore the only security lies in a bonanza or a patron. This is why the founding of Brasília had such a profound psychological effect throughout the interior: not only did the city offer employment to an army of unskilled laborers, largely from the Northeast, but it served as a tangible guarantee that the super-patron, the federal government, did not propose to abandon the rural areas.

However, an analysis which emphasizes the functions of patronage does not have explanatory value only for rural Brazil. It would be possible to argue that the influence of the masses in the political process of the more industrial states had been exaggerated. It could be argued that only candidates for offices such as the presidency of the republic or the governorship of such states were elected for their programs and that the majority of deputies in both state and federal chambers, even from the advanced states, still owed their seats to old-style patronage politics. . . . This point of view does elucidate some of the malfunctions of bureaucracy.

The bureaucracy, be it state or federal, is well known among the Brazilians for its inefficiency, inertia, and swollen size. Newspapers regularly excoriate its shortcomings, and even government ministers complain about it. Yet politicians have been unable to do much about it. Even Jânio Quadros, who was twice elected to high office, once as governor of São Paulo and once as president of the republic, on a "new broom" platform aimed at corruption of all sorts and at bureaucratic malpractice in particular, found that he could not clean out the Augean stables. . . .

This bureaucracy soon developed in ways over which the executive branch of government had little control. Positions in the tiny pre-1930 bureaucracy had been distributed as patronage, and it was inevitable that the practice should continue after [Getúlio] Vargas came to power. Brazil was still a cartorial state dominated by patronage politics. Now there were more clients than ever competing for the spoils of patronage, and it was therefore convenient that there should also be more jobs to be distributed. Governmental bureaucratic control was rapidly extended to areas of public life that had previously been free from it and that might have got along better with less of it. Bureaucrats were appointed with little or no consideration of their ability to do their job or, indeed, of their abilities in general. The unintended consequence of this was that bureaucratic agencies gradually lost sight of their ostensible functions. Their jobs became incidental. The important thing was who got appointed, and little attention was paid to what he was appointed to do. In fact, many jobs were sinecures, and their incumbents never went near their offices. This custom hardly made for efficiency. After the end of the Vargas era, when Brazil faced a concatenation of social, economic, and political problems requiring decisive governmental action for their solution, not the least of the country's difficulties lay in the immobility of the administrative apparatus. The bureaucracy had become a modified, urban form of *coronelismo*; or, to be more accurate, the patronage relations which formed the basis of Brazilian society in the heyday of *coronelismo* came to dominate the bureaucracy.

36 *Thomas G. Sanders* ◆ The Social Functions of *Futebol*

Thomas G. Sanders received his doctorate in religion from Columbia University in 1958. A former professor of religious studies at Brown University, Sanders was also a foreign area specialist stationed in Brazil for Universities Field Staff International (UFSI), a nonprofit consortium of American universities. For over twenty years, Sanders, as UFSI's associate in Latin America, wrote a series of interpretive reports on Brazilian political, economic, and social conditions. This selection is taken from a report on soccer. In 1994, Brazil became the only nation to win four World Cup championships.

From "The Social Functions of Futebol," *Fieldstaff Report* TGS-7–'70 East Coast South America Series (Hanover, NH: American Universities Field Staff) 14, no. 2 (July 1970): 1–2, 6–9. Reprinted by permission of Thomas G. Sanders.

An observer who deals with Brazilian economics and politics may feel himself in contact with issues relevant to history, but he who neglects *futebol* [soccer] overlooks what is important for the Brazilian people. The average Brazilian, who does not understand the complexities of his country's economic and social problems and ignores his political leaders, is far more interested in his *futebol* team. He knows intimately the playing styles and personal lives of stars like Pelé. . . .

In Brazil, *futebol* is more than a sport and lucrative occupation for the players and numerous hangers-on. It is even more than a psychological experience by which individuals detach themselves from their unexciting lives to participate collectively in the thrill of victory, to share the prestige of the nation, or to identify mystically with the players. *Futebol* serves clear social functions in a large and potentially powerful country that suffers from national disorientation, confusion about its image, and the pangs of overcoming underdevelopment. . . .

Futebol in Brazil helps bolster myths that contribute to national unity and self-definition. All societies create interpretations of what they are, what distinguishes them from other peoples, why they are significant. In this process they often resort to exaltation of traditions and characteristics that are partly mythological or to symbols with which the citizenry only imperfectly identifies. *Futebol* helps gloss over such myths as the following: (1) Brazil is a nation unified by an effective set of political symbols. (2) It is a mixed society which provides equal opportunity for all races, including blacks. (3) Through economic development the standard of living of Brazilians is becoming better. . . .

The current *futebol* success has promoted a pride in being Brazilian and a unifying symbol without precedent. Even the lower classes of the cities, thanks to television, felt a sense of participating in something representing national life. They know that Brazil is now internationally significant, not necessarily for reasons of interest to the scholar or public figure, but of importance to the common man. . . . The Englishman in his pub, the French worker, the German with a Volkswagen all know that Brazil is not just another large "tropical country," but the homeland of the world's best *futebol* and a legend named Pelé. . . .

The second myth which *futebol* helps validate is that of equal opportunity for all races. Brazilians often point to themselves as having created the most nearly perfect racial democracy in the world, a country which has mixed white, black, Indian, and Oriental without rancor and discrimination.

Perceptive analysts . . . have pointed out the flaws in this image. Brazil does have an easy-going acceptance of different races, visible friendships, respect for the educated black, and extensive interracial courtship and marriage. But as former slaves in a country with restricted social mobility and at least half the population functional illiterates, blacks occupy a disproportionate role in such low-prestige occupations as sugarcane workers, common laborers, maids, and as dwellers in urban slums. . . . Far less than the United States has Brazil provided the descendants of slaves with opportunities to overcome their economic and educational handicap. Power is overwhelmingly in the hands of the whites. . . . The Brazilian national consciousness is permeated by the assumption that Caucasian characteristics are attractive and negroid characteristics unattractive. . . .

Futebol, however, provides the clearest proof of the myth. Even though it is very difficult for the poor and relatively uneducated black to improve his status by working within the system, through *futebol* he can acquire both wealth and fame. Every humble child in Brazil with a flair for *futebol* hopes that he can make the leap from misery to affluence by becoming a star. In June of 1970, prosperous and powerful Brazilians were screaming hysterically for blacks from poor backgrounds, like Pelé, Paulo César, and Evaraldo, and light-colored mulattoes, like Carlos Alberto and Jairzinho. In fact, they would have been flattered to shake their hands. Brazil's racially mixed team which was observed by millions of spectators, the ascendance of black stars in *futebol*, and the popular idolatry surrounding them nourish the myth and obscure for the average Brazilian the tough reality of racial discrimination. And this is more comforting and easier than providing educational facilities and decent jobs, or expunging from the national consciousness the bias for Caucasian characteristics.

A final social function that *futebol* seems to serve is enabling the poor to forget partially the harshness of their life amid the optimistic aura of development. In the past two years, Brazil has begun to repeat the phenomenal economic growth records of the 1950s. . . . On the public level and among businessmen one finds a new attitude of confidence that Brazil's population and economic growth will project it by the year 2000 into a position among the "giants," but this picture of development appears different to the masses.

Development has actually led to a reduction of the standard of living in the poorer sectors of the population. The austerity measures undertaken by the government to check inflation since 1964 have fallen heavily upon them. . . . In effect, real wages declined, and this in a country which . . . has the most inequitable distribution of income in Latin America. . . . This inequity is not new, and observers have often noted the capacity of the Brazilian lower classes to maintain a charm and tolerance amid their poverty. *Carnaval*, a four-day-long outburst of dancing, music, costumes, and parades, and passion over *futebol* are usually cited as "safety valves" for releasing popular tensions. . . .

Sitting in his bleacher seat or listening to his transistor radio, the worker lives in another world and can forget that in the midst of development his life is hard and his salary, if he has a regular one, scarcely provides for his family. Underneath he knows that he is watching the world's best *futebol* and that the players are himself. . . .

Not all Brazilians have this consolation, however. It is often said that Brazil has ninety-five million fans (the entire population of the country [in 1970]). The nation's number one fan discovered that this was still another myth. Visiting the interior of the Northeast, devastated by one of its periodic droughts, President [Emílio Garrastazu] Médici asked a group of peasants who Pelé was. Only one of the men knew, and when asked what position he played, [incorrectly] replied: "Goalie."

37 *Anani Dzidzienyo* ◆ An Obsession with Whiteness and Blackness

Anani Dzidzienyo was born in Ghana in 1941, studied in the United States, Great Britain, and Brazil, and has traveled in Brazil regularly. He was a research fellow at the Institute of Race Relations in London in the 1970s and has been a professor at Brown University since the 1980s, attached to its Center for Luso-Brazilian Studies, teaching courses on Afro-Brazilians and on Brazilian politics. In this selection, first published in 1971, Dzidzienyo brings an African viewpoint to bear on the reality of race relations in contemporary Brazil.

In Brazil, there is no racism: The Negro knows his place.
(A popular saying)

Brazil has been described as the one country in the world where people of different races live together in harmony and where opportunities are open to all, irrespective of racial background. That description is definitely misleading, if not completely inaccurate.

Another widely held opinion is that the races have intermingled successfully for so long that one cannot say for certain who is black and who

From "The Position of Blacks in Brazilian Society," in *The Fourth World: Victims of Group Oppression*, ed. Ben Whitaker (New York: Schocken Books, 1973), 5–8, 14–15. Reprinted by permission of Anani Dzidzienyo. Adapted by G. Harvey Summ. Footnotes omitted.

is white in Brazil. In fact, a sizeable proportion of Brazilians—approximately 10 percent of 96 million people [1971 figure]—are recognizably black or distinctly dark. Their presence does not belie the extent of racial intermingling. However, it does bring out the bias which is a hallmark of much-vaunted Brazilian "racial democracy"—that white is best and black is worst, and, therefore, that the nearer one is to white, the better.

This view has an all-pervasive hold on Brazilian society, affecting stereotypes, role playing, job opportunities, and life-styles. Even more important, it serves as the cornerstone of the closely observed "etiquette" of race relations in Brazil. This etiquette dictates strongly against any discussion of the racial situation, especially if controversial, and helps perpetuate the pattern of relationships since slavery. Traditionally, blacks are expected to be grateful to whites for kindnesses shown them, and to continue to depend on whites acting as their patrons and benefactors. Blacks are also expected to continue to accept the whites as the nation's official mouthpiece, explaining to outsiders the "unique" nature of Brazilian race relations. Official platitudes used to describe the Brazilian situation, like racial democracy, are to be accepted without question. Critical analysis or open discussion of this delicate subject is strongly discouraged.

The black man's position in Brazil can only be described as being virtually outside the mainstream of society. He is almost completely unrepresented in any area involving decision making. With relatively few exceptions he is not to be seen in government, administration, business, or commerce, except at the lowest levels where manual labor is required. The only areas where he plays a significant rather than menial role are in football [soccer] and entertainment. This implies more parallels between the Brazilian racial situation and that of other multiracial countries than is generally acknowledged.

Since social control mechanisms have traditionally been used very effectively to ensure that one group remains dominant over another, Brazilians have not had to enact rigid rules to ensure continuance of the dominant-dominated relationship. Were legal precepts alone proof that racial justice and harmony exist, it would be a completely different story. The distinction between theory and practice is very important in assessing the black Brazilian's position, since no legal provisions force him to remain disadvantaged. There is, in fact, no need for them, because Brazilian economic, social, and political structures, by their very nature, operate against the interests of blacks. This politico-socio-economic structure can effectively handle the rare black person who manages to succeed despite all the odds against him, because his example does not threaten to upset the fixed nature of existing unequal relationships. If anything, because he has managed to "make it," he will be used by the society as a "pin-up" to support the contention that Brazil is indeed a racial democracy.

The term "people of color" is itself probably the greatest single factor contributing to the myth of racial democracy, for it is used to describe all nonwhite people or "mixed-bloods"—a group ranging from those completely black to those almost white. In practice, Brazilians make extremely fine distinctions between subtle variations in skin tone. Lighter-skinned Brazilians do not consider it a compliment to be classified with dark or black people. To group all of them together under a blanket term is to distort the real situation. Because of this Brazilian obsession with whiteness and blackness and shades in between, there are further race and color breakdowns. Brazilians have more than twenty different expressions to distinguish color variations between the extremes of black and white. The claim that Brazil has always offered the person of color or of mixed blood equal opportunity is deceptive. It lumps together all people not generally considered in the same racial/color category, and not accorded the same treatment.

Denying the existence of significant racial similarities between Brazil and the United States also contributes to creating a false impression about Brazil. Emphasizing certain points about the Brazilian racial scene invariably brings out its better aspects, while the worst aspects of the American racial situation are stressed. Brazilians argue that in Brazil there is "prejudice against appearance," while in the United States one finds "prejudice against origins." Testing this claim by applying it to Brazilians who look black, we find that appearance and origin cannot meaningfully be separated. The distinction is therefore false.

A further element in this distinction admits the existence of "prejudice" but not the action to which it leads, that is, "discrimination." In the Brazilian case, although a certain amount of prejudice is admittedly felt against dark persons, such prejudice, it is claimed, does not involve actual discrimination. Since prejudice is a state of mind, people can be prejudiced without translating their prejudices into discriminatory action. Where overt discrimination is considered inadvisable, the explanation is that prejudice, not discrimination, exists.

This prejudice, it is further argued, is not really directed against darker people as such (that is, not on the basis of their color), but rather against their low position in society (that is, their socio-economic standing). The blacks, having originally been brought to Brazil as slaves, were of course at the very bottom of the socio-economic and—by implication, political—pyramid. With the abolition of slavery in 1888 they were immediately thrown into a competitive socio-economic situation for which they were quite unprepared. They were handicapped even before they could begin.

Thanks to the system of promoting individuals as they begin to move up economically, blacks and dark people who began to acquire technical and professional skills could gradually move away from the base and edge upwards on the socio-economic pyramid. If the majority of blacks and dark-skinned people remained at the very base, as has happened, this would not necessarily be regarded as having a connection with their appearance and racial origins; instead, the assumption would be that they were suffering because they were poor. The expression generally used in Brazil to characterize this phenomenon is "money whitens," meaning that once an individual of dark color acquires money he can literally buy himself out of the black category and into the white; because, the argument goes, along with money come all the social benefits which are commonly associated with whiteness and success in Brazil.

Once again the reality is more complex. For blacks, professional qualifications and economic status are not always synonymous with social success as is normally the case with near-white and light-skinned people. The truth is, of course, that an individual's blackness does not suddenly become invisible simply because he has acquired some wealth.

Not many blacks are likely to accumulate wealth, and therefore some of the exceptional few who do may be accepted within the white fold. Because of their small numbers and because they have achieved a certain measure of success within the existing system, such people are not likely to upset the overall pattern of relationships between whites and blacks. Indeed, if anything, these people are more likely to conform to than to challenge the patterns of the group to which they have been admitted: first, because their success and inclusion in white society is proof of their personal abilities; and second, because they are unlikely to criticize the system which has just accorded them so signal an honor. Thus, they become captives of the situation and are often called upon to testify to the efficacy of the racial democracy which has enabled them to reach their relatively high positions.

The black Brazilian's position in white-dominated Brazil differs from that of blacks in similar societies elsewhere only to the extent that the official Brazilian ideology of nondiscrimination, by not reflecting the reality and indeed by camouflaging it, achieves without tension the same results as do overtly racist societies. Black and dark Brazilians have been encouraged to believe that they are the most fortunate blacks in the New World—especially in comparison with the "poor black North American." An essential element in this attitude is the black's long-term subjection to racial stereotypes promulgated by whites. Having been imposed upon the black man for so long, these negative images of himself have come to be accepted by him as true.

Those blacks and dark people who have been successful are regularly cited as evidencing the equality of opportunity which is said to exist in Brazil. Thus, because of his acceptance of the orthodox line, Pelé, the "King of Football," is an invaluable ally of the Brazilian authorities, and he is constantly used to demonstrate the validity of their racial democracy propaganda. He himself claims that there is no racism in Brazil and that he personally has never experienced any acts against himself which could be construed as racist. Pelé happens to be the best known of these "honorable exceptions" but he is by no means the only one. Others in the world of football and entertainment, having themselves succeeded, avoid making controversial pronouncements about race. It is not that these people lack racial consciousness; it is rather that they prefer not to place themselves on the firing line. Pelé can talk about racism in the United States and declare his agreement with the politics of Muhammad Ali, yet at the same time he cannot see that similar tactics might be equally applicable in Brazil.

It has been said of Pelé that "no black person in the whole world has done more to break racial barriers. He who claps hands for Pelé claps hands for black people." It is difficult to see how this statement could be justified: applause for a black football player disproves in no way the existence of racist or discriminatory practices in society. A black sportsman or musician may be required to play for audiences from which blacks have been deliberately excluded; the players themselves are present to provide entertainment for the white audience who, in return, may deign to admit the black players to their clubhouse and might even fete them as "symbols." None of this will affect the basic relationship between the white and black races.

38 *Wayne A. Selcher* ◆ Brazil in the World

Wayne A. Selcher is professor of political science at Elizabethtown College in Pennsylvania. He is the author of books and articles on Brazilian domestic as well as foreign politics, and his topics include political liber-

From "Brazil in the World: Multipolarity as Seen by a Peripheral ADC Middle Power," in *Latin American Foreign Policies: Global and Regional Dimensions*, ed. Elizabeth G. Ferris and Jennie K. Lincoln (Boulder, CO: Westview Press, *alization, Brazil's multilateral relationships, and the country's Afro-Asian policies. He has lived in and traveled to Brazil often. This selection examines how, in adjusting their diplomatic style to foreign policy objectives and domestic realities, the Ministry of Foreign Affairs and its career diplomats follow patterns similar to those manifested in other aspects of Brazilian life.*

More than is the case with any other Latin American country, Brazil's foreign relations must be analyzed in the global context. . . . Brazil is involved in a wider range of issues and with a greater number of partners beyond the Western Hemisphere than any other Latin American country . . . Brazil has one of the more developed foreign policies in the region, in that its interests are flexibly framed on operational case by case terms rather than based on philosophic abstractions, and they are then backed up with sophisticated diplomatic and organizational skill. Furthermore, there has been more policy continuity between administrations than is typical for a Latin American country. . . .

Brazil's international position shapes its foreign policy interests and sets out some strategic and tactical imperatives, which by constituting parameters for action result in regular patterns of behavior. In explaining these observable patterns in Brazilian foreign policy, the concepts of "national role" and "diplomatic style" are particularly insightful. . . . Role conceptions derive from a wide variety of national and systemic sources and provide broad policy guidelines for specific types of foreign policy behavior, often carried out within a diplomatic style characteristic of that particular state. . . .

Compared with the full range of roles expressed by states, Brazil fell toward the bottom of a passive category characterized by a narrow and restricted view of the world, with no sense of direction or commitment beyond reaction to specific issues, and with a tendency to deal either in sweeping generalizations or specific commercial problems. This unassertive role image contained little reference to national function in the international system beyond noninvolvement and minding one's own business, but with a willingness to cooperate with other states. A state characterized by this "law-abiding good citizen" posture of modesty, with no tradition of really serious engagement, would not, of course, be out to make a name for itself in influencing other states or reforming the system.

As Brazil became more seriously engaged in the international economic system during the 1970s, it took on a more active and complicated set of participationist roles. Remnants of the traditional self-perception,

---

1981), 81, 98–101. Reprinted by permission of Elizabeth G. Ferris and Jennie K. Lincoln. References omitted.

however, continue to affect its attitude toward exercising political influence, its style, and its international image. Because Brazil is not an advanced industrial society, and has some considerable capability weaknesses despite its size, and because it has pursued a development policy which lacks really integrated national depth, it is still largely inner-directed and is building infrastructure rather than being concerned with (or being really capable of) exerting influence abroad. Brazil is still consolidating its internal front, so foreign policy concerns are turned heavily to economic matters rather than to matters usually considered political. In the absence of strong security concerns in the military sense ("high politics," implying conflict), the "low politics" of commercial competitiveness, attracting foreign investments and technology, and access to raw materials and energy supplies have become the chief foreign policy concerns. To these ends, success is aided by projection of a benign image as a self-confident but unassuming, a rising but not threatening, intermediate power pursuing a responsible policy of prudence and restraint with an air of quiet competence.

Brazil would like to play the role of a serious and reliable partner in bilateral dealings with a wide range of states, and so pursues compromise-prone and noncombative multilateral policies aiming at broad political acceptability extending over lines of international tension. The Foreign Ministry is careful to avoid taking sides in others' disputes, whether among the great powers or within South America. Its policies stress coexistence and plurality rather than alliances and exclusivity. Brazil can achieve these multiple identifications by capitalizing upon its membership in diverse international groupings without regarding any single affiliation as definitive across all issues or as constraining flexibility in any given case. The image of ambiguity caused by this "responsible pragmatism" or resistance to alignments has occasionally been criticized as unprincipled opportunism by diplomats from ideological states or those heavily committed to one side of an issue, but, in general, the strategy has worked favorably for Brazil and has been respected by its numerous partners.

Brazil's geopolitical location and status as an ADC [advanced developing country] middle power have given rise to and reinforced a diplomatic style which is technically oriented, particularly active in functional questions, nonideological, reasonable and gradual in approach, limited to matters directly affecting the country, and predisposed to disclaim any leadership or influence attempts or ambitions. Brazil purposely avoids taking a political lead because most major international issues are divisive and polarizing; it does not wish to alienate any of the diverse and demanding constituencies on which it depends. . . .

Citing the country's "delicate position" in international affairs, Brazilian diplomats are well aware of their national limitations and of the common counterproductivity and unpredictability of influence attempts by major states. They are not yet ready to play in that bigger league, and in fact are quite critical of the principles of the current international political system which are determined largely by the conduct of the powers above Brazil in the hierarchy. Brazil consistently condemns hegemonies, interventionism, and the use of force (supposed prerogatives of the great powers) and disavows having hegemonic pretensions of its own or designs to gain predominance in South America. Nor has it demonstrated any interest in playing the role of surrogate gendarme, or in replicating the relations of force practiced by the current great powers. In relations with other developing countries, Brazilian officials speak of "horizontal relations of cooperation" rather than "vertical relations of domination," and of constructing a new kind of international relationship different from the paternalistic or colonial relationships which characterized interaction between the West and former colonial areas. With the progress of political liberalization in Brazil, the theme of "democratization" of the international system with equitable distribution of its benefits became a part of foreign policy statements.

Brazil's diplomats give themselves maximum political maneuvering room and fully utilize advantages of the country's position by observing the following principles of cautious statecraft:

1. Avoid isolation, conspicuous exposure in a controversial position, and precipitous action. Shun rhetoric and grandstanding.

2. Play the best option without absolute (ideological or dogmatic) commitment, overextension, or unnecessary risk-taking. Maintain national freedom of action.

3. Keep all options open by not alienating important actors; avoid being drawn out, labeled, or pinned down.

4. Be particularly cautious about attempts at leadership or initiatives which imply responsibilities, outlays, or sacrifices that may burden future flexibility or allocations of resources. Practice selective engagement.

5. Trust bilateral relationships over multilateral and national over collective self-reliance. Diversify relations on a global basis to balance dependencies and multiply alternatives with states at all levels of development.

6. Maintain the LDC [less developed country] classification as long as possible, to safeguard preferential status and to avoid

premature promotion to DC [developed country] ranks. Follow the Group of 77 consensus in rhetorical terms and defend group solidarity, but separate the national interest in application.

7. Work for incremental gains in international economics, being willing to take a conciliatory approach to established interests rather than frontally attacking them in the name of creating a new order.
8. While economic interests are concrete, worth defending, and risking attrition over, beyond abstract declarations little is likely to be gained in trying to change the course of political currents. Therefore separate economic from political matters whenever possible.
9. Vital national political and security interests are limited to South America, with global political events crucial only as they affect Brazil directly.
10. When pushed to take a political stand on a distant question (Beagle Channel dispute, Nicaragua, Korea, Egypt-Israel, the Palestine Liberation Organization), finesse and avoid commitment for as long as possible. Statements on such matters should be typically mild and justified in terms of universal values, principles of international law, or an international organization consensus. Avoid the appearance of giving in under pressure.

In putting these moderately reformist policy guidelines into practice, Brazil is not presently exercising all the political capabilities it can marshal and will not gain greater status recognition until it does exert more influence. Although this reticence to appear influential may be a continuation of a long-standing national self-image as a subject rather than a participant, a diplomacy of restraint is quite understandable for a middle power in Brazil's peripheral geopolitical position. Overt exercise of one's full capabilities may stir up resistance which would make future attempts to exert influence much less successful because of antagonisms created. . . .

The approach to influence which Brazil has adopted [is] one which has not abandoned aspiration to greater significance in the future, but one based on the belief that this enhanced influence is best cultivated gradually without provoking concomitant and troublesome startle reactions from neighbors or the topdog states (which Brazil may not yet be in a position to overcome). Such a strategy is facilitated domestically by both the low level of radicalism in national politics and the low levels of social awareness and concern about national foreign policy. Should either of these internal conditions change markedly, or should the success of gradual advancement falter, the viability of accommodationism could be seriously questioned—hence Brazil's ascension could take a more conflictful turn. Meanwhile, as in the case of Japan, the case of Brazil cautions that political influence does not flow inexorably from economic size, nor do all economically significant countries seek political importance.

39 *David T. Haberly* ◆ Three Sad Races

After receiving his doctoral degree in Romance languages from Harvard University, David T. Haberly taught there from 1966 to 1973. Since 1973 he has been a professor of Portuguese and Spanish at the University of Virginia. Haberly's research interests are in Brazilian literature, Afro-Brazilian and Afro-Hispanic literature and culture, and comparative literary history of the Americas in the nineteenth century. He has written "Captives and Indians: The Figure of the Cautiva *in Argentine Literature" (1979); and "Women and Indians: The Last of the Mohicans" (1976). In this selection from his analysis of the work of six leading Brazilian poets and novelists—four of whom were nonwhite—Haberly examines the interweaving by these authors of the dual themes of sadness and multiracial culture.*

The Brazilian poet Olavo Bilac declared, in the second decade of the twentieth century, that the music of his nation was the "loving flower of three sad races" ("*flor amorosa de três raças tristes*"). Bilac was in many ways the epitome of fin de siècle Brazil—diligently superficial in his literary creations and in his cultural judgments, fervently if fuzzily patriotic, and resoundingly bourgeois in his attitudes toward art and society. His dictum was hardly the product of a radical consciousness, and it was widely accepted by his contemporaries as both deeply poetic and profoundly true. Most Brazilians, then and now, would unhesitatingly extend it to describe the nation's literature as well as its music.

Two discrete concepts coexist in Bilac's summation of this national consensus: the multiracial nature of Brazilian culture, and the sadness inherent in the national soul. The Portuguese, in Bilac's interpretation of Brazil's musical—and cultural—history, sang songs filled with nostalgia

From *Three Sad Races: Racial Identity and National Consciousness in Brazilian Literature* (New York: Cambridge University Press, 1983), 1–8. Footnotes and references omitted.

for the homeland they had left behind. The Indians joined in to mourn the world the white man had taken from them. The Africans, brought to Brazil in chains, wept for the freedom they had lost.

But Bilac was not referring simply to the first decades of Brazilian history, for the theme of national sadness—an existential sense of suffering, of exile, and of loss—survived the assimilation of the Portuguese, the virtual disappearance of the Indian, and the abolition of African slavery; by Bilac's day, it was deeply embedded in the consciousness of the independent Republic. One decade later, in 1928, Paulo Prado suggested that this sadness was fundamental to the national character, subtitling his *Portrait of Brazil* (Retrato do Brasil), *An Essay on the Sadness of Brazil.*

The idea that Brazil—and Brazilian literature—is the end result of the interaction of these three racial groups is even more of a commonplace in the national consciousness than this conviction of sadness. It must be admitted, moreover, that the idea is firmly based, at least for literature, upon reality. . . .

The multiracial character of Brazilian literary history, however, goes far beyond genetics. . . . Much of Brazil's literature has been preoccupied with an anguished search for a viable racial identity—a search that has been both personal and national in scope. In this endeavor, Bilac's two themes of race and of suffering have been joined again and again; the most emotional example, perhaps, is Guilherme de Almeida's 1925 description of the nation [in his narrative poem *Raça*] as a "cross in whose shadow / three races crossed and mixed, three different bloods dripped from three crucified victims."

This Brazilian tradition is particularly striking when set against the generally optimistic North American belief in the inherent viability and perfectibility of social and cultural institutions. And, despite the essential similarity of the racial backgrounds of the United States and Brazil, Americans have illogically but decisively defined themselves and their nation in terms of the white majority alone. American literature, with pitifully few exceptions, has been written by whites, for whites, and about whites. Nonwhite characters have been marginal at best, serving only to highlight the white heroes or heroines, the only conceivable national symbols.

The gap between this American tradition of whiteness and optimism and Almeida's tortured vision of three victims of different colors is the result of contrasting definitions of the nature of race and of the function of literature. In the United States, racial identity has been simply and clearly defined as almost entirely a question of genetics. Although there is some evidence that this ancestry-based system of racial classification has been applied to Indians and to other minorities, its operation can best be understood in its application to black Americans. A black, in the American tradition, is a person with at least one African ancestor—however convoluted the family tree. The genetic basis of racial categories in the United States can be clearly seen in American English: the term "mulatto" has traditionally been applied to individuals with one white and one black parent; the now obsolete "quadroon" (one black grandparent) and "octoroon" (one black great-grandparent) were even more mathematically precise.

The far more complex Brazilian system operates in a very different way, but a system of racial categories, equally founded upon prejudice toward nonwhite peoples, does exist. Briefly stated, this system functions on several distinct but closely interconnected levels. Simple genetic ancestry, the single focus of the North American system, is but one level. Equally important in Brazil are physical characteristics associated with race—skin pigmentation, hair color and texture, and the contours of the nose and lips—and such cultural patterns as dress, religion, education, and speech. All three levels—ancestry, somatology, and culture—form a continuum, founded upon prejudice-based value judgments, that ranges from African or Indian to European, from ugliness to beauty, from barbarism to civilization.

The racial identity of any individual—his or her position on the continuum—is not necessarily fixed and immutable, as it so often is in the United States, but is constantly redefined by the perceptions of others, perceptions that can vary greatly from region to region and within different social settings. . . . Each Brazilian, therefore, whatever his own feelings about the reality of his racial background, daily presents himself for careful inspection and classification by those he meets. And even the elite, very sure of its own whiteness, has tended to view the national population as a whole as nonwhite and, therefore, inferior.

This conviction of national inferiority does not depend upon statistics (the very subjectivity of racial categories in Brazil makes census figures on race highly unreliable) but upon perception and, ironically, upon the elite's need to justify its own privileged position. If one group within Brazil is to define itself as genetically, somatically, and culturally superior, it must believe implicitly in the inferiority—that is, the nonwhiteness—of most of the rest of the population. And yet this justification of superior status, however comforting in personal terms, has had profoundly negative effects upon the Brazilian elite's vision of the nation and its future possibilities, a vision clouded by feelings of pessimism, of frustration, of alienation. For the elite, Almeida's Calvary expressed the reality of this vision: the Indians and Africans have been tortured by whites, but are also crucified by their own inferiority; and the whites themselves are tormented by the knowledge that they are condemned to share their land with beings viewed as hopelessly and permanently inferior.

Within the context of this interplay of individual pride and national despair, literature has had a very special function for the Brazilian elite, a function that is quite alien to the American conception of the purpose and nature of literary activity. The goal of the white literature of white America has been to reach as many of the nation's readers as possible, to create a broad-based national culture, to elevate the level of that culture, and—not entirely incidentally—to sell a great many books.

Literature in Brazil, on the other hand, has been almost exclusively the creature of the elite. The proportion of the Brazilian population classed as minimally literate has not changed greatly over the last half-century, and the proportion of Brazilians who are active consumers of literature—the cultural elite of the nation—probably remained constant, from 1822 to at least 1950, at less than 1 percent. As Brazilian society is structured, moreover, this cultural elite, set apart by education and inclination, as well as by the financial ability to purchase books, is also the political, social, and economic elite of the nation. And the very act of reading a literary work, for upper-class Brazilians, is therefore an act of social self-affirmation, since that action and the abilities it presupposes are proof of membership in the elite.

The consumption of literature is not merely a ritual of class distinction, however, but a declaration of whiteness as well: the education and intelligence required to read a work of literature, after all, are part of the prejudice-based cultural and genetic definitions of race. And nonwhites who somehow manage to become consumers of literature thereby whiten themselves, in their own eyes and in the eyes of others. . . .

A further peculiarity of the Brazilian literary tradition is its narrow circularity: those who consume literature are, to a surprising extent, its producers as well. The classic example of this identity of producers and consumers is Tobias Barreto, a nonwhite intellectual from Pernambuco, who wrote and published an erudite and highly specialized philosophical journal in German; Barreto was also almost the only Brazilian reader capable of wading through this esoteric publication. What might appear to us an absurd exercise in futility, however, was for Barreto a vital affirmation of cultural whiteness, concrete proof of his intellectual and social superiority. Although Barreto's case is clearly an exaggeration, it does symbolize the ritualistic nature of literature in Brazil. The creation of a literary text is an act even more refined, even more aristocratic, even more whitening than the consumption of literature, and most consumers of Brazilian literature have attempted seriously, generally during adolescence, to perform this highest ritual of social and racial self-affirmation.

Because, once again, the cultural and genetic components of the racial continuum define intelligence, literary ability, and education as inherently white traits, nonwhites who produce texts of merit have some real possibility of moving themselves along the continuum toward the escape hatch of perceived whiteness. In the case of the great mulatto novelist Machado de Assis, for example, some of his white contemporaries appear to have been fully persuaded, by his talent and culture, that he was literally white.

In less extreme cases, however, we do find a general tolerance of nonwhite writers of talent, at least before about 1900. Recognition of the progress of such writers along the racial continuum, after all, in no way negated the harsh and instinctive prejudice that is as much the basis of race relations in Brazil as it is in the United States; the achievements of those of mixed blood could always, in the final analysis, be explained away as the triumph of white genes over African or Indian genes. This system, in fact, was severely tested only once in nineteenth-century Brazil, in the case of João da Cruz e Sousa, a figure whose racial origins and appearance placed him irrevocably at the extreme black end of the continuum.

The creation of literature, however, is more than merely a ritualistic declaration of whiteness and elite status. As I have suggested, most educated Brazilians have traditionally endeavored to produce literary works—primarily poetry—during adolescence. Such efforts are seen as entirely natural, as well as laudable, because of the almost universal conviction that although literature may presuppose inborn talent and a vocation, it is above all the result of some sort of creative crisis, a by-product of the kind of suffering, marginality, and alienation considered typical of the passage from youth to maturity. The creative crisis, though most common during adolescence, may nonetheless occur at any stage in life. Old José Bonifácio de Andrada e Silva, the "Patriarch of Brazilian Independence" and as tough a political infighter as the nation's history has seen, published a little book of poems while exiled from the land he had helped make free. Exile almost moved Dom Pedro II—emperor of Brazil from 1841 to 1889—to turn his hand to verse (1898).

This, then, is the ultimate irony of Brazilian literature: literary creativity is public proof of genetic and social superiority; it is also, simultaneously, the result of a private crisis of misery and alienation. By logical extension, great texts presuppose uncommon suffering. The idealized, even sentimentalized, image of the tragic writer was a Romantic commonplace throughout Western culture; Brazilian literature of the nineteenth century had more than its share of brilliant young poets who suffered greatly—or who convinced themselves that they suffered greatly—and who died in their late teens or early twenties. The tradition of the creative crisis of sorrow and exile, however, can be traced back to the seventeenth century in Brazil, and has survived into our own time.

This tradition helps explain Brazilian acceptance of a handful of non-white writers as central figures in the nation's literature. If one accepts the hypothesis that literary creativity derives from suffering and alienation, and if one also accepts Brazilian ideas and expectations about race, it is only reasonable to conclude that nonwhiteness itself can be viewed as a supreme creative crisis of physical misery, psychological exile, and social marginality.

The relationship I have noted between literature and the relatively brief creative crisis of adolescence, and between literary achievement and the far more profound and enduring creative crisis of nonwhiteness itself, not only serves to define the origins and nature of the production of individual writers, but also, by extension, determines the character and the purpose of Brazilian literature as a whole. Brazilians have always tended, even in this century, to look at their nation and its culture in terms of the model of human psychological and physical development, defining Brazil itself as an adolescent—weaned from Portuguese colonialism, but still dependent upon external influences and not yet ready to stand alone as an adult member of the family of nations.

Critical to this self-definition of Brazil as an adolescent is the widespread recognition of the lack of a clear-cut, fully accepted racial and national identity, and the complementary conviction that such a single, unifying identity can and must be found. This conviction has been particularly intense in Brazil precisely because the culture that gave birth to the nation, that of Portugal, has appeared to possess just such an identity, forged by the Reconquest and by maritime expansion. A single text, the *Lusiads* of Luis de Camões—the product of the poet's long exile from Portugal—has seemed to Brazilians to provide Portugal with a supreme national text, an act of self-definition that has both expressed and reinforced that vital unity and identity.

The Portuguese identity, however comforting to white Brazilians, has generally been rejected since the early years of the nineteenth century as part of the colonial childhood of the nation; its loss is a major factor in the sadness and frustration of the Brazilian elite. The lack of the sort of coherent and cohesive self-image Brazilians attribute to Portugal has been a major factor, moreover, in the definition of Brazil and its culture as adolescent, filled with uncertainty and self-doubt. Yet the adoption of any unifying identity that is entirely white would serve only to deny the reality of the nation. Such a self-image could not be truly Brazilian. At the same time, the racial prejudice that allows white Brazilians and those who manage to be perceived as members of the elite to justify their own superior status inevitably leads to profound disquiet about the implications of any national identity that is less than totally white.

This paradox is the crux of the creative crisis of Brazil-as-adolescent, the source of the anguish and alienation that have served to form the nation's literature. Brazil's writers, by definition themselves the victims of personal misery and marginality, have ironically been charged with a central and heroic role in the formation of a new national identity; it has been their function, and their responsibility, to fuse their own creative crises with the psychological crisis of the nation in order to present possible solutions to the paradox, to point out possible pathways to maturity and self-confidence.

40 *Phyllis A. Harrison* ◆ Behaving Brazilian

A folklorist and the director of the Community Arts School of Tacoma, Washington, Phyllis A. Harrison received her Ph.D. from Indiana University. She taught folklore and nonverbal communication there and at Colorado College. She has also worked in arts administration. This selection examines influences on and aspects of Brazilian behavior, including class and status, relations between the sexes, family, friendship, and concern for smoothing things over. When in print, her book was given to American foreign service personnel assigned to Brazil.

Social Organization

The concepts of class and status are strong in Brazil, influencing many other aspects of Brazilian life. Jobs are accorded a particular status, and an upper- or middle-class person would not perform a lower-class job. . . . Upper-class children and young adults generally do not work, partly because they are expected to put their efforts into their studies, and partly because of the jobs that would be available to them. Jobs such as babysitting or waiting tables, so often filled by students in the United States, are considered lower-class jobs in Brazil, the status being determined by the wages. . . . Upper- and upper-middle-class women who go to work after or instead of college would probably not take a secretarial position, as such a position lacks status. . . .

From *Behaving Brazilian: A Comparison of Brazilian and North American Social Behavior* (Rowley, MA: Newbury House Publishers, 1983), 3–4, 6–12, 14–15, 17–19. Reprinted by permission of Phyllis A. Harrison.

Interaction between classes is not great, except within specific roles such as employee/maid, customer/sales clerk, or customer/waiter. . . . One phrase that is heard frequently in cross-class situations is "Você sabe com quem está falando?" ("Do you know who you're talking to?"), used when the speaker senses a lack of respect. A lower status person (whatever his specific status) may use *doutor* (doctor) when addressing a person of higher status. The title shows social deference and may have nothing to do with educational degrees or specific professions. . . .

Machismo

The Brazilian man demonstrates his strength through aggressive pursuit and courteous respect. He must be the aggressor in all senses (or, as some women say, must think he is the aggressor), so he must be the one to take the initiative in a business deal, in problem solving, in courtship. . . . A Brazilian woman initiates flirtations through subtle but effective means like eye contact. Men are expected to make passes at women, and a man may very well make a pass at a woman he has no interest in and whom he expects will refuse him. Men—particularly young men or men from lower socio-economic classes—may stare at, whistle at, and comment upon women they see in public. At the same time, the man's superior strength means he must show courtesy to women, particularly to women of an equal class or status. Men open doors, help with coats, carry packages, and always pay the bills. Such actions demonstrate strength and respect for women. They are viewed as social courtesies in Brazil and most Brazilian women expect them. . . . The macho man shows his strength by the way he interacts with women. At the same time, he is much freer than the North American man to express his emotions—to laugh, to cry, to hug a friend—and less concerned with maintaining a calm, controlled exterior.

The Brazilian woman displays her femininity through feminine beauty and grace, accentuated by tighter fitting and more revealing clothes than the North American is used to seeing or wearing, frequent and lavish use of cosmetics and jewelry, and a concern for a graceful appearance when sitting, standing, or walking. These concerns stem in part from an awareness of being watched closely and constantly by men and other women. While a woman is expected to display her charms, she must not take any direct or obvious initiative in approaching a man. Doing so risks being labeled "fast" or "loose," as the second component in traditional Brazilian femininity is dependence on the man. Displays of physical strength detract from a woman's femininity, so Brazilian women expect the courtesies like door-opening. . . . Women often do not plan careers (at least, not long-term careers) in the business world, as the majority will marry, after which their primary responsibilities will be home and family. . . .

Within this system, perhaps because of the expectations of teasing and flirtatious behavior, jealousy can be a problem. The line between complimentary flirting, expected by women of men, and overly aggressive or overly direct behavior, grounds for a jealous reaction especially from husband or boyfriend, is often a fine one. Men and women often form separate groups at a party, as do married couples and dating couples. The explanation for the separation is that "they have nothing in common," but it helps to ease possible jealous tensions. . . .

Romantic relationships tend to be more possessive in Brazil than in North America. Couples go everywhere together and do everything together, and for a woman, this often means that her boyfriend's circle of friends becomes her circle of friends. Couples keep in daily contact through visits, dates, and telephone calls. Women rarely go out alone, so the woman without a boyfriend may find her social life rather curtailed. "Your whole life revolves around that relationship. When it ends, you have nothing." Romantic attachments often form between members of the extended family, such as second, third, and fourth cousins, and more distant cousins often marry. Such attachments strengthen the family unit and the marriage bond by making the family sphere the social sphere as well. . . .

Family and Friends

The Brazilian family network is much larger and much closer than in North America. "Family" means parents, children, grandparents, aunts, uncles, cousins, second, third, and fourth cousins, plus spouses and siblings of all of these. . . . Several generations may live under one roof, and when family members leave the home, they try to settle within close proximity. Children and young adults remain at home until marriage, and after marriage make frequent visits home—at least one a week if possible. Perhaps because the network is so large, one finds little rivalry and many close relationships in a Brazilian family. Most Brazilians feel a strong sense of family loyalty and consider it an automatic duty to help family members in any way possible. One's closest personal friends are likely to come from this extended family network. . . . The family network may be further extended through a system of godparents, *compadres* and *comadres*, which entails much closer involvements than does the North American system of godparents.

"Friend" likewise means something very different to a Brazilian. . . . North Americans . . . often assume that Brazilians feel close friendship with nearly everyone, but this is not precisely the case. Brazilians do form friendly relationships easily, but they also distinguish levels of friendship. . . . *Colega* translates as fellow or colleague. . . . *Colega* names a much closer relationship than what the North American intends by "acquaintance," perhaps nearer to what the North American intends by "friend," since *colegas* do share obligations and responsibilities. . . . Brazilians do not understand the American concept of casual friendship or acquaintanceship without mutual obligations.

In Brazil a real friend, an *amigo(a)*, is "somebody you can really count on who is with you always." While all friends are called *amigos*, all Brazilians know the distinction between an *amigo(a)* and a *colega*. An *amigo(a)* is "like family" and may well be family—a second cousin or a family member through the system of godparents. . . . A person has only one or two true *amigos*. . . . It is often a lifelong relationship and creates a degree of mutual involvement that few North Americans find outside the immediate family. Friends are absolutely at home in one another's houses, and friends know all about one another's lives. . . .

Privacy

The extended family living situation, the general concern for the group rather than the individual, and an appreciation for the human world around them, all create situations in which Brazilians are rarely alone. A person who wants to be alone is assumed to be sad. . . . However, to say that Brazilians have no sense of privacy is far from accurate.

Little privacy exists between family members, and little exists between friends, between *amigos*. Between *colegas*, a greater degree exists, and until one enters the relationship of a *colega*, Brazilians can be very private people indeed. . . . Home and family are very private matters. . . . Upper- and upper-middle-class homes often sit behind a high fence, a solid and tangible proof of the separation a Brazilian wants to maintain between his family and the world at large. . . .

Doing Favors

Brazilians often ask favors of friends, especially of close friends, but also of acquaintances. . . . Small things not requiring much responsibility or time are not considered favors, but just part of normal interaction. The request for a favor might be in the form of an indirect hint rather than a direct question, and many Brazilians are hesitant to ask unless they feel fairly sure they can be accommodated. . . . Because the concern for human feelings and human relations makes the refusing of favors difficult, some Brazilians may agree to do a favor even though circumstances make their performance of it impossible. Knowing this, Brazilians might ask several friends for the same favor, so that one, at least, should be able to comply.

Brazilians do not "balance" favors . . . and do not feel obligated to repay a favor immediately. Depending upon the amount of time and trouble a person has taken, a Brazilian might do something nice as a gesture of appreciation, but too marked an insistence on repaying might give offense. Brazilians do, however, feel freer to ask favors of those they have done favors for in the past. . . .

Personal Relations

One finds less competition for jobs in Brazil, where many jobs are gained through friends and family connections, and people are frequently judged on personal standards rather than abstract (i.e., prompt, efficient) or job-specific (i.e., typing, previous experience) qualities. Brazilians . . . may view an ambitious person as one who tries to keep others down for his own benefit. The means to the end are very important to a Brazilian. . . .

Concern for smoothing things over has marked Brazilian history as relatively peaceful. . . . The same concern for smoothing things over marks daily life, meaning that business deals, job recommendations, or the asking of a favor might all be approached slowly and indirectly. . . . Brazilians regard an indirect approach as gracious and as a way of sparing the other's feelings, a way to avoid putting the other on the spot, in a potentially awkward situation. . . . One must always consider the personal relations involved in a situation. To ignore those relations is to invite delay, frustration, and often failure in communicating with Brazilians.

41 *Riordan Roett* ◆ The Patrimonial State

Riordan Roett, a political scientist, is professor of international relations and director of the Center for Brazilian Studies at the School of Advanced International Studies, Johns Hopkins University, Washington, DC. He has written books on Brazilian foreign and domestic politics as well as on Paraguayan and Mexican foreign relations; his works include The Politics of Foreign Aid in the Brazilian Northeast *(1972);* Paraguay: The

From *Brazil: Politics in a Patrimonial Society* (New York: Praeger Publishers, 1984), 17–19, 35, 37–43, 45.

Personalist Legacy *(1991); and* Political and Economic Liberalization in Mexico: At a Critical Juncture *(1993). Here, Roett examines the way political elites manipulate power flexibly and resourcefully to maintain domination of the traditional and hierarchical "patrimonial state."*

One of the leading attributes of the Brazilian political system is its elitist nature. Regardless of the time period, politics in Brazil have been dominated by a relatively small group of individuals who have been able to manipulate the mass of the population and define the goals of the state in their own terms. Most members of the elite have been drawn from groups such as the landowning oligarchy, the public bureaucracy, the export-oriented and commercial interests, the military, and the industrial and banking groups. The elite nature of the political system has been reinforced by the traditional and hierarchical nature of Brazilian political culture. Through history, there has been a high degree of similarity and congruence in the political ideas, attitudes, and action patterns of the elites. Similarly, there has been a notable lack of opposition to this prevailing political culture by other groups and classes in Brazil. Emerging social groups have chosen to emulate existing elites and their codes of political conduct, rather than to challenge or confront them.

Elite domination is further aided by the oft-noted propensity for compromise and the peaceful settlement of disputes among elite members and the expectation among the masses that accommodation and bargaining are sufficient to settle disputes. . . . What has emerged in Brazil is a pattern of elite interaction that assigns great value to pragmatism in policymaking, displays little ideological fervor, endorses flexibility in interpersonal relationships, and stresses highly personal or charismatic forms of leadership. . . .

The Patrimonial Regime

Our use of the term "patrimonial" refers to the creation and maintenance of a highly flexible and paternalistic public order, dedicated to its own preservation and the preservation of the unity of the nation-state, whether under imperial, republican, or military tutelage. . . .

The power of the few has characterized Brazilian society from its founding (with due allowance for different actors in different historical periods). In periods when the concept of representative government has emerged in the political process, the constitution and the popularly elected delegates of the people have been a superficial cover for the continuing influence of the patrimonial regime. . . .

The patrimonial state represents the "minority power" of the few in Brazilian society. Most Brazilians, the "majority power" of the state, have never been involved in policymaking or governance. When the people have been allowed to elect their representatives freely, the latter have been successfully co-opted into the orbit of the patrimonial regime. . . .

The patrimonial state is perhaps best described as a residual state in terms of power application: through custom as well as usage its preeminence is accepted and safeguarded. To accomplish its purposes in Brazil, the state was—and is—willing to allow limited political activity as long as the actors adhere to the established rules. This provides for a flexible and resourceful system of control. It allows for diversity—social and economic—which is a dominant characteristic of Brazil. In exchange for political support from the dominant social factors in society, the patrimonial state confirms and supports their local socioeconomic hegemony.

The concern of this type of state is its authority and the unfettered exercise of that authority. It possesses the capacity to control society coercively but prefers to utilize the techniques of persuasion, tradition, and co-optation. While it is insistent on dominating, it is not insistent on regulating, and this is a decisive difference from totalitarian states. Regulation of many issues is left to local initiative, with the understanding that local initiative, regardless of its diversity, will be supportive of the general system of power previously established.

What is to be stressed is that the state is not monolithic, nor is the national elite which manipulates its political system. The key characteristics, in addition to survival, are adaptability, resiliency, and omnipresence in every activity of the society. Working through and with the complicity of the political elite, the state penetrates and dominates the nation. But the consolidation and extension of its power is explicable in terms of its own interests, which may or may not coincide with the interests and needs of the citizenry. . . .

Elites in Brazil

Real power today is exercised by the political elite, whose power is built on its influence with the institutions of the patrimonial state, of which the bureaucracy and the military are the most important. While there is a certain amount of social cohesion that characterizes the ruling class, this is not so of the political elite. The driving force behind the political elite is its desire for public power. The two groups have cooperated effectively for generations; their goals have complemented each other. For the ruling class, the primary objective has been to prevent any reorganization of land tenure, the basis of its wealth and influence. It also opposes all efforts to organize the rural workers to introduce the benefits of modern society into rural areas. The political elite, concerned primarily with gaining public office and access to the patronage benefits of political power, cares little about real reform. Its interests are in holding power, whether appointive or elective. . . .

The elite is permeable, susceptible to infiltration by new members as long as the aspirants are willing to accept and defend the basic rules and prerogatives of the patrimonial state. . . . These rules are, principally, to avoid the political mobilization of the masses, especially in the countryside; to maintain a ban against illiterates' voting (in support of the first objective); to leave land tenure and land utilization patterns untouched; to smother any originality and proclivity for independence in the labor movement; to foster industrialization and economic diversification by importing advanced technology, expanding exports, and attracting foreign investment; and to subordinate overall economic development programs to the needs of national security. . . . These are the objectives to which the national elite has been consistently loyal. Even regime changes have not altered (although personnel have changed) the commitment to a traditional and tutelary patrimonial state. . . .

The national elite succeeds because it is united; it survives because it is flexible and adaptive; it serves the interests of the patrimonial state while it serves its own through unalterable but muted opposition to potentially disruptive systemic inputs such as "basic reforms" (João Goulart) and personal power exercised independently of the framework of the authoritarian state (Getúlio Vargas in 1945). Its subtle presence is often overlooked because it is so pervasive; its power becomes readily apparent when we examine the crises leading to changes in regime in Brazil. . . .

The level of psychological membership of the average Brazilian citizen in the nation-state remains low. . . . While, to the average Brazilian, "Brazil" has symbolic value in that it is real in a legal and geographical sense, his feeling of participation and involvement is shallow. . . . Political cultural factors work to support the patrimonial order. Even *favelados* (urban slum dwellers) see the government "not as an evil but as doing its best to understand and help people like themselves.". . .

The policy of the patrimonial state to identify its goals without consultation with the people, and to act independently of any expressed opinion of the people is a long-standing and venerable tradition in Brazil. This tradition, combined with little, if any, sustained political mobilization of a majority of the population, provides an uncomplicated and relatively efficient means for the political elite both to survive and to govern the nation.

42 *Lauro Moreira* ◆ Living Avidly in the Present

Lauro Moreira is a Brazilian career diplomat who has been stationed in Argentina, Switzerland, and the United States, principally performing cultural and commercial duties. After his tour as counselor for cultural affairs, Brazilian Embassy, Washington, DC, from 1983 to 1987, he served in Brasília. His most recent assignment is to Barcelona, Spain, as consul general. This selection, drawn from a videotaped interview at the Foreign Service Institute of the Department of State, explores various facets—both positive and negative, according to Moreira—of the Brazilian character in terms of adolescence.

I think that we can compare the psychology of the Brazilian people to that of an adolescent. If we examine these people more closely, we see that they are young. They are in full development, just like adolescents. They are in a stage of transition, with unmistakable traits from their colonial childhood, mixed with elements that indicate a certain maturity, exactly like an adolescent. The Brazilian brings traits from childhood and already shows traits of adulthood, but he is not yet strictly one thing or another.

This, in my opinion, is the Brazilian. He does not consider himself tied to or subject to any past. No adolescent feels himself tied to the past. The Brazilians are people with an extremely short historical memory. Yesterday in Brazil is almost the last century, in contrast to other countries, where the last century still appears to be yesterday. The Brazilian does not think about the past, but he does not think about the future, either. What he really thinks about is the present. He lives avidly in the present. To him, the future is something without definite boundaries, but which he knows is going to be very brilliant and very important. He knows that intuitively, like an adolescent who does not know if he is going to be a doctor or a lawyer or a dentist, but he knows he is going to be a great doctor, a great lawyer, a great dentist. He has the naïveté of an adolescent who thinks that his brilliant future is necessarily going to be assured. This, among other things, makes Brazil always the country of the future.

The Brazilian is rebellious and undisciplined—as the adolescent is rebellious and undisciplined—toward any order or system imposed arbitrarily, although he is docile and easy to lead when an appeal is made to

From "The Brazilian National Character," videotaped interview in Portuguese recorded at the Foreign Service Institute, U.S. Department of State, March 22, 1986. Translated by G. Harvey Summ.

his reason or above all to his sentiments. President [José] Sarney's [economic stabilization] program is all that one could ask for in identifying the subject I have been talking about. During twenty years of an authoritarian regime in Brazil, we did not succeed in stamping out or reducing inflation. Institutional Act No. 5, which gave practically unlimited powers to the executive, did not succeed in resolving this economic problem. Suddenly, in a regime that is absolutely democratic, where obedience is not demanded or imposed but support of the people is asked for, 91 percent of the country, according to a survey, are entirely caught up in the government's program, which demands great sacrifice from all of society. It is not a program that is going to distribute goodies to everybody. It is a program that, in the final analysis, involves taking very bitter medicine. All of the people are aware of this and are caught up in the possibility of participating. This is what I mean when I say that Brazilians are docile and easy to lead, especially when their reason, and above all their feelings, are appealed to.

The Brazilian, as do all adolescents, lives in a state of psychological transition and instability, which alternates between euphoria and depression very easily. It is very simple to recognize euphoria in Brazil. If we win the World Cup, Brazil becomes euphoric. I have been told by sociologists and economists that productivity in factories in São Paulo increases noticeably in a week when the Corinthians [soccer team] win a game in São Paulo. The Brazilian is very mercurial in this sense. Since he reacts to variations in external events, he plunges easily into great depression. This is neither good nor bad; this is the Brazilian. It's the same as asking: Is it good to be an adolescent, or not? Every age in life is a phase. Adolescence is a phase. Childhood is a phase; maturity is a phase.

The Brazilian is profoundly individualistic. He rarely succeeds in identifying constructively with the suffering of others, exactly like an adolescent. But at the same time he is profoundly sentimental and generous, above all in relation to his friends, and he is very hard to rouse to fanaticism. This, in my view, is one of the most important aspects of the Brazilian psyche. As an irreverent Brazilian humorist used to say, Brazil will never be a communist or socialist country. Can you imagine a samba school, run by the state or by public officials, parading at Carnival time?

Brazil is an individualistic country. Brazilians will never allow themselves to be treated like sheep. This is a most important trait, which I consider Portuguese rather than Iberian. The Spaniard can be aroused to fanaticism much more easily. We do not have this in common with our Latin American brothers. In my opinion, they have a greater propensity toward fanaticism than the Brazilian, who is much too individualistic to be a fanatic.

The Brazilian is distrustful. An adolescent is distrustful, insecure, and engages in self-criticism to excess. The Brazilian is very self-critical. He always has "one foot behind." He does not have confidence. He does not feel secure. The American is the opposite. Americans are quite self-confident; they are an open, secure, tranquil people. The Brazilian is much more insecure, although in appearance very much an extrovert.

The Brazilian is averse to disciplined thinking, and there is nothing premeditated or effective in his actions. He doesn't prepare anything. He improvises. But this is very interesting: every one of these characteristics has a positive as well as a negative side. Obviously, the ideal is not to improvise; the ideal is to plan. But we have so often seen people who plan so much that they have lost the capacity to improvise and can no longer get out of difficulties as easily as a country like Brazil succeeds in doing, precisely because it is always using this capacity to improvise. This is not an ideal situation; it is also a passing phase.

The Brazilian does not know what lasting hatred is. He may have momentary outbursts of anger. He is very emotional. But lasting hatred is not part of the Brazilian psyche.

Apparently, the Brazilian has a certain disrespect for symbols. This used to be a very serious matter. Starting in 1964 there was a serious debate about this in Brazil, because the military thought that the attitude of the Brazilian toward symbols of the nation, the flag, the anthem, etc., represented a lack of civic consciousness and a lack of respect for things that ought to be objects of respect. But for the Brazilian, at bottom this basically means not lack of respect but great wisdom, because it means not confusing the symbol with what it is supposed to symbolize. The nation is one thing; the flag, the anthem, are symbols of this nation.

To use a current example, suppose you are at a soccer game in a crowd of two hundred thousand at Maracanã stadium [in Rio de Janeiro] on a hot, glorious, sunny Sunday afternoon, in a game against a foreign team, and they play the national anthem. When they play the first part of the anthem, everybody puts up with it and thinks it's fine and feels emotion and goose pimples. But if they play the second stanza, people won't feel the same emotion. This means no lack of respect for the national anthem; it just means that it's enough. What's important is life; at that moment, what's important is soccer, the game being played, the presence of other people, not the national anthem. This ability to separate one thing from another is a very interesting aspect of the Brazilian. And symbols are only symbols, and do not represent all of life.

In summary, then, in my opinion, we have a portrait of an adolescent, with all his perplexities, dogmatisms, doubts, instabilities, generosities, timidity, insecurity, and, above all, an enormous will to live, which is fundamental and dominant in the character of the Brazilian.

---

43 *Daphne Patai* ◆ Vera: A Woman Speaks

Daphne Patai is professor of women's studies and of Spanish and Portuguese at the University of Massachusetts. She has also taught at Rutgers University. Her works include Myth and Ideology in Contemporary Brazilian Fiction *(1983);* The Orwell Mystique: A Study in Male Ideology *(1984);* Looking Backward: Essays on Edward Bellamy *(1988);* Women's Words: The Feminist Practice of Oral History *(1991); and* Rediscovering Foreign Radicals: Brazilian Women Writers, 1889–1939 *(1993).*

In the early 1980s, Patai conducted a series of interviews with twenty "ordinary" women in what she called a "patriarchal society"—northeastern Brazil and Rio de Janeiro. She interviewed domestic servants, secretaries, factory workers, nuns, hairdressers, prostitutes, seamstresses, students, businesswomen, and homemakers. This selection is from her interview with "Vera," a woman in her midforties and leader of an Afro-Brazilian cultural group in a working-class neighborhood in Rio. Vera, who believes that she is living at "the most important time" in her life, describes her own rise from humble beginnings and comments articulately on race, class, and gender relationships.

I'm the daughter of an unmarried mother. I only started to have a closer relationship with her, more mother-daughter, after my marriage, and just recently when she came to live with me. I never knew my father.

When I was a baby, my mother lived in a tenement in São Paulo, and she used to leave me in a room alone while she went out to wash clothes and do cleaning. And when I was six months old, my mother says that I got my head caught in the bars of the crib, and that someone passed by, heard my crying and wondered about it, and came in and saw me stuck. A few more minutes and I would have died. Maybe that would have been better, who knows? Afterward, when I was nearly two—I'd already started to walk—my mother was advised by some people to put me in the care of a friend of hers, and this family then moved to the interior in the state of São Paulo. That's where I was raised, loose in the street, running around barefoot, with no idea of cleanliness, no manners, nothing. . . .

From *Brazilian Women Speak: Contemporary Life Stories* (New Brunswick, NJ: Rutgers University Press, 1988), 80–83, 85–87, 90–93, 98, 107–8. Reprinted by permission of Rutgers University Press. Footnotes omitted.

At five I already knew how to read. For that town and that time, I was a genius, but it did me no good because . . . I was a little black kid wandering the streets, with ugly skin, circulation problems, always going around with open sores. . . . Later, my mother had a rooming house in São Paulo, for prostitutes, and that's how she had the money to support me. When I was eleven my mother got me into the best school in the state. . . . I was the only black there, but I didn't get bent out of shape because of the racism, no. I was above all that. I always had a strong character, and I didn't let it affect me or my work at school. But a time came when it began to get to me, so then I decided to really be the black sheep. I thought, "I can't stay here being discriminated against, being mistreated even by the nuns." But I also couldn't tell my family about it, because they didn't understand me. . . .

I was in that school for just eight months. When I left I went back to my foster family, but I couldn't really adapt to life there again, because all that I wanted to be—this is what I thought—was what I could be only at the school, among the people there. . . .

~ One of my aunts used to prepare banquets at the home of the richest family in town. . . . I would deliver the laundry to their house. . . . I didn't dress like their daughters. I didn't have those beautiful manners that they knew about, their way of behaving at the table or even the rest of the time. When they played, they never shouted. I used to shout a lot. I fought a lot. They didn't. They would work things out quietly. One had a doll and the other would take it perfectly calmly. There was no trouble, nothing. And it all got my head muddled. I used to say, "But why are they like that?"

And then I discovered the reason: because they used to sit in their father's lap, their mother's lap, their grandfather's, grandmother's, and they had that permanent support from all the members of the family. Those girls had all that intimacy within their family. . . . My foster parents never took me into their laps, and I was becoming more and more withdrawn, more cut off. Then one day I thought, "When I get to their house, I'm going to sit on my aunt's lap." And to my amazement she liked it. I was really too big by then, and I'd never done it before because I didn't live with them and by the time I was old enough to want to I was afraid of their reaction. . . . But that day I sat on [my aunt's] lap, and she began to stroke my hair. And then I started to become more manageable. . . . People began to notice that I was changing, because when I first came back from school I felt discriminated against. My whole life was that discrimination—because I was black, had poor manners, behaved differently from the other kids. . . .

~ [My mother could not] continue to pay for my education. She tried to get me into a public school, but couldn't; . . . she put me in this other place, . . . an asylum, run by nuns. There was one wing for old people who could pay, men and women, and another for those who couldn't pay, indigent people. And there was a wing for children with disabilities—spastics, mental retards, all kinds of problems. I was already thirteen years old. It was a huge place. . . .

I started having problems, not with the institution—because there I was extremely useful, in all kinds of ways. But my relationship with the disabled children began to trouble me. I'd keep thinking, "That girl is fourteen, just like me, and she can't even talk. How long can she live like that?". . . There was a retarded girl there who had a marvelous voice. She sang in the choir, she had perfect pitch, and this retarded girl gave me a slap. She was blonde, blind but with such eyes—one was deformed, but the other was a perfect clear blue. And I didn't see a retarded girl hitting me. I saw a *white* girl hitting me. She hit me and I hit her back. Then I panicked. I went to a sister and told her what I'd done, and she didn't reproach me. My head got even more muddled. I actually wanted to be punished for what I'd done. But the sister wasn't in the least concerned about it. And so I started to think, "My God, I've been looking upon this girl as an enemy, but that's not what she is at all. She's as needy, as discriminated against, as I am. . . ."

A lady was looking for someone to keep her company . . . not just to help with the housework but also with some embroidery that she did at home . . . and to help her with the accounting for a restaurant she had. So I went to stay with her. It was a real experience for me, because I went through the greatest trials with her—of honesty, dishonesty, conflicts of interest, exploitation, everything. Not that I was exploited in my work, but she was exploited by her daughter and son-in-law. . . .

I was already engaged by then, and one day my employer came to me and said, "Look, Vera, you want to get married just so you can have your own house, but you don't really love your fiancé. . . . It would be better if you went back to school, got a degree, and thought about having a family in the future. I see a gloomy future for you, even in setting up a family, because this boy can't provide you with a good standard of living, nor can he match that thirst for knowledge that you've got.". . . I said, "No, *Senhora*, you don't want me to marry because you want me to stay here, putting up with your daughter, solving your problems.". . . In fact she was right about my husband, and years later—when I told him, "I want to go to university"—he said, "University? With two kids? What for? You should be taking care of your children."

Ah. my husband. . . . Things were going from bad to worse. . . . And then he got very sick and spent nearly a year in the hospital. . . . When he got out, he decided to take up with someone else. He met a woman and started a relationship with her. He wanted to have that relationship and keep on living at home, but I . . . I don't accept that sort of thing. . . . So we separated. . . . We lived together for eighteen years. Today I look on our separation as a perfectly natural thing, but at the time I felt a lot of turmoil that I hadn't been able to keep my family together. I judged myself to be a terrible wife, a terrible housewife, a terrible mother.

Because of my husband's poor health I had this fear of having children, and so I had two abortions. I already had one child—now I have two—and between the first and second, I had two abortions. . . . No, I didn't go to a doctor. It was a really unpleasant situation. I felt brutalized . . . because they stuck in what they call a sound [probe]. . . . They caused a hemorrhage. I got really sick both times. . . . My husband said . . . that whatever happened to me was my own responsibility. . . . I hadn't told him in advance because I knew he wanted to have those children, but he was very sick. He used to stay for ages in the hospital, ages at home. So I was the one who had to take care of everything. . . . I thought there was no way we could raise four children, on top of everything else and the financial problems, too, there was no way. With the standard of living that we had, two children were fine, but if we had more than two I thought we wouldn't have been able to maintain that standard. . . .

If it happened today, if I had the financial stability that I had in those days, I'd have my four children. It was stupidity really, lack of information, fear, insecurity. But today I'm not against abortion. I think women ought to decide, they ought to choose. Nothing should be forced on them. But, you know, the legalization of abortion here in Brazil is the subject of lots of disagreement, because the women of the lower class, proletarian women, they haven't been consulted about this. There's a law already in the works in Brasília, and nobody's asked if we want it or don't want it. . . . There's a great deal of opposition to it, a great deal. On the part of women, too. It's interesting, because they all do it; but when it's time to legalize it, they're opposed. But also, to legalize abortion so that a minority has access to hospitals, to conditions for doing an abortion, I'm against that. It ought to be available to everyone, through the medical care programs, that's how it ought to be done. But, on the other hand, that frightens me a lot, because our medical care is awful, so we're in a bind. Lots of women die from illegal abortions. If it's not legalized, women do it anyway and die; and if it is legalized, you still can't trust in the care that poor women are going to get. You're damned if you do and damned if you don't. The medical care that's provided by the government is stratified. If a patient, a worker from the slums, goes to the public clinics, he's treated one way. If he's middle class, suddenly, wham! He goes to the same doctors and they treat him in a different way. . . .

~ Black women are exploited starting with the samba schools [samba groups that perform during Carnival], which parade them half naked, and this attracts the attention of another kind of exploiter, the nightclub owner who puts on shows. We've got one here who's an incredible exploiter of black women. He's gotten rich by staging a show with black women, whom he calls *mulatas*—that old sexual mystique of the *mulata*. You see, we're *black* or *white*, and this label of *mulata* and *mulato* was created to hide the truth. *We are blacks*, and black women, when they go into these clubs, these shows, are labeled *mulatas* and, even worse, "the *mulatas* of so-and-so." They start having an owner, a master. And they are prostituted on the stage. . . . Black women have few options, and lots of these women who go on the stage and expose themselves have hardly any education. They don't need to talk, just to wiggle. And when they get old, they beg. Those that make it. Lots of them die young—sick or murdered. . . .

I think that laws in this country . . . should come about in response to a necessity, and not the necessity mold itself to the law! To my mind, that's not right. We have a law here against racial discrimination. I'm telling you frankly, I've never stopped to read that law, to study it, because to me it's a joke. . . . What I want is to fight for a law that would really address this problem of racial discrimination. . . .

We have to fight for equality. Whites don't. They have their rights, all their rights. We want our rights, in proportion to the duties that we have in this country. Because we're overloaded with duties, and we're blamed for everything that goes wrong in society. A holdup? A black did it. If three people are standing on the corner talking, two whites and a black, the police won't search the whites; they'll go directly to the black. . . . Burglars, drug dealers, and everything else—they've necessarily got to be black! On principle it's the black who's the rapist, who's the mugger. It's the black woman who's the prostitute—and also the maid, because people have this image of domestic servants. . . . If a black woman appears at an apartment house here, she has to go in by the service entrance because that's what all the servants use. . . . Of course, I don't do it. I argue with the doorman, threaten to make a scene in front of the building. And I get in. I don't understand why a maid has to go up by one elevator and the lady of the house by another. . . .

In schools—I have personal experience of this—there's discrimination against blacks. My son was studying in a public school, and he was discriminated against by the teachers themselves, and also by his classmates who already brought this discrimination from home with them, that's what they learned at home. . . . One mother in the *favela* not far from here told me about a case. The teacher turned to her son and said, "Look, you're a *favelado*"—the boy was having a hard time with some subject—"You're not learning, you're stupid, you're a *favelado*. You'll end up on the streets.". . . If a man is a Nordestino [northeasterner], he's discriminated against here for being Nordestino and for being black. But, on the other hand, the Nordestinos themselves discriminate against blacks, too. . . . If it's a woman, she suffers three kinds of discrimination. . . . At the bottom of the whole social ladder are the blacks, us. If a black reaches a high professional level, or cultural, he doesn't stop being discriminated against on that account. It's racial discrimination here, not class discrimination as they say—though they try to pretend that's it. But we know perfectly well it's not that.

In the mass media you find the greatest discriminators, in terms of both employment and the message. All day long you're bombarded by endless commercials and appeals to buy, but the people who make this appeal, who are selling you these products, are all white. They're blond. They seem to belong to the middle class, they represent that class. The children who ask other children to buy chewing gum, cookies, a toy, to use a certain toothpaste, they're all children getting out of a comfortable bed, leaving their room and going into a luxurious bathroom, with a father who's also very well nourished, well groomed, successful, sending messages to the *favelados* to buy that particular brand of toothpaste.

There's a newspaper that advertises its classified pages on television. The commercial shows a head of the family who's unemployed. His wife's really sad, his kids look worried—they're sitting in a comfortable living room, watching a color TV. . . . The next day he goes and finds a job. Right away. . . . Well, the *favelado* goes out with his paper under his arm and looks for work, but he doesn't find it. . . . The reality of blacks in this country isn't what they're trying to convey on TV.

Sometimes I feel like I'm going to explode, there's so much going on inside me. All around me I see our problems placed in the hands of people who are—they're not incompetent, they just have bad intentions. When people say our legislators are incompetent, they're wrong. They've just got bad intentions. And in their hands the problems just continue. These things are suffocating us. . . .

São Paulo is a state where there's a lot of discrimination against blacks, more than in Rio. It's apparent at all levels, all the time. It's not camouflaged. As you go farther south—São Paulo, Paraná, Santa Catarina, Rio Grande do Sul—discrimination gets worse and the blacks more silent.

Because Cariocas [residents of Rio], Bahianos [residents of Bahia] are more outgoing. They show what they feel. But farther south, I think blacks are often ashamed of even being black. Sometimes they're not even conscious of this racial discrimination because of the notion, the image that people try to create, that there's no discrimination in Brazil.

It's been demonstrated that the majority in this country are racially mixed, not black or white. But blacks can have light skin; that makes no difference. If my daughter gets home soon, you'll see that she's light-skinned, but she's still black. My husband looks white, but he's descended from blacks. In my family we're 100 percent black, with no miscegenation. My husband, no, he's the grandson of Italians, the son of a Nordestino who married the granddaughter of a black woman here in the South. So in my children's heredity, the black race predominates. . . . This whole story of mulattoes, mestizos, is nonsense. For us, mulattoes are blacks. . . .

~ My story, this life, this struggle—if I had the opportunity to live, to choose a certain number of years of life with good health, a clear mind, I'd like forty more years, because until now I haven't taken part. I haven't contributed in any way. . . . When you're a mother you think, "Wow! Now I'm fulfilled. The best thing in my life is being a mother." It is very important, but to be an alienated mother, to be a mother separated from everything that's happening, to be mother only to your own children—that's very little. . . . We have to be mother to all children, sister to them all, companion to them all. And we have to be mother to our ideas and defend them as if they were children of our flesh and blood that someone was trying to hurt. . . . My God, forty years of idiocy, of watching the clouds drift by.

I'm just beginning to make a contribution. This is the most important time in my life.

---

44 *Nancy Scheper-Hughes* ◆ The Everyday Violence of Life

Nancy Scheper-Hughes is professor of anthropology at the University of California at Berkeley. A native of Brooklyn, NY, she first went to Brazil with the Peace Corps and served from 1964 to 1966 as a public health

From *Death without Weeping: Mother Love and Child Death in Northeast Brazil* (Berkeley: University of California Press, 1992), 90–91, 98, 108–9, 115, 229–31, 429–30, 433–37, 440, 473–74, 505, 507–8.

worker and community organizer in the sugar plantation zone of the northeastern state of Pernambuco. In the 1980s she returned four times, for a total of fourteen months of anthropological fieldwork, to the place that she interchangeably calls "Alto do Cruzeiro" or "the Alto," a hillside shantytown of about five thousand rural workers in the larger town of Bom Jesus da Mata. She also did fieldwork in Ireland, and in 1979 published Saints, Scholars, and Schizophrenics: Mental Illness in Rural Ireland, *for which she received the Margaret Mead Award in 1981.*

The material that follows is taken from her book Death without Weeping *(1992). Prof. Scheper-Hughes provides an extraordinarily perceptive view—mainly that of rural migrant women shantytown dwellers of Northeast Brazil—on many of the themes dealt with by other foreign and Brazilian authors in this volume.*

The people of the *mata* [forest] who have come to reside in the hillside crevices of Bom Jesus look very different from the bronzed Europeans who are their bosses and *donos* [masters]. The *matutos*' faces are browner; their bodies are smaller and slighter. One might see them as tough and sinewy, but that would be at variance with their own image of themselves as weak, wasted, and worn-out. One can see both the Amerindian and the African in their eyes, cheekbones, hair, and skin, although it is the African that predominates. . . .

These people are the descendants of a slave- and runaway slave-Indian (*caboclo*) population. Yet they do not think to link their current difficulties to a history of slavery and race exploitation. Racism is a disallowed and submerged discourse in Northeast Brazil. . . . These are a people "without a history." They call themselves simply *os pobres* [the poor], and they describe themselves as *moreno* (brown), almost never as *preto* or *negro* (black). They are "brown," then, as *all* Brazilians, rich and poor, are said to be brown. In this way the ideology of "racial democracy" goes unchallenged. . . .

Allow me to refer momentarily to the people of the Alto do Cruzeiro as the "foresters," if nothing else a quaint rendering of *matutos* that lends a feudal, almost medieval, but also dignified character to the term. In so doing I want to link these rural migrants to a not-so-distant, yet almost mythological, past when these "good country people" did indeed live in small clearings in dense woodlands as "conditional squatters," as peasant-workers on peripheral lands of sugar plantations, before these marginal lands, too, were claimed for sugar.

But just as the *zona da mata* is today without *mata*, so are the *matutos* stripped of their fields and woodlands and forced into life in the shantytowns and *mocambos* [shacks] on the edges of urban life. But the culture of the foresters, the ethos and the ethic that define and guide their actions, is still largely that of the *mata*. Meanwhile, to the somebodies of Bom Jesus the foresters are the little people, the humble people, those without names, possessions, and family connections, in short, the nobodies. . . .

Rural and illiterate, the foresters operate in a world of gifts and favors, barter and cunning, loyalties and dependencies, rumor and reputation. They live by their wits, not by the book. In the world of the *rua* [street] they are anathema—neither modern individuals with rights . . . nor yet persons, people "of family," reputation, substance, and influence, respected and cherished because they are the children of somebody. . . .

Although the foresters could be described as a "displaced rural proletariat" or even as a newly formed "urban underclass," they are both of these and yet a good deal more. They are poor and exploited workers, but theirs is not simply a "culture of poverty," nor do they suffer from a poverty of culture. Theirs is a rich and varied system of signs, symbols, and meanings. The *matutos* have brought with them into the urban environment ways of seeing, knowing, and reacting to the world around them that bear traces of their former lives in the *mata*. . . .

The people of the Alto act, because they must, within a dual ethic. . . . One guides behavior toward family, kin, *compadres* [godparents], coworkers, and friends who are *pobres* like themselves. The other guides behavior toward *patrões* [patrons], bosses, *donos*, superiors, and benefactors. Whereas the first siphons off the most minimal surplus to redistribute it among those even worse off, the other locks the foresters into relations of servility, dependency, and loyalty to those who oppress and exploit them. The one enhances class solidarity; the other contains within it the seeds of class betrayal. The first is the ethic of open and balanced reciprocity. It is the ethic of the *mata*. The other is the ethic of patronage, of *paternalismo*, of misplaced loyalties and self-colonizing dependencies. It is the ethic of the *casa grande*, of the big house and the sugar barons, the *senhores de engenho*. Both ethics coexist in a tense dialectic on and around the sugar plantations; both are transformed when the foresters come to reside as *moradores*, as squatters, along the muddy paths of the Alto do Cruzeiro. . . .

Between the foresters and their variously described bosses, patrons, and owners, an altogether different image of the impoverished *morador* emerges, that of a fawning, "humble" man or woman, hat in hand, eyes cast downward, as unctuous and dishonest and conniving as Dickens's Uriah Heep. The history of the sugar plantation, slavery, peonage, paternalism, and *coronelismo* can weigh heavily on the demeanor and the behavior of the rural workers, who throughout their lives put up with humiliating gestures and postures and with unequal exchanges that obligate them to people who would only take further advantage of them. The squatters behave toward their bosses in ways that end up angering and disgusting themselves, so that later and in private they rain forth invectives on the head of their bad boss or greedy patron. . . .

Although when disillusioned the people of the Alto will and do "give up" on one or even on a whole series of bad bosses and disappointing patrons, they do not give up on the idea of patronage and the persistent belief that there are good bosses to be had: kind, just, noble, generous, caring, strong, and charismatic. A good boss is a rescuer and a savior, one who will swoop down at a precarious moment and snatch a dependent worker and his or her family from the clutches of disease, penury, death, or other forms of destruction. For people who live their lives so close to the margins of survival, the idea of a benefactor is soothing. To admit the opposite, to entertain the idea that patronage itself is exploitative, is to admit that there is no structural safety net at all and that the poor are adrift within an amoral social and economic system that is utterly indifferent to their well-being and survival. It is to suggest that hope is absurd and that "good fortune" is an illusion. . . .

[The difficulties of Lordes, a poor black laundress, with her employer are described.] And so Lordes left that household but soon took up a position with the adult daughter of Dona Rita, where she fared no better. The structural and psychological hold of patron-client relations is such that a break with a particularly bad boss often leaves the client stranded so that she is virtually forced to take up where she left off, sometimes (as in this instance) going to work for another member of the same family. In addition, there is the "lure" of even marginal involvement in the lives of the wealthy. The rise and fall of fortunes in the *patroa*'s extended household and family often provide the "high drama" missing in one's own seemingly impoverished and lackluster life. These affective ties and points of reference and identification are difficult to sever. . . .

~ What makes the political tactic of disappearance so nauseating—a tactic used strategically throughout Brazil during the military years (1964–1985) against suspected subversives and "agitators" and now applied to a different and perhaps an even more terrifying context (i.e., against the shantytown poor and the economic marginals now thought of as a species of public enemy)—is that it does not occur in a vacuum. Rather, the disappearances occur as part of a larger context of wholly expectable, indeed even anticipated, behavior. Among the people of the Alto, disappearances form part of the backdrop of everyday life and confirm their worst fears and anxieties—that of losing themselves and their loved ones to the random forces and institutionalized violence of the state.

The practices of "everyday violence" constitute another sort of state "terror," one that operates in the ordinary, mundane world of the *moradores* both in the form of rumors and wild imaginings and in the daily enactments of various public rituals that bring the people of the Alto into contact with the state: in public clinics and hospitals, in the civil registry office, in the public morgue, and in the municipal cemetery. These scenes provide the larger context that makes the more exceptional and strategic, politically motivated disappearances not only allowable but also predictable and expected. . . .

Similarly, the *moradores* of the Alto speak of bodies that are routinely violated and abused, mutilated and lost, disappeared into anonymous public spaces—hospitals and prisons but also morgues and the public cemetery. And they speak of themselves as the "anonymous," the "nobodies" of Bom Jesus da Mata. For if one is a "somebody" and a "person" in the aristocratic world of the plantation *casa grande*, and if one is an "individual" in the more open, competitive, and bourgeois world of the new market economy, the *rua*, then one is surely a nobody, in the anonymous world of the sugarcane cutter (the *mata*). . . .

~ Of no account in life, the people of the Alto are equally of no account in death. On average, more than half of all deaths in the *município* are of shantytown children under the age of five, the majority of them the victims of acute and chronic malnutrition. But one would have to read between the lines because the death of Alto children is so routine and so inconsequential that for more than three-fourths of recorded deaths, the cause of death is left blank on the death certificates and in the ledger books of the municipal civil registry office. In a highly bureaucratic society in which triplicates of every form are required for the most banal of events (registering a car, for example), the registration of child death is informal, and anyone may serve as a witness. Their deaths, like their lives, are quite invisible. . . .

Alto women generally face child death stoically. No one on the Alto do Cruzeiro criticizes a mother for not grieving for the death of a baby. . . . She is not told that crying is a healthy (and womanly) response to child death or that it is "natural" to feel bitter and resentful or that she must "confront" her loss and get over her unhealthy emotional "numbness.". . .

Instead of the mandate to mourn, the Alto mother is coached by those around her, men as well as women, in the art of resignation and "holy indifference" to the vagaries of one's fate on earth and a hopefulness of a better life beyond. In this cultural milieu a deficit of emotion is not viewed as unhealthy or problematic; rather, an excess is. To experience strong emotions and passions—of love and lust, envy and anger, ecstasy and joy, grief and longing—is for most Brazilians, rich as well as poor, urban as well as rural, the most "natural" and expected occurrence. It is what being human is all about. But if allowed to run riot, these emotions are understood as the harbingers of much misery and suffering. Excessive emotions can bring down large and powerful households as well as small and humble ones. They can ruin lives and livelihoods. They can destroy relationships. They can cause physical as well as mental sickness. . . .

The strong mandate *not* to express grief at the death of a baby, and most especially not to shed tears at the wake, is strongly reinforced by a Nordestino folk piety, a belief that for the brief hours that the infant is in the coffin, she is neither human child nor blessed little angel. She is something other: a spirit-child struggling to leave this world and find its way into the next. It must climb. The path is dark. A mother's tears can impede the way, make the road slippery so that the spirit-child will lose her footing, or the tears will fall on her wings and dampen them so that she cannot fly. . . .

In all, what is being created is an environment that teaches women to contain their affections and hold back their grief during the precarious first year of the child's life. The question remains, however, whether these cultural "conventions" actually succeed in producing the desired effects or whether the dry-eyed stoicism and nonchalant air of Alto mothers are merely "superficial" and skin-deep, covering up a "depth of sorrow," loss, and longing. . . . Although I have no doubt that the local culture is organized to defend women against the psychological ravagings of grief, I assume that the culture is quite successful in doing so and that we may take the women at their word when they say, "No, I felt no grief. The baby's death was a blessing.". . .

The *moradores* of the Alto are passionate people who express their emotions with freedom and with a range of nuances in sentiment and sensibility. . . . Brazilians, they say of themselves, are sensual, vibrant, alive, also deeply sentimental, heavy, melancholy, sad. They describe themselves, above all, as a people of feeling. . . . It is not true that Northeast Brazilians generally "express painful topics" in a "blank" or an emotionless way. Quite the opposite is the case. No, the absence of grief, the emotional indifference to infant death, is something else and is perhaps in a class by itself. . . .

The notion of *saudades* [nostalgic longings] offers a key to understanding "death without weeping" on the Alto do Cruzeiro. Infant death is the one context of loss in which people, mothers in particular, never refer to their *saudades*. . . . There were *saudades* for a loved one who was gone or for a love that had turned sour or bitter. But one could also have *saudades* for particular smells, foods, colors, or sensations from the past that were associated with poignant events and loved ones. . . . Alto women did not refer to *saudades* when talking about the death of their infants and young angel-babies. In these contexts, it was not sadness, sorrow, or wrenching, tortured, yet sweet, longing that they felt; it was pity. . . .

Saudade and *pena* [pity] are contradictory emotions: where *saudade* unites and attaches, *pena* distances and separates. . . . *Saudade* has been described as the ultimate nourishment of love. *Pena* is evoked for creatures who are assumed to be preconscious and presentient: infants and dumb animals. *Saudade* is a positive emotion; it is linked with pleasurable and satisfying past experiences. *Pena* is linked with painful and conflicted memories; it carries only negative meanings. . . .

~ When my Alto friends refer to finding a *jeito* or *jeitinho*—that is, a quick solution to a problem or a way out of a dilemma—they are speaking the language of tactics. *Jeitos* entail all the mundane tricks for getting by and making do within the linear, time-constrained, everyday, uphill struggle along the suffering *caminho* [road]. The Brazilian *jeitoso* is an ideal personality type connoting one who is attractive, cunning, deft, handy, and smooth. When the word *jeito* is invoked to imply a "getting away with murder" or a "taking advantage" of a situation at someone else's expense, it is closely related to *malandragem*, a term without an English equivalent, although "swindling" comes close. *Malandragem* is the art of the scoundrel and the rascal: a "badness" that entails an enviable display of strength, charm, sexual allure, charisma, street smarts, and wit.

The *malandro* (rake) and the *jeitosa* (one who operates around and outside the law and who lives by her wits) are products of the clash of competing realities and social ethics in contemporary Brazil. As social personalities and distinct interactional styles, they are culturally derived defenses against the rigidity of the race-class system, the complexity of Brazilian laws, and the absurdity of an unwieldy, inflated, and corrupt state bureaucracy. . . .

Although among middle-class Brazilians *malandragem* is a characteristically male, sex-linked trait, in the rougher context of shantytown life, women, too, can survive as rakes and scoundrels. . . . Staying alive in the shantytown demands a certain "selfishness" that pits individuals against each other and that rewards those who take advantage of those even weaker. *Moradores* admire toughness and strength, and they point with pride to those who show a knack for life, including a seductive charm and a "way" with words that can move, motivate, and fool others. And they pity those who are *sem* [without] *jeito*—that is, weak, hopeless, without the "right stuff," altogether graceless and deficient beings.

And so *moradores* try to work the traditional *patrão* system to their advantage. They try to make alliances with the strong, the beautiful, and the powerful. They will vote for the local, regional, and national candidates who are most likely to win, and they will avoid associating with likely losers, even if the "weaker" candidate has expressed solidarity with their class. . . . Some *moradores* rejected Lula, the Socialist Workers' Party presidential candidate, not only because he was unlikely to win but because he was too *ugly*: "Lula is too much like us: weak and defective [referring to his injured fingers], and his speech is rough, not beautiful.". . .

Moradores treat their spiritual patrons with similarly undisguised pragmatics. As folk Catholics they "work" the spirit world using the familiar, everyday tactics of barter, blackmail, debt, and shifting loyalties. An ineffective patron saint is of no more use than a drunken, unemployed husband, and he or she is just as easily dismissed or exchanged for another. . . .

~ They endure and they get by, the women and men of the Alto, "making do" as best they can, relying on their wits, playing the odds, and engaging in the occasional *malandragem* of deceit and white lies, gossip and rumor, feigned loyalty, theft, and trickery. But can we speak of resistance, defiance, opposition—themes that are so privileged in critical circles today? My friends on the Alto do Cruzeiro do not deceive themselves any more than do the few, discouraged members of the surviving radical left in Bom Jesus, who now speak only with irony and bitterness of when, "come the revolution," things will be different. . . .

The people of the Alto, like [the] rural poor of the Northeast more generally, understand human nature to be flawed and inclined toward treachery. They expect their popular leaders to turn against them if the rewards for doing so are great enough, and they are not self-righteously indignant or outraged on discovering self-serving political deception. Such events only confirm their worst suspicions and reinforce a well-grounded pessimism. Far from rebels or revolutionaries, the rural workers of the Northeast are by social temperament patient, long-suffering, and nonviolent people. They generally keep their peace despite the everyday violence of drought, hunger, sickness, and unnecessary death. And they are gentle in the face of the aggression of local bosses and big men, with their hired thugs and gunmen. . . . [Morever], the people of the Alto swallow and deflect their anger by means of an ironic, absurdist black humor. . . . Their nonviolence, humor, [and] display of compliance do not mean, however, that the poor of the Alto are passively accepting of the situation in which they are trapped. The *moradores* understand and freely comment on the evils of the local political economy in the traditional, folk Catholic idiom of the seven deadly sins. Little escapes their devastating, running critique of human culpability, in particular the greed, pride, lust, and sloth of their political bosses and of the planter class. . . .

Nonetheless, despite their understanding of the social sources of their collective misery, the people of the Alto remain skeptical of radical and revolutionary proposals and do their best to survive in the cracks and crevices of daily life in Bom Jesus da Mata through the charade of "learned helplessness," breached only by their biting humor and by the occasional, sometimes quite daring, act of trickery or cunning. And in these latter instances their silence and feigned ignorance serve as their cover. Nor shall I blow that cover here by giving specific illustrations of what I am alluding to!

Suggested Readings

General and Background Information

Suggestions for supplementary reading include a basic fact book, *Brazil: A Country Study* (Washington, DC: U.S. Government Printing Office, 1982). Other books of general interest include Eric N. Baklanoff, *New Perspectives of Brazil* (Nashville: Vanderbilt University Press, 1966), which contains interpretive essays on politics, the economy, society, national character, religion, and literature. Thomas C. Bruneau and Philippe Faucher, *Authoritarian Capitalism: Brazil's Contemporary Political and Economic Development* (Boulder, CO: Westview Press, 1981), includes a series of essays on contemporary economic and political development.

Rollie E. Poppino, *Brazil: The Land and the People* (New York: Oxford University Press, 1968), emphasizing social and economic topics, is the best history of the country for the beginner. E. Bradford Burns, *A History of Brazil*, 2d ed. (New York: Columbia University Press, 1980), deals comprehensively with politics as well. Another general history is Donald E. Worcester, *Brazil: From Colony to World Power* (New York: Scribner and Sons, 1973). Michael L. Conniff and Frank D. McCann, eds., *Modern Brazil: Elites and Masses in Historical Perspective* (Lincoln: University of Nebraska Press, 1991), contains a series of essays on the history of political, economic, cultural, and social elites. Ronald M. Schneider's *"Order and Progress": A Political History of Brazil* (Boulder, CO: Westview Press, 1991) is a recent comprehensive political history. Sérgio Buarque de Holanda, *História geral da civilização brasileira* (São Paulo: Difusão Europeia do Livro, 1971), provides the most complete history from a Brazilian source. Burns, *A Documentary History of Brazil* (New York: Alfred A. Knopf, 1966), contains valuable basic historical documents. Raymundo Faoro, *Os donos do poder: Formação do patronato político brasileiro* (Porto Alegre, Brazil: Editora Globo, 1977), is a penetrating two-volume analysis of the formation of the patrimonial state. Victor Nunes Leal's classic, *Coronelismo* (Cambridge, England: Cambridge University Press, 1977), examines local political bosses. Conniff's *Urban Politics in Brazil: The Rise of Populism, 1925–1945* (Pittsburgh: University of Pittsburgh Press, 1981) is an analysis of populist movements since the 1920s.

The Colonial Era and the Empire

Robert Southey, *History of Brazil*, 3 vols. (New York: B. Franklin, 1970), provides very detailed colonial history. Charles R. Boxer, *The Golden Age of Brazil: Growing Pains of a Colonial Society, 1695–1750* (Berkeley: University of California Press, 1962), deals with the gold-rush days. João Pandiá Calógeras, *A History of Brazil* (New York: Russell and Russell, 1963), covers, from the Brazilian viewpoint, both the colonial period and the empire.

A. J. R. Russell-Wood, *From Colony to Nation: Essays on the Independence of Brazil* (Baltimore: Johns Hopkins University Press, 1975), examines the independence period. Roderick J. Barman, *Brazil: Forging of a Nation* (Stanford, CA: Stanford University Press, 1988), focuses on the struggle for independence and the establishment of the nation. Clarence H. Haring, *Empire in Brazil* (Cambridge, MA: Harvard University Press, 1958), is an incisive history of the imperial period, while Emilia Viotti da Costa, *The Brazilian Empire: Myths and Histories* (Chicago: University of Chicago Press, 1985), emphasizes the role of the political elite in the nineteenth century. Stanley J. Stein, *Vassouras: A Brazilian Coffee County, 1850–1900* (Princeton: Princeton University Press, 1985), is an insightful examination of coffee-growing in the Rio de Janeiro-São Paulo area in the last half of the nineteenth century. Pelham H. Box, *The Origins of the Paraguayan War: The Struggle for Liberty in Brazil and Paraguay* (Urbana: University of Illinois Press, 1929), is a solid study of that war. Neill Macaulay's *Dom Pedro* (Durham, NC: Duke University Press, 1986) is a biography of the first emperor, and Harry Bernstein, *Dom Pedro II* (New York: Twayne Publishers, 1973), of his son. Leslie Bethell, *The Abolition of the Brazilian Slave Trade* (Cambridge, England: Cambridge University Press, 1970), and Carolina Nabuco, *The Life of Joaquim Nabuco*, ed. and trans. Ronald Hilton in collaboration with Lee B. Valentine, Francis E. Coughlin, and Joaquin M. Duarte, Jr. (Stanford, CA: University of California Press, 1950), cover the abolitionist movement.

From the Republic through the Military Period and After

The republican period is the subject of José Maria Bello, *A History of Modern Brazil, 1889–1964*, trans. James L. Taylor (Stanford, CA: Stanford University Press, 1966). Thomas E. Skidmore, *Politics in Brazil: An Experiment in Democracy, 1930–1964* (New York: Oxford University Press, 1967), deals ably with politics between the presidencies of Getúlio Vargas and João Goulart. Peter Flynn, *Brazil: A Political Analysis* (London: Ernest Benn Ltd., 1978), examines the 1889–1964 period carefully and comprehensively. John W. Dulles and Karl Loewenstein have both written biographies of Vargas: *Vargas of Brazil: A Political Biography* (Austin: University of Texas Press, 1967) and *Brazil under Vargas* (New York: Russell and Russell, 1973), respectively. Robert J. Alexander, *Juscelino Kubitschek and the Development of Brazil* (Athens: Ohio University Press, 1991), is a biography of that important president, who was elected in 1955.

The political role of the military is the subject of Skidmore's *The Politics of Military Rule in Brazil, 1964–1985* (New York: Oxford University Press, 1988); Alfred Stepan, *Authoritarian Brazil: Origins, Policies, and Future* (New York: Yale University Press, 1973); and Ronald M. Schneider, *The Political System of Brazil: Emergence of a "Modernizing" Authoritarian Regime* (New York: Columbia University Press, 1971). Maria Helena Moreira Alves, *State and Opposition in Military Brazil* (Austin: University of Texas Press, 1985), examines the so-called national security state of the military period. *Torture in Brazil: A Report by the Archdiocese of São Paulo* (New York: Vintage Books, 1986), studies the excesses of the repressive military regime, while Amnesty International's two volumes, *Brazil: Authorized Violence in Rural Areas* (London: Amnesty International, 1988), and *Torture and Extrajudicial Execution in Urban Brazil* (New York: Amnesty International, 1990), look at human rights violations.

Wayne A. Selcher, ed., *Political Liberalization in Brazil: Dynamics, Dilemmas, and Future Prospects* (Boulder, CO: Westview Press, 1986), contains several essays examining the country's transition from military rule to representative political institutions, while Stepan, ed., *Democratizing Brazil: Problems of Transition and Consolidation* (New York: Oxford University Press, 1989), similarly looks at the economic and social impact, including the effect on women, labor, and religion, of the transition.

The Economy

Corporativist control of the labor movement is analyzed by Kenneth P. Erickson, *The Brazilian Corporative State and Working-Class Politics* (Berkeley: University of California Press, 1977). Youssef Cohen, *The Manipulation of Consent: The State and Working-Class Consciousness in Brazil* (Pittsburgh: University of Pittsburgh Press, 1989), focuses on state control of the working class through authoritarian manipulation of their beliefs and values. Margaret E. Keck, *The Workers' Party and Democratization in Brazil* (New Haven: Yale University Press, 1993), examines the 1989 elections, presidential candidate Luis Inácio ("Lula") da Silva, and his relatively new labor party.

The best single text on the economy is Werner Baer, *The Brazilian Economy: Growth and Development* (New York: Praeger Publishers, 1991). Celso Furtado, *The Economic Growth of Brazil: A Survey from Colonial to Modern Times*, trans. Ricardo W. De Aguiar and Eric C. Drysdale (Berkeley: University of California Press, 1963), and Caio Prado, Jr., *The Colonial Background of Modern Brazil*, trans. Suzette Macedo (Berkeley: University of California Press, 1967), are both excellent economic histories from the Brazilian point of view. Nathaniel H. Leff, *Economic Policy-Making and Development in Brazil, 1947–1964* (New York: John Wiley and Sons, 1968), and *Underdevelopment and Development in Brazil* (Boston: Allen-Unwin, 1982) cover economic development since 1822.

Particular aspects of the economy include Sylvia A. Hewlett, *The Cruel Dilemmas of Development: Twentieth Century Brazil* (New York: Basic Books, 1980), contrasting the nation's impressive aggregate economic development with the painful costs to the wealth, health, and freedom of many of its inhabitants. Edmar L. Bacha and Herbert S. Klein, eds., *Social Change in Brazil, 1945–1985: The Incomplete Transition* (Albuquerque: University of New Mexico Press, 1989), is a series of essays analyzing uneven industrialization and urbanization since 1945. Peter B. Evans, *Dependent Development: The Alliance of Multinational, State, and Local Capital in Brazil* (Princeton: Princeton University Press, 1979), examines that alliance in the industrialization process. Judith Tendler, *Electric Power in Brazil: Entrepreneurship in the Public Sector* (Cambridge, MA: Harvard University Press, 1968), is an excellent case study. Samuel A. Morley, *Labor Markets and Inequitable Growth: The Case of Authoritarian Capitalism in Brazil* (New York: Cambridge University Press, 1982), examines inequitable income distribution perceptively. Thomas W. Merrick and Douglas H. Graham, *Population and Economic Development in Brazil: 1800 to the Present* (Baltimore: Johns Hopkins University Press, 1979), takes an in-depth look at the demographic dimension of economic development.

Social and Cultural Themes

T. Lynn Smith, *Brazil: People and Institutions* (Baton Rouge: Louisiana State University Press, 1972), is a detailed sociological study that includes a discussion of immigration. Maxine L. Margolis and William E. Carter, eds., *Brazil: Anthropological Perspectives* (New York: Columbia University Press, 1979), is a series of essays interpreting Brazilian society. Specific social and cultural themes are analyzed in Janice Perlman, *The Myth of Marginality: Urban Poverty and Politics in Rio de Janeiro* (Berkeley: University of California Press, 1975), a close look at organized, productive, and politically moderate "marginal" Rio shantytowns. June E. Hahner, *Emancipating the Female Sex: The Struggle for Women's Rights in Brazil* (Durham, NC: Duke University Press, 1990), is a fine history of that struggle. Carolina Maria de Jesus, *Child of the Dark* (New York: New American Library, 1962), is the diary of an observant black woman in the São Paulo *favelas*. Conrad Phillip Kottak, *Assault on Paradise: Social Change in a Brazilian Village* (New York: McGraw-Hill, 1992), documents change in a northeastern fishing village.

A. J. R. Russell-Wood, *The Black Man in Slavery and Freedom in Colonial Brazil* (New York: St. Martin's Press, 1982), is the story of black slaves and freedmen. Artur Ramos, *The Negro in Brazil* (Philadelphia: Porcupine Press, 1980), gives a Brazilian view of the history, culture, and status of Afro-Brazilians. José Honório Rodrigues, *Brazil and Africa* (Berkeley: University of California Press, 1965), studies the African contribution to Brazilian society. Katia Mattoso, *To Be a Slave in Brazil, 1550–1888* (New Brunswick, NJ: Rutgers University Press, 1986), examines slavery from the point of view of the slave. Florestan Fernandes, *The Negro in Brazilian Society* (New York: Columbia University Press, 1969), studies the role of blacks, especially in São Paulo, from 1880 to 1960. Carl L. Degler, *Neither Black nor White: Slavery and Race Relations in Brazil and the U.S.* (New York: Macmillan Company, 1971), compares race relations between those two countries.

Roger Bastide, *The African Religions of Brazil: Toward a Sociology of the Interpretation of Civilizations* (Baltimore: Johns Hopkins University Press, 1978), provides perspective on religious behavior of African origin since the time of the slave trade. Thomas C. Bruneau, in *The Political Transformation of the Brazilian Catholic Church* (New York: Cambridge University Press, 1974), and *The Church of Brazil: The Politics of Religion* (Austin: University of Texas Press, 1982), examines Catholicism. Scott Mainwaring, *The Catholic Church and Politics in Brazil, 1916–1985* (Stanford: Stanford University Press, 1986), pays particular attention to the radical role of segments of the Catholic Church during the military period. Rowan Ireland, *Kingdoms Come: Religion and Politics in Brazil* (Pittsburgh: University of Pittsburgh Press, 1991), and Cecília Loreto Mariz, *Coping with Poverty: Pentecostals and Christian Base Communities in Brazil* (Philadelphia: Temple University Press, 1994), analyze recent religious change, including fundamentalist movements.

Samuel Putnam, *Marvelous Journey: A Survey of Four Centuries of Brazilian Writing* (New York: Alfred A. Knopf, 1948), surveys literature. David Brookshaw, *Race and Color in Brazilian Literature* (Metuchen, NJ: Scarecrow Press, 1986), focuses on black writers and Brazilian attitudes toward blacks. João Cruz Costa, *A History of Ideas in Brazil: The Development of Philosophy in Brazil and the Evolution of National History* (Berkeley: University of California Press, 1964), includes nineteenth-century positivism. John Nist, *The Modernist Movement: A Literary Study* (Austin: University of Texas Press, 1967), examines the seminal Modern Art Week in São Paulo in the 1920s.

A quick reference guide to the educational system is provided by Jerry Haar, *The Politics of Higher Education in Brazil* (New York: Praeger Publishers, 1977). Alma Guillermoprieto examines the relationship of the samba to drugs, crime, poverty, and race in a Rio *favela* in *Samba* (New York: Random House, 1990). Janet Lever, *Soccer Madness* (Chicago: University of Chicago Press, 1983), studies the social significance of that sport, and Conrad Phillip Kottak explores the influence of television in *Prime-Time Society: An Anthropological Analysis of Television and Culture* (Belmont, CA: Wadsworth Publishing, 1990).

The Amazon

Two sound histories of the Amazon are Barbara Weinstein, *The Amazon Rubber Boom, 1850–1920* (Stanford: Stanford University Press, 1983), and Warren Dean, *Brazil and the Struggle for Rubber: A Study in Environmental History* (New York: Cambridge University Press, 1987). Charles Wagley, *Amazon Town: A Study of Man in the Tropics* (New York: Macmillan Company, 1953), is a landmark community study of a small town in the region. Notable recent publications include John H. Hemming, ed., *Change in the Amazon Basin* (Dover, NH: Manchester University Press, 1985), a two-volume series of essays assessing the human impact on the environment; Dennis J. Mahar, *Government Policies and Deforestation in Brazil's Amazon Region* (Washington, DC: World Bank, 1989); Andrew Revkin, *The Burning Season: The Murder of Chico Mendes and the Fight for the Rain Forest* (Boston: Houghton Mifflin Company, 1990); and David Goodman and Anthony Hall, eds., *The Future of Amazonia: Destruction or Sustainable Development?* (London: Macmillan and Company, 1990).

Foreign Policy

Foreign policy works include E. Bradford Burns, *Unwritten Alliance: Rio Branco and Brazilian-American Relations* (New York: Columbia University Press, 1966), an analysis of the first decade of the twentieth century. Frank McCann, Jr., *The Brazilian-American Alliance, 1937–1945* (Princeton: Princeton University Press, 1973), explores military relations between the two countries during World War II. Phyllis R. Parker, *Brazil and the Quiet Intervention* (Austin: University of Texas Press, 1979), studies U.S. policy toward Brazil prior to the 1964 coup d'état. Wayne A. Selcher, ed., *Brazil in the International System* (Boulder, CO: Westview Press, 1981), contains a series of essays examining the nation's foreign relations and its world power ranking.

Latin American Silhouettes
Studies in History and Culture

William H. Beezley and
Judith Ewell
Editors

Volumes Published

William H. Beezley and Judith Ewell, eds., *The Human Tradition in Latin America: The Twentieth Century* (1987). Cloth ISBN 0-8420-2283 X Paper ISBN 0-8420-2284-8

Judith Ewell and William H. Beezley, eds., *The Human Tradition in Latin America: The Nineteenth Century* (1989). Cloth ISBN 0-8420-2331-3 Paper ISBN 0-8420-2332-1

David G. LaFrance, *The Mexican Revolution in Puebla, 1908–1913: The Maderista Movement and the Failure of Liberal Reform* (1989). ISBN 0-8420-2293-7

Mark A. Burkholder, *Politics of a Colonial Career: José Baquíjano and the Audiencia of Lima*, 2d ed. (1990). Cloth ISBN 0-8420-2353-4 Paper ISBN 0-8420-2352-6

Kenneth M. Coleman and George C. Herring, eds. (with Foreword by Daniel Oduber), *Understanding the Central American Crisis: Sources of Conflict, U.S. Policy, and Options for Peace* (1991). Cloth ISBN 0-8420-2382-8 Paper ISBN 0-8420-2383-6

Carlos B. Gil, ed., *Hope and Frustration: Interviews with Leaders of Mexico's Political Opposition* (1992). Cloth ISBN 0-8420-2395-X Paper ISBN 0-8420-2396-8

Charles Bergquist, Ricardo Peñaranda, and Gonzalo Sánchez, eds., *Violence in Colombia: The Contemporary Crisis in Historical Perspective* (1992). Cloth ISBN 0-8420-2369-0 Paper ISBN 0-8420-2376-3

Heidi Zogbaum, *B. Traven: A Vision of Mexico* (1992). ISBN 0-8420-2392-5

Jaime E. Rodríguez O., ed., *Patterns of Contention in Mexican History* (1992). ISBN 0-8420-2399-2

Louis A. Pérez, Jr., ed., *Slaves, Sugar, and Colonial Society: Travel Accounts of Cuba, 1801–1899* (1992). Cloth ISBN 0-8420-2354-2 Paper ISBN 0-8420-2415-8

Peter Blanchard, *Slavery and Abolition in Early Republican Peru* (1992). Cloth ISBN 0-8420-2400-X Paper ISBN 0-8420-2429-8

Paul J. Vanderwood, *Disorder and Progress: Bandits, Police, and Mexican Development*. Revised and Enlarged Edition (1992). Cloth ISBN 0-8420-2438-7 Paper ISBN 0-8420-2439-5

Sandra McGee Deutsch and Ronald H. Dolkart, eds., *The Argentine Right: Its History and Intellectual Origins, 1910 to the Present* (1993). Cloth ISBN 0-8420-2418-2 Paper ISBN 0-8420-2419-0

Jaime E. Rodríguez O., ed., *The Evolution of the Mexican Political System* (1993). ISBN 0-8420-2448-4

Steve Ellner, *Organized Labor in Venezuela, 1958–1991: Behavior and Concerns in a Democratic Setting* (1993). ISBN 0-8420-2443-3

Paul J. Dosal, *Doing Business with the Dictators: A Political History of United Fruit in Guatemala, 1899–1944* (1993). ISBN 0-8420-2475-1

Marquis James, *Merchant Adventurer: The Story of W. R. Grace* (1993). ISBN 0-8420-2444-1

John Charles Chasteen and Joseph S. Tulchin, eds., *Problems in Modern Latin American History: A Reader* (1994). Cloth ISBN 0-8420-2327-5 Paper ISBN 0-8420-2328-3

Marguerite Guzmán Bouvard, *Revolutionizing Motherhood: The Mothers of the Plaza de Mayo* (1994). Cloth ISBN 0-8420-2486-7 Paper ISBN 0-8420-2487-5

William H. Beezley, Cheryl English Martin, and William E. French, eds., *Rituals of Rule, Rituals of Resistance: Public Celebrations and Popular Culture in Mexico* (1994). Cloth ISBN 0-8420-2416-6 Paper ISBN 0-8420-2417-4

Niblo, Stephen R., *War, Diplomacy, and Development: The United States and Mexico, 1938–1954* (1995). ISBN 0-8420-2550-2

Summ, G. Harvey, ed., *Brazilian Mosaic: Portraits of a Diverse People and Culture* (1995). Cloth ISBN 0-8420-2491-3 Paper ISBN 0-8420-2492-1

N. Patrick Peritore and Ana Karina Galve-Peritore, *Biotechnology in Latin America: Politics, Impacts, and Risks* (1995). Cloth ISBN 0-8420-2556-1 Paper ISBN 0-8420-2557-X